Colonel G. J. BURNAGE, C.B., V.D.

Lt.-Col. D. G. MARKS, D.S.O., M.C., (Serbian Order).

Lt.-Col. H. W. MURRAY, V.C. C.M.G., D.S.O.
(and Bar), D.C.M., C. de G.

Lt.-Col. J. M. A. DURRANT, C.M.G., D.S.O.

The History of the Thirteenth Battalion, A.I.F.

BY

THOMAS A. WHITE, (Captain, 13th Bn., A.I.F.)
(Author of "DIGGERS ABROAD.")

TO

"THE GAMEST OLD MAN"

OUR

Honoured and Beloved COLONEL GRANVILLE JOHN BURNAGE, C.B., V.D.

Our FIRST COMMANDING OFFICER

AND TO

The Memory of our GALLANT YOUNG COLONEL

The Late DOUGLAS GRAY MARKS, D.S.O., M.C., (also Serbian Eagle),

who after continuous Glorious War Service from the beginning to the end of the GREAT WAR, gave his life in an attempt to rescue a stranger from the undertow at Palm Beach on the 25th January, 1920, at the age of 24,

the author respectfully dedicates this Story, knowing that, in so doing, he represents the wishes of all ranks of the "FIGHTING THIRTEENTH," who knew them.

TWO ORIGINALS.

The Naval & Military Press Ltd

Published by
The Naval & Military Press Ltd
5 Riverside, Brambleside, Bellbrook
Industrial Estate, Uckfield, East Sussex,
TN22 1QQ England
Tel: +44 (0) 1825 749494
Fax: +44 (0) 1825 765701
www.naval-military-press.com
www.military-genealogy.com
www.militarymaproom.com

*In reprinting in facsimile from the original, any imperfections are inevitably reproduced
and the quality may fall short of modern type and cartographic standards.*

FOREWORD

MANY and varied have been the opportunities with which I have been favoured, of associating myself with the published records of the Arms and Units of the Australian Imperial Force; but on no occasion have I esteemed it a greater pleasure and privilege than to have been invited to write a few lines to commend this book to the indulgent reader. For the 13th Battalion of the A.I.F. was dear to me in an especial degree, as is the first-born to the patriarch. It was the senior Battalion of the Fourth Australian Brigade, with the responsibility for the raising and training of which I was honoured in the earliest days of the Great War. The 13th led the way and set the standard for the whole of that famous Brigade, and history now testifies to the very high standard of efficiency and performance which that Brigade achieved, first in Gallipoli, and later on the Western Front.

In no Unit of the A.I.F. was the spirit of Unit consciousness stronger than in the 13th Battalion. It is a golden example of devotion to patriotic duty. Its record for service, for discipline for distinguished achievement stands second to none other. This book is the story of its birth, its training, and its war life. Battle scarred as is its record, it came out of the ordeal with the highest battle honours, and with an imposing contribution from its own ranks to the long list of individual officers and men who gained great distinction during the war.

The story of this Battalion rests upon the pride in their Unit, the concern for its prestige, the ardour for its reputation, and the zeal for its traditions, which were, from first to last, fostered and cherished by every man who entered its ranks.

JOHN MONASH,
Lieut.-General.

5th February, 1924.

"The 13th was a fighting unit to be proud of, and reflected great credit upon the State which raised it."
—Col. Burnage.

"Can anyone show me a Battalion with a finer record than the 13th?"
—General C. H. Brand.

"Tres bons soldats, et vous etes si gentils."
— A French Lady.

"I always take off my hat to the 13th."
—Sir Walter Davidson.

"Leur valeur grandit l'Australie."
—Aulneau.

"True gentlemen, one and all, in every way."
—Maire d'Hansinelle, Belgium.

Lt.-Col. TILNEY, D.S.O.

Major T. WELLS, M.C.

Lt.-Col. A. S. ALLEN, D.S.O., C. de G.

Sgt. MAURICE BUCKLEY V.C., D.C.M.
(Generally known in the 13th as Sgt. Gerald Sexton.)

THANKS.

I must first of all thank C. E. W. Bean for the use of his very valuable notes on the Somme battles and Bullecourt. I have also used his "Story of Anzac" as a source-book for the first days on Gallipoli and copied several of his maps of that period. He and all connected with the historical part of War Records in Melbourne have been the essence of courteous helpfulness. General SIR JOHN MONASH graciously allowed me the full use of his 4th Brigade records, for which I am very grateful. The ex-members of the 13th who have helped me are too many for individual thanks, but I thank them one and all, not only for obliging me as they have by replying to my hundreds of questions, but especially for the honor of selecting me as their historian. I must however, specially thank Lt. B. Blythman for the very considerable amount of work he has done so willingly for me as Hon. Secretary of our Battalion Committee, General S. C. E. Herring and Colonel J. M. A. Durrant for copious notes, maps, and valuable advice. To Mrs. M. Marks, the worthy mother of our late worthy Colonel, I am more than deeply grateful for the free use of her son's records. The Mitchell Library authorities helped me most obligingly and considerably. To all the above I have the honor of conveying my own and the unanimous gratitude of the 13th Battalion Committee. I have also to thank "Aussie," "The Bulletin" and "Smith's Weekly" for permission to re-use some of my yarns published in these journals, and Tyrrell's Ltd. for their very valuable and gratuitous interest and advice concerning publication.

T. A. WHITE.

FOREWORD.

THE 13th Bn., A.I.F., first saw active service at the Dardanelles, taking part in the famous Landing, the defence of Anzac, the attack on the Chessboard, and the Anzac evacuation. It was also actively engaged in the Battle of Sari Bair, which formed part of the battles of Suvla in August, 1915.

In France and Flanders the 13th took part in the Battle of the Somme (1916), experiencing hard fighting in the battles of Pozieres, Mouquet Farm, and Stormy Trench. It also participated in the Battles of Arras (1917), the first attack on Bullecourt on 11th April, being of a desperate character. Further part was taken in the 1917 offensive at Messines, and in the battle of Ypres at Polygon Wood. The German offensive in 1918 brought the battalion again to the Somme, the stubborn defence of Hebuterne in March and April helping to stem the tide. The 13th also assisted in the brilliant capture of Hamel on 4th July, 1918.

Finally, this battalion took part in the Advance to Victory, experiencing strenuous fighting at the Battle of Amiens (8th August, 1918) and the battles of the Hindenburg Line.

The foregoing is a summary of the fighting admirably described by Captain T. A. White in the following pages, from which every reader is certain to learn something, since no one knows all about the Great War.

The "Fighting Thirteenth" is a "family" history, intended to remind officers and men of all they went through and how they suffered adversity or gained victories in the tremendous struggle of 1914-19, but it also has a great historical value as a faithful record of the accomplishments of an Australian battalion. Further, it is a memorial to the work of our fallen comrades, and a record of traditions to be handed down to, and be an inspiration for, the 13th Battalion of the Citizen Forces.

The 13th formed portion of the famous 4th Brigade, organised and first commanded by Lieut.-General Sir John Monash, G.C.M.G., K.C.B., V.D., whose training and administration built an initial foundation so secure as to stand magnificently the supreme test of four years' campaigning. We can never forget the extent of our indebtedness to our Brigadier.

The Battalion enjoyed further good fortune in obtaining such an excellent start under its first C.O., Colonel Burnage, C.B., V.D., who so courageously guided us through our first baptism of fire. From the Anzac Landing until the moment of receiving his severe wound he set an example which influenced all ranks, and thus early established an ideal from which we later Commanding Officers derived constant inspiration.

The outstanding character in our history is Lieut.-Colonel H. W. Murray, V.C., C.M.G., D.S.O. (and bar), D.C.M. He also received the French Croix de Guerre. He was known to the men as "Mad Harry," but there was considerable method in his madness. No officer took more care to avoid losing men, and he took astonishing risks while personally reconnoitring, with the sole object of saving his men. A quick thinker in times of danger, he displayed extraordinary energy, resolution and courage. A Lance-Corporal at the Anzac Landing, his record of promotion and honours is one of the most brilliant in the British and Dominion Forces.

The Battalion was a large and happy family, a self-contained community, to an extent not realised outside the A.I.F. We had a doctor for our sick, a qualified dispenser, and men trained in first aid. The Medical Officer trained a squad in sanitation, also men whose duty it was to test the purity of the water supply. Our Supply Department included a butcher and a baker, although these were rarely required, and we had an excellent staff of cooks. Bootmakers mended and remodelled boots, and a tailor was kept busy at his machine altering and mending clothes. The watchmaker was fully employed, since every man had at least one watch. The barbers were busy men, shaving, hair-cutting and setting razors. We had a post office with a busy postman. Our Pioneers included carpenters, blacksmiths, painters, and handy-men of all kinds. At one time there was a shortage of solder, so we built a kiln and salvaged solder from all our meat and jam tins. The Signallers supplied us with a telephone service, or sent messages by cyclists or orderlies. We had our own Transport, which boasted a farrier, wheelwright, saddler, veterinary first-aid man, and grooms. Also an excellent band. We had our own police, and the Orderly Room was a Court of Justice. In the Orderly Room, too, were our records, and the staff there included an expert typist and stenographer. For a considerable time we had a chiropodist. Each new country we journeyed to provided us with an interpreter; also we had our own expert linguists, who were specially trained in the work of billeting. We possessed a branch of the Brigade Canteen, from which we purchased extras. We were more than fortunate in possessing our own Battalion Comforts Committee —our devoted lady helpers in Sydney. There were fire-piquets, which corresponded to a fire brigade, guard rooms, which represented the lock-up armourers, scouts, salvage men (the material salvaged represented many tens of thousands of pounds; concert artists, physical training instructors, and personnel for dealing with the prevention of casualties from enemy gas attacks. To some of the machine gunners was assigned the responsibility for anti-aircraft defence. We had sports organisers, and on several occasions there were attempts at a trench newspaper. The Orderly Room was our bank. When light railways existed we were even able to provide engine-drivers; and we often furnished miners for mining operations. A sign-writer was a useful man for notice boards. The officers censored the men's letters. Last, but not least, we had a Chaplain (Padre) who attended to our spiritual needs and buried our dead.

Thus the Battalion was everything to us. I remember Colonel Murray (then Company Commander) saying to a delinquent, in a surprised tone of voice: "You don't seem to realise we only live for the Battalion." Men coming back from leave or hospital would say: "It is like coming home."

The demeanour of the men was marked by a great confidence—in themselves, their comrades, and their leaders. Confidence was the result of the careful attention given by the officers to the welfare of their men; for instance, throughout the dreadful Winter of 1916-17 the 13th supplied two hot meals a day to the men in the most advanced trenches, and this despite the difficulties of snow, ice and mud.

The N.C.Os. and men were wonderful. Their unfailing cheerfulness in all times of difficulty or danger always strengthened the fortitude of the officers, who would have been unworthy indeed if their hearts had failed to respond to the devotion so evident in the men they commanded. An appeal to their honour was never made in vain; to remind them of the good name of the Battalion always sufficed to ensure good conduct.

The discipline of the Australians has often been adversely criticised, but they undoubtedly possessed the greatest soldierly quality, viz.: battle discipline.

In the 13th special efforts were made to explain forthcoming operations to all ranks; company and platoon commanders were frequently seen before an attack explaining the plan to their men by means of chalk on a barn door, or drawing a sketch in charcoal on the side of a house. This enabled the men to make full use of their initiative and intelligence, bringing success to their arms and honour to the race.

The "esprit de Corps" of the "Fighting Thirteenth" was real, and carefully fostered by every possible means throughout the war. It was early noticed that although the men were keen to make a great name for New South Wales, they were even more determined to make Australia famous. They charged, shouting, "Come on, Australia!" and died with the name of their country on their lips.

On behalf of the 13th Btn., I have great pleasure in expressing our deep gratitude to Captain T. A. White for writing this book, which he has undertaken as a labour of love, and on which he has sacrificed tremendous time and energy.

11th November, 1923.

J. M. A. DURRANT,
Lt.-Colonel.

INTRODUCTION.

IF one were to write the life of any individual hero of the 13th, naturally he could not deal with the splendidisms of the thousands of other members. So with a battalion history. To a reader from another unit it may seem that an undue share of the Allied victory is given to the 13th, or that the Battalion is made the centre of A.I.F. activities. Such is not the case. No member of the "Two Blues" but salutes as a token of the highest honor the colors of any unit of the A.I.F.

In his introduction to his splendid "Official History of Australia in the War," the gallant and able Bean says: "At the beginning of the war the British Army, small though it was, nevertheless by the tenacity of the retreat from Mons profoundly affected the course of the struggle. Similarly there were occasions at the end of the war when the Australian forces engaged as they were in the very centre of the conflict at one of its most critical stages, were not without a conspicuous influence upon the result."

So it was with the 13th. There were occasions when their initiative, gallantry and devotion to duty were such that they affected the movements of the whole 4th Division.

In common with several other battalions, the 13th throughout its history, among all ranks, aimed at being the finest battalion in the A.I.F. Its members never claimed that it was the finest, but they felt that their record, in or out of the line, in attack or defence, was second to none. And surely even so great a pride is justifiable. Consider the glorious names that are wreathed together in its laurels! The GALLIPOLI LANDING, ANZAC, POPE'S HILL, THE CHESSBOARD, BLOODY ANGLE, QUINN'S POST, AUSTRALIA VALLEY, HILL 60, THE EVACUATION, BOIS GRENIER, POZIERES, MOUQUET FARM, STORMY TRENCH, BULLECOURT, MESSINES, POLYGON WOOD, PASSCHENDAELE, YPRES, HOLLEBEKE, HEBUTERNE, VILLERS BRETONNEUX, HAMEL, EIGHTH OF AUGUST, LE VERGIEUR, HINDENBURG LINE. Consider the Battalion's wonderful list of heroes, including such a name as that most distinguished fighting soldier of the A.I.F., Lt.-Colonel Harry Murray, V.C., C.M.G., D.S.O. (and bar), D.C.M., also Croix de Guerre; and others like Sgt. Maurice V. Buckley, V.C., D.C.M.

But although its aim was so high and its record so splendid, the 13th is, and will always be, proud to be regarded as a typical Australian Battalion, proud that by "doing its bit," as told hereinafter, it helped to make the fame of the A.I.F., and in a smaller way that of the British Army, and that it helped to win the final hard-won victory.

Though typical, the 13th, like other battalions of the 4th Brigade, more perhaps than of any other Australian Brigade, had its own well-marked characteristics. The writer, like officers of the battalion with whom he discussed the matter and who recognised the difference, is unable to define these characteristics. It was remarked on several occasions by Colonels Durrant and Marks. The former once asked us our opinions as to what the differences really were and the reasons for them. Murray replied: "I can't just say what the differences really are, or why, but march a section of each battalion of the brigade before me with their color-patches off, and I'll guarantee to tell the battalion they belong to." And we all agreed with him. The difference was more noticeable among the officers of the 4th Training Battalion, where one found half-a-dozen of each battalion of the brigade in close contact.

The reasons for the differences were most probably geographical, the 13th belonging to New South Wales, the 14th to Victoria, the 15th to Queensland and Tasmania, and the 16th to South and Western Australia, for it could be noticed in groups of reinforcements newly arrived from Australia; but the influence of the Commanding Officers on Gallipoli and in France accentuated the geographical differences. Where could one find among four strong personalities greater differences than among Colonels Durrant, Peck, McSharry and Brockman, taking for example the four Commanders at any special time? It is interesting to note that the average age of these four C.Os. was only 30.

Unfortunately, three years passed after the Armistice without any attempt being made to collect data for this history. No one felt that it was his job, and those who did think about it at all felt that our late gallant and respected C.O., Col. D. G. Marks, was the one to write our story, he having been an Active Service 13th officer from the formation of the battalion to the Armistice. Col. Marks certainly thought and spoke seriously either of writing the history himself or of collaborating with others in the matter. He had asked for and had been promised the valuable assistance of Col. J. M. A. Durrant, but his sad and untimely death on the 25th of January, 1920, while gallantly attempting to rescue a drowning woman from the waves at Palm Beach, left the matter in the air for almost the next two years.

Col. A. S. Allen, D.S.O., the last C.O. of the battalion, who became C.O. of the 13th Regiment A.M.F. on his discharge from the A.I.F., feeling that it would be good for the young Australians of this regiment, who were being trained for the defence of their country, to know the story of their parent battalion, then moved and asked the author to take it in hand, and Lt. B. Blythman to convene a meeting of ex-members of the Battalion to form a committee as required by Commonwealth Regulations before the use of official documents would be granted.

The author, a very humble member of the 13th, refused the honor of becoming the battalion historian, believing there were several others with stronger claims to the appointment. However, the committee was unanimous in its wish that he should accept the position.

The committee does not desire this history from any sense of self-glorification. It is felt that it is due to the relatives of our fallen and maimed comrades to place on record the work of their loved ones; it is due to the future members of the 13th Regiment to have a record of the doings of their parent battalion to look to as an example of what Australians were during those years of the world's agony.

It is not for the purpose of making "Prussians" of our future citizens, so much as to show them the horrors Prussianism wrought upon the civilised world, and how decent, dutiful, loyal Britishers were able not only to stand against, but to defeat Prussianism utterly.

Gen. S. C. E. HERRING, C.M.G., D.S.O.,
(C. de G., L. d'H.).
First C.O. of our Sister Battalion—the 45th.

CONTENTS.

Chapter.		Page.
	Foreword	4
	Thanks	6
	Foreword	9
	Introduction	11
I.	The Call	15
II.	Overseas	21
III.	Egypt. Hard Training, Lemnos	23
IV.	Anzac	27
V.	Bloody Angle and Chessboard	32
VI.	May, 1915	37
VII.	Reserve Gully	43
VIII.	A Wonderful Night March	46
IX.	Australia Valley and Hill 60	49
X.	Durrant's Post and Sarpi Camp	52
XI.	The Evacuation	55
XII.	Ismailia, Moascar, Tel-el-Kebir, Serapeum	58
XIII.	Flanders, Bois Grenier	62
XIV.	Pozieres	64
XV.	Mouquet Farm	72
XVI.	Second Period up North, Voormezeele	77
XVII.	(A) Flers and Gueudecourt. ("The cruellest winter for fifty years, Monsieur")	80
XVIII.	(B) Christmas, 1916	82
XIX.	(C) Stormy Trench, Murray's V.C.	85
XX.	Bullecourt	91
XXI.	Messines, Ploegsteert, Gapaard	101
XXII.	Polygon Wood, Ypres, Passchendaele	107
XXIII.	A Miscellany. Winter Again	115
XXIV.	Hollebeke and the Canal Area	117
XXV.	Darkest Days. Hebuterne	120
XXVI.	Villers Bretonneux	132
XXVII.	Efficiency	139
XXVIII.	Hamel	142
XXIX.	A Happy Interlude	148
XXX.	The 8th August, 1918	149
XXXI.	The 23rd August	153
XXXII.	The 18th September, Le Verguier	155
XXXIII.	From Picquigny to Charleroi and Home	163
	Envoi	168

Chapter I.—The Call.

AUGUST, 1914, saw, on every road and track throughout Australia, serious men moving towards its capitals; trains moving citywards packed with men of all classes, conditions, trades, professions and religions. The city roads and trams carried the accumulated crowds towards the various military headquarters.

Victoria Barracks, Sydney, resembled a disturbed ant colony with its streams constantly hurrying in eagerly to volunteer, and after acceptance, many hurrying out again to make final arrangements to leave their businesses and families before entering camp a day or two later. Doctors by the score were examining the stripped bodies of men by the thousand, while clerks, newly pencilled, by the hundred wrote particulars as if their lives depended on the number of forms they could fill in in a given time, and Staff-Sergeants took charge of more men than they had ever dreamt of handling and showed them how to turn, stand to attention, stand at ease, and form fours in a rough way before marching them off to the Showground, Randwick, Kensington or Rosebery Racecourse.

The New Guinea Expedition was fitted out; the State's quota for the First Division, and complete Light Horse Regiments and other special units, was quickly obtained; and still volunteers came pouring in. It was the same in all the capitals. Too many volunteers for the 20,000 offered by our Commonwealth!

A 4th Brigade was decided on, and Colonel John Monash, V.D., approved by the Minister for Defence as its commander on the 12th September. New South Wales' quota was called the 13th Battalion. (See Appendix i.)

Had it been thought at the time that the volunteers would have been sufficient for a Second Division, and that the war would have lasted long enough for such division to be prepared and transported overseas, the 4th Brigade would not have been formed as a distinct unit, but as part of the Second Division.

So constant remained the rush of volunteers that the medical officers were more than particular in their examinations, and thousands who later on were eagerly accepted, were now rejected.

Still, because of General Bridges' anxiety that the 1st Division should sail within a month, many were accepted for that division who would have been postponed had they offered a little later.

Hence the men who were accepted in September, 1914, and assembled at Rosehill Racecourse (many of them from Rosebery Depot), first of all as four companies of reinforcements for the 1st Division, and then as the 13th Battalion, were among the pick of the biggest and healthiest Australians, and the 13th became known generally as the Battalion of Big Men. And, indeed, how splendid they looked drilling in their shirt sleeves or singlets, and later on, in dungarees and white hats, while awaiting their uniforms, although several from far out had no change of clothes for a fortnight, having, in anticipation of an immediate issue of uniform, brought nothing but what they stood in !

And how the Ordnance Stores Staff had to ransack their stores to find sufficient "outsizes" for the Battalion!

"Here's a bag of elevens!" someone would call out.

"Send them to Rosehill," was the curt reply.

"Half-a-dozen O.S. tunics!"

"Put them in that 13th Heap."

On arrival in Egypt the 13th Guards were looked upon by the Allied soldiers as giants, for, on several occasions they averaged well over 6 feet in height and 14 stone in weight.

Later on we often spoke of those early guards as what guards ought to be.

At Rosehill the 13th received its first Commanding Officer, Lieut.-Col. Granville John Burnage, V.D., of Newcastle. He had had meritorious Boer War experience.

Serious and organised training commenceed, and the Battalion gradually developed into a uniformed unit, commencing from the feet and working up, for boots were the first issue; then followed breeches and puttees, and, still later tunics, hats and caps and equipment.

Although the metamorphosis from civilian to soldier (in looks) took weeks, there was no gorging or sleepy chrysalis stage. Stew and bread for breakfast, bread and stew for dinner, and bread and marmalade for tea, prevented the desire for the former, while physical "jerks" and doubling an hour each morning before breakfast, parades from 8.45 to 5, with a three hour route-march often after tea, allowed little enough time to sleep after one's shaving, bathing and cleaning were done.

Later recruits grumbled at much shorter hours, but these early officers, N.C.Os., and men were so keen to get themselves thoroughly fit and trained that a 16-hour day was very often ended with cheerful singing and joking as they sardined themselves up to 23 into an ordinary bell-tent.

Even at Rosehill that company and regimental self-confidence which helped the Battalion so much in the serious times to follow was noticeable. Although many had never before seen a service rifle or a fixed bayonet, still, in things of active service value, the early 13th was soon the pride of its members of all ranks and their relatives, who every week-end, visited the camp loaded up with dainties for their soldier husbands, sons, sweethearts or brothers. But these strong and freedom-loving individuals were apt to take unwillingly to what they, in their ignorance of the value of many irksome details of the new military life for which they had voluntarily given up the freedom of the freest citizens of the world, believed to be unnecessary, or in which they could see no training benefit.

There were in Australia, comparatively speaking, very few officers who had learnt the art of commanding men. Some there were who had had commissions in the old regiments, on the Instructional Staff, or in the Senior Cadets. But all those given commissioned or non-com. rank in those early days took their duty so conscientiously that, even in the few cases where newly-acquired mannerisms or unconscious rank affectation, so earnestly cultivated from "What N.C.Os, Should Know," "Points for Platoon Commanders," etc., amused or irritated, the men good-naturedly regarded the sincerity as out-weighing everything else.

The battle discipline for which the Diggers were soon to become world-famous was acquired only on the fields of Gallipoli and France.

Among our original N.C.Os., at least one sergeant had never before seen a rifle. Another addressed his squad: "I'm supposed to give you chaps an hour's Fixing and Unfixing. Does anyone know anything about it?" Sergeant Laseron, an Original, in "From Australia to the Dardanelles," tells of a case in which a newly-formed company was asked, "Is there anyone here who would like to be a sergeant?" Our first R.S.M., H. MacDonald, had plenty to do indeed to train such raw material. So conscientious and efficient was his work that the results of it were noticeable even to the end of the Battalion's history. He conducted special classes for N.C.Os. at Rosehill and Liverpool, and ended each course by a three-days' severe practical test.

Having such a splendid start with big men, the Colonel determined to keep the standard up, and in this he was cordially assisted by Major Baxter, O.C., Depot, at Liverpool, to where the Battalion moved from Rosehill. On one occasion, when we wanted one man a hundred were paraded; on another 250 were selected from over 5000 in camp in order that the 13th might choose 80 from the selected. Major W. Ellis, our first Adjutant and then Second-in-Command, who did the choosing was as keen as the Colonel on getting the best stamp of men possible and on building them up to even greater health-efficiency. He it was who got Captain Cook-Russell, the best of our Physical Training Staff, to supervise our physical training and to train our officers and N.C.Os. in the work.

The 13th's standard of behaviour was also high, and any man failing to keep up to it was rejected. We also combed the Depot for the most suitable men for our Transport, Signals, Band, Machine-guns and Clerks.

The move from Rosehill to Liverpool was an agreeable one, for not only was Rosehill unhealthy as a camp, but we experienced so much wet weather while there, that hundreds developed the "Rosehill Cough." At Liverpool we had green fields, good weather, showers and swimming, and a thoroughly clean camp. Here, near the river, our first Pioneer Sergeant, W. T. Brown, built such an excellent incinerator that it was adopted as the standard, not only for the Camp, but, later on, at Broadmeadows, Heliopolis and Anzac. Also at Heliopolis officers of the Imperial staff, hearing that its fire never went out no matter how it rained, and that it burnt everything put into it, examined Sgt. Brown's incinerator and had it copied by many Imperial units. Sgt. Brown's work was an example of the splendid work of our Pioneers throughout our history. Inventors of less important things have received big rewards. Sgt. Brown's reward was the feeling of pride in work done efficiently.

After musketry training the Battalion fired practices at Randwick, and, again, men failing to reach the standard were changed for those who could satisfy the test.

Col. Monash, on his visit to Liverpool on 6th November, to inspect the 13th, expressed himself astonished and pleased beyond measure. Preparations for our move to Broadmeadows were then expedited, a small advance party in charge of the Adjutant, Captain J. M. A. Durrant, going across on 21st November.

The march out of the Battalion took place on the 23rd November. The Union Jack, presented to Col. Burnage for the Battalion by the Ulster Association of New South Wales at their annual banquet on the 22nd October, was taken to Melbourne, and after hanging in the vestibule of the "Ulysses" for the voyage, remained with the Battalion even on Gallipoli, whence it was returned to Newcastle, where it now hangs in the Cathedral. Our band was already one to be proud of. The instruments had been most generously and patriotically presented by Miss Harris, of "Littlebridge," Ultimo. The left-half of the Battalion had the misfortune to be thoroughly drenched by a terrific thunderstorm while waiting to entrain, and to them the journey was rather a miserable one. Still it is officially recorded that, on its departure from Liverpool, the 13th was a model of smartness and soldierly bearing. What pale civilian flabbiness there may have been in a few had given way to bronzed wiriness; drawling footsteps to elastic freedom; and pocketed hands had learnt to swing or hold rifles regularly.

Morning of the 24th gave wide views of the golden wheatfields of Eastern Riverina, and whistling engines brought farmers and their families as well as townspeople out to wave and shout "Good Luck!" Those who had gone to camp from these parts—for every district of the Mother State was represented in the 13th—were forced to impart information concerning wheats, soils, rainfall, amusements, etc., of the Riverina to those who had never before been over the range. Then the gardens and vineyards of the Murray came into view.

At Albury refreshments were provided by the ladies of the picturesque border town, after which the Alburians gave us an enthusiastic send-off.

Arriving at Broadmeadows, 10 miles north of Melbourne, just after a heavy downpour, we found mud everywhere; and the advanced party had not been able to obtain tents in time to erect them for all. By nightfall, however, we had them erected on the damp, muddy ground. Our early days here, and our last, were muddy and miserable, although the four weeks in between were generally hot and dusty. Few of the Original 13th have pleasant recollections of Broadmeadows.

The 14th turned out to see the 13th march in from the platform two miles away. Our men, although weary and still sodden from the Liverpool downpour, held up their heads and forced such a swinging soldier-like march that one of the 14th was compelled to ejaculate: "Poor blanky Kaiser!"

With such an unhealthy start, our first Medical Officer, Captain Shellshear, had a busier time than at Liverpool, and, in addition to ordinary camp ailments, we had a typhoid inoculation at Broadmeadows, which affected many severely. Captain Shellshear will not mind, I feel sure, a story or two against himself going into our history.

One of his earliest orderlies at Liverpool became very puffed-up with the importance of his job. After handing out pills and mixtures for a week under the Doc's orders, he began to feel that he knew as much as the doctor, and often had to be remonstrated with for having prescribed for serious cases, or cases that afterwards became serious, on his own. A broken collarbone was brought in one day and "His Nibs" took charge.

"Discolated 'umerous; nothing serious," he informed the party. "Lay down on yer abdomen an' I'll do the rest." The poor patient's roars brought the M.O. at the double. He found "His Nibs" astride his man with his arm screwed up behind his back. "A little painful, that's all; but I'll soon 'ave it back now," he was telling the man and his mates encouragingly. Shellshear found himself unwanted. "It's all right, sir; I can fix 'im." But Shellshear soon bundled him out. He had repeatedly wanted to get rid of "His Nibs," but didn't know how to

A

do it in the military. "His Nibs," however, did the trick himself. Still suffering from offended dignity, he had one of his own prescriptions sharply countermanded by the doctor next morning. He immediately reported at the Orderly Room and charged Captain Shellshear with a "Breach of Perfessional Ethiquets." "It's pure perfessional jealously," he told Captain Durrant. The latter found him another duty, to the great joy of the M.O.

Another day, Burnage saw a 13th man on Liverpool Station without authority. On being questioned he said he was ill and was going to Sydney to see a doctor.

"Why didn't you go to Captain Shellshear?" asked the Colonel.

"He's only a Medical Officer; I want to see a doctor."

While awaiting embarkation strenuous training was carried out, and a musketry course fired at Williamstown. On 17th December the brigade marched to, through and back from Melbourne, with all its First-Line Transport, the first time such a completely-equipped body had passed through any Australian city. The 4th Brigade had everything "almost to the last button." The Governor-General took our salute at Federal Parliament House. Although the Melbournites were naturally proud of the appearance of the 14th, representing their own State, their cheers and greetings were none the less hearty and cordial for the other battalions. Our band, under the baton of Sgt. P. Copp (selected in Melbourne as bandmaster by Durrant) was the band of the day. Our Pioneers looked terrifically efficient, carrying their polished axes in front of the band, and out transport was, without doubt, one of the finest any battalion ever had. Every man and horse had been carefully tested and selected by our First Transport Officer, Lieut. G. D. D. Macarthur, a member of the well-known station family of that name. "Mac." himself was a magnificent horseman—one of those "tall, lithe Australians," born in the saddle, and a past-master at trading, begging, borrowing or contriving to get the best horses in the brigade or division.

Bde. Order 37 referred to this march:

"The Governor-General was very much impressed by the condition, discipline and marching of the men of the 4th Brigade. Their physique and steadiness gave to the regiments the appearance of a corps of veterans."

In promulgating the above, the Brigadier desires to convey to all ranks his great satisfaction with the excellent turnout, the efficient execution of the March Orders in all details, and the fine spirit displayed by all.—(Signed) J. P. McGlinn."

Intense rivalry prevailed over the inter-battalion tug-of-war contests and great was the 13th's enthusiasm when our team won the Brigade Championship, and the cup we never received.

Whatever the 13th lacked, we never lacked coolness combined with a little bit of "hide." It was probably the first time we put it over the Brigadier. Lieut. Locke was Officer of the Guard, and, wanting a photo, had his guard at its very best. The photographer was just ready to snap when the sentry was heard: "Stand-by, the guard! Headquarters' car!" Locke hustled the photographer with his camera unceremoniously behind the tent and took post. It looked to Monash a perfect turn-out. He stopped his car and complimented the guard and Locke. "I have never known a better turn-out on such short notice," he added. And Locke and his guard didn't even smile—until afterwards.

On the night of the 21st December rain fell heavily, and, when the Battalion marched out of camp to entrain for Port Melbourne we walked through mud a foot deep at the main gate. This mud was singularly tenacious, for men were seen in Egypt, and even at Anzac, with Broadmeadows' mud marks still on their uniforms.

The train trip to the boat was marked by the enthusiastic manner in which the population turned out to bid farewell. Flags waved all along the route, and thousands congregated at the entrance to the wharf. Although a guard was placed as the troops began to file aboard, the crowd broke down all barriers and guard and police were helpless to prevent soldiers and relatives intermingling. We arrived on the wharf at 11 a.m., but it was 6 p.m. before all were aboard, and 7.30 before we moved out into the Bay. The evening meal, a big one, for no one had had anything to eat since the early hasty breakfast, was not over until 9.30. The C.O. and his officers then sat down to theirs.

We had taken four emergencies to the wharf, but finding none required, had detailed them to return to camp. They repeatedly attempted to board, but were refused admittance. Determined not to be left behind, they hired a boat, pulled out to the "Ulysses" and climbed aboard by ropes let down by mates. The weary essayed their hammocks early, roars of laughter greeting the clumsy attempts to get into them. Many watched the bright line of lights extending for miles along the shore for hours before seeking their "beds." Several were busy all night, for it was not till 5 a.m. on the 23rd that final arrangements were completed, and the "Ulysses" steered towards the Heads and the open sea.

The "Ulysses" (Captain Barber) was a 10,000-ton Blue Funnel liner, fitted up to carry troops. In addition to the 13th, she carried the 14th Bn., 4th Field Ambulance, 4th Bde. Hqrs., and a few details. Col Monash was O.C. Troops of the Fleet to accompany the "Ulysses," and Lt.-Col. Courtney of the 14th Bn. was O.C. Troops on the "Ulysses."

APPENDIX I. [Copy.]

BRIGADE ORDER No.1, by Col. John Monash, V.D.
17th September, 1914. Victoria Barracks, Melbourne.

(1) Composition of Brigade.—The following Units will be raised:—

    (a) Headquarters in 3rd Military District (Victoria).

    (b) 13th Battalion in 2nd Military District (N.S.W.).

    (c) 14th Battalion in 3rd Military District.

    (d) 15th Battalion, less 2 Companies, in 1st Military District (Q.).

    (e) G and H Companies, 15th Battalion, in 6th Military District.

    (f) 16th Battalion, less 3 Companies, in 5th Military District.

    (g) A, B, and C Companies of 16th Bn. in 4th Military District.

    (Note.—A battalion then contained 8 companies.)

2. The organisation, equipment and training of each of the above units will be carried out by the Senior Officer with the Unit. The question of concentration of the whole Brigade at Melbourne for training has not yet been decided.

3. Commanders of Units will, immediately upon appointment, proceed to the selection, for recommendation to the Brigadier, through the Commandant, of the whole of the Officers of the Unit. Especial care is to be taken to allocate officers to those duties for which they are most fitted.

5. Commanders of Units will act throughout considering the best interests of the Brigade as a whole before the interests of the Unit.

6. More will depend upon the judicious selection of officers than upon any other factor. Therefore, while not an unnecessary moment is to be lost, sufficient time is to be taken over this task to ensure that the recommendations shall be the very best under all the circumstances.

In Brigade Order No. 2, signed by Lt.-Col. J. P. McGlinn, as the first Brigade Major of the 4th Brigade, the appointment of officers for the battalions was placed in the hands of District Selection Committees by the Minister.

In "Amended Table as Affecting 4th Infantry Brigade, of 30th September, 1914, the 13th Battalion was detailed to supply the original unit of 32 officers and 991 other ranks, plus its first reinforcement of 1 officer and 99 others, and to concentrate at Melbourne as soon as its quota was complete.

APPENDIX II.

THE FIRST 4th BRIGADE LIST OF 13th OFFICERS.

C.O.: Lt.-Col. Granville John Burnage, V.D.

Second-in-Command: Major W M. Ellis.

Adjutant: Captain J. M. A. Durrant.

Q.M.: Lieut. F. V. Thompson.

Sig. Officer: Lieut. F. H. Faddy.

Transport Officer: Lieut. G. D. D. Macarthur

M.G.O.: Lieut. R. G. Legge.

M.O.: Captain C. Shellshear, A.A.M.C.

"A" Company: Captain J. N. Edmonds.
    Lieut. W. J. M. Locke.
    Lieut. R. H. Crowe.

"B" Company: Captain W. O. Brache.
    Lieut. C. B. Hopkins.
    Lieut. G. G. Gardiner.

"C" Company: Captain W. A. Forsythe.
    Lieut. H. Hartnell-Sinclair.
    Lieut. H. T. Watkins.

"D" Company: Captain R. G. E. Kellick.
    Lieut. A. F. Smith.
    Lieut. S. L. Perry.

"E" Company: Captain S. C. E. Herring.
    Lieut. F. M. Barton.
    Lieut. H. J. Salier.

"F" Company: Captain H Norton-Russell.
    Lieut. F. G. Granger.
    Lieut. G. W. Binnie.

"G" Company: Captain J. W. A. Simpson.
    Lieut. F. G. Wilson.
    Lieut. D. Marks.

"H" Company: Captain R. T. Hunt.
    Lieut. J. E. Lee.
    Lieut. K. A. Macleod.

Several Company changes of officers were made before sailing, but all the abovenamed sailed. The Colonel and Captain Forsythe had seen service before in South Africa and had there distinguished themselves. Captain Durrant was a permanent officer of the Administrative and Instructional Staff; Lieuts. Legge, Locke, Hopkins, Granger, Lee and MacLeod were young Duntroon graduates, all of whom proved themselves heroes and leaders; and most of the other officers had belonged to the Citizen Forces.

It will be seen that a Battalion then contained 8 companies, each of two half-companies. On arrival in Egypt these companies were grouped into four companies—A, B, C, and D, and each half-company became a platoon, the platoons being numbered from 1 to 16. Thus we became uniform with the new Imperial Army Battalions. At Colombo Col. Monash received a copy of this new establishment and immediately prepared his battalions for the change, so that we were ready for it before we reached Egypt.

Chapter II.—Overseas.

BEFORE sunset, although the sea was comparatively calm, many felt their first touch of seasickness. Be it remembered that, before enlistment, several of the 13th had never even seen the sea.

For some reason or other, the 14th Bn. rank and file, patronised the 13th. Their attitude caused a good deal of friction between the two units which later on became bosom friends. At the first assembly of officers the 14th withdrew themselves to the starboard side of the smokeroom, leaving the port to the 13th; which arrangement became the recognised habit for all subsequent meetings on the voyage. Later on, in France, the camaraderie among the Brigade members was such that all ranks of the four battalions mixed as freely together as men of the same platoon. This rivalry and ill-feeling had started at Broadmeadows, but it was greatly exaggerated by many.

The reasons for it were mainly: 1. Australians had not yet come to think as Australians, the pre-federation jealousy between Sydney and Melbourne being still alive. 2. The 14th, having been in the camp for two months, had flourishing regimental institutions, such as canteens and messes when the 13th arrived and had to pitch their tents on the bleak fields of Broadmeadows. We felt envious of the 14th's prosperity and comfort as well as of their crowds of visitors. 3. The "patronising air" on the part of the officers of the 14th, but this, also, was exaggerated.

By Christmas Day all had settled down to the new life and were in great heart. Very few were unable to enjoy the splendid dinner of roast pork, vegetables, plum pudding, fruit, tinned fruit, biscuits, nuts, cigars and cigarettes. Divine service was held in the morning, and a good concert in the evening, while our band gave a programme in the afternoon. Indeed, our band played at least every second day during the voyage. Copp's piccolo and Durrant's cornet solos always being special favorites.

"Australia Will be There" was then quite new, and to our band must be given the credit or blame not only of popularising it throughout the fleet to such an extent that everyone was constantly whistling, or humming it, but also of introducing it to the A.I.F. in Egypt. Sgt. Rogers' songs were the favorite vocal items.

At Albany, which we reached before daylight on the 28th, the Brigade waited in the Outer Harbour for the rest of the Convoy—19 transports in all—with a solitary submarine the AE2, nicknamed "The Baby," itself having to be towed by a transport, to guard it—a proof of the efficiency of the British Navy. It was here that the 13th and 14th became on slightly improved terms. The newness of cramped personal contact with strangers and the horribleness of seasickness began to disappear in spite of the very turbulent waters of Outer King George's Sound.

Then, at 8 a.m. on the 31st December, the "Ulysses," as part of the second great convoy carrying 10,500 Australians and 2,000 New Zealanders, set sail from Australia. The Australian ships of the convoy were: Ulysses, Ajama, Ayrshire, Vestala, Themistocles, Port Macquarie, Ceramic, Suevic, Persic, Berrima (towing AE2), Borda (assisting in towing AE2), Hobart, Boonah, Bakara, Boorara and Barunga. The New Zealand transports were Willochra, Verdala and Knight of the Garter.

The Ulysses, being the Flagship, was at the head of the centre line of the fleet, which was now arranged in three parallel lines with about a mile between lines and a mile between ships. The Convoy travelled at the speed of the slowest ships—about 10 knots. Commander Brewis was the Naval Officer-in-Charge of the Convoy, his headquarters being also on the Ulysses, where he was generally referred to as "Admiral Nelson," because of the telescope he constantly carried under his arm.

"C" Company will remember the amusement caused by one of their number sneezing his false teeth overboard at Albany, and "Gummy's" discomfort for the rest of the voyage. They will also remember, amongst others, the outbreak of ptomaine poisoning at Albany, and the second which followed shortly after, several being serious cases. These outbreaks made the men more critical of their food than they would perhaps otherwise have been, and before Colombo was reached many complaints were made.

No leave was given at Albany, but a great deal of intercommunication between ships and shore was necessary. Forsythe was O.C. Launch Communication Parties, and was specially mentioned in a letter by the Principal Transport Officer to Col. Monash "for the highly satisfactory manner in which he carried out his duties in very heavy seas."

On the 8th January a unique sight was presented to all. The whole fleet ceased steaming, and the "Ceramic," from the left, and the "Suevic" from the right, came quite close to the "Ulysses." In mid-ocean, in the unrippling doldrums, three huge ships close together, small boats in between, and as far as the eye could see a succession of big ships. And someone called out to the neighbouring ship, "Do you want a chief steward cheap?"

During the voyage, in spite of the crowded ships, physical training, games, boxing and wrestling, as well as lectures, were carried on. Several sports meetings were also held. Officers attended lectures regularly and gave them in their turn, while twice a week the N.C.Os. were lectured to by the Company Commanders in the Sergeants' Mess. Among the junior officers, Binnie shone out as a lecturer of wide reading and deep study. Col. Monash was generally regarded as equal to the finest military lecturer Australia possessed. After his first lecture—on Reconnaissance—all felt he had set a standard to be aspired to. Forsythe wrote: "I have never in my 20 years' experience met an officer who could lecture as effectively as he. It was a distinct pleasure to listen to him."

Before sailing, Burnage had got Durrant to spend £30 on text-books and instructive devices such as signalling cards, landscape targets, aiming targets, and so our battalion library was the best in the fleet. Lieuts. Binnie and Barton were our librarians. This material was splendid for Officers, N.C.Os., and thoughtful men, and helped considerably to make the six-weeks' voyage less weary. "The Defence of Duffers' Drift" was studied and discussed by all with great interest. A big supply of dummy cartridges enabled all to get that practice in rapid loading for which we remained famous throughout our history, and which enabled us, perhaps as much as anything else, to retain our precarious advanced positions at various critical times on Gallipoli.

At sports tugs-of-war were generally well contested, but blindfold boxing created most amusement. For the latter, one competitor arranged with a mate to instruct him. Col Monash was a most interested spectator and was standing well in front, when "One yard front! Low!" was heard. The blind boxer lashed out mightily as instructed, and caught the Colonel fair in his stomach. We wondered what he would say when the boxer appeared later for his trophy, but he pretended to have forgotten it.

Apart from several wireless alarms concerning enemy cruisers, the most definite of which proved, after much excitement and a threatened attack by "The Baby," to be an Indian transport also suspicious of us, the voyage was uneventful. At Colombo, reached early on the 13th January, no official leave was granted, but 200 from the fleet took French leave and got ashore by the most hazardous means, such as climbing down anchor-chains on to native boats. Twenty of these were still ashore when the fleet sailed the next day; so piquets were left to collect them. By sunset the majority had been rounded up and the "Ulysses" weighed anchor, but waited outside the breakwater until daylight of the 15th for the last party of the "scrags" to be brought aboard. According to the numbers breaking ship, the 13th proved itself to be the best disciplined unit in the fleet. Here again Forsythe was mentioned by the P.T.O. in orders for his work as O.C. of a launch. "He had been on duty for 30 hours without a meal, and, although surrounded by distractions, gave absolute attention to his work, kept his boat ready at all times, carrying out his duty in a thorough, steady and soldier-like manner."

The 23rd was spent at anchor several miles off Aden, and Suez reached on the 28th. Here all day and night the boats with bridges flour-bagged with 200lb. bags of flour for barricades, the Brigade acted as Reserve for the British defending the Canal against a Turkish attack. On the 29th, in the Canal, crowds of British war vessels, transports, batteries, encampments, Indian troops and New Zealanders were passed, cheery greetings being extended to and by all, the New Zealanders performing a war-dance in our honor. Near El Kantara the first actual "scrap" even seen by most Australians was witnessed in the distance by a few from the bridge.

At Port Said the "Ulysses' anchored near the monument of the famous Canal engineer, de Lesseps, but during the night sailed for Alexandria, which was reached at 5 p.m. on Sunday, 31st January.

The next day the Battalion entrained for Heliopolis, whence a most tiresome two-mile march across the desert brought the dusty, tired, sea-weak Battalion to Aerodrome Camp. Here the 4th Brigade became part of the shortly-to-be famous New Zealand and Australian Division, which consisted of the N.Z. Inf. Bde., N.Z. Mtd. Rifle Bde., First Australian L.H. Bde., and our own 4th Bde., the whole under the command of General Godley.

Chapter III.—Egypt. Hard Training. Lemnos.

AERODROME CAMP was situated a short distance from Heliopolis, a new town in the irrigated area on the fringe of the desert, about five miles S.E. of Cairo. The Palace Hotel, a huge, wonderful building which had been erected with the intention of making Heliopolis a second Monte Carlo, was used as an Australian hospital.

After reorganising into a Headquarters and four Companies by amalgamating "A" and "H," "B" and "G," "C" and "F," "D" and "E," under the respective commands of Major Edmonds, Captains Brache, Forsythe and Herring, and equipping and a week's light training, the Brigade was taken on its first desert march, and during smoke-ho, met their first tribe of "Gypo" camp-followers, who seemed to spring from nowhere all at once with loud, wailing cries of "Eggs is cook! Lemonata! Oringhes!" producing extraordinary stores of boiled eggs, fruit, cakes and drinks from the folds of their voluminous dirty garments. Then came bivouacs, more strenuous field training and manoeuvres, using ball cartridges in conjunction with artillery.

On March 3rd eventuated "Corporal X's Battle." It was a big field day in which the New Zealanders, Australians and Lancashires took part, the 13th covering 22 miles between 1 and 8 p.m. Our "Corporal X," possessed of a wonderful imagination, wrote home to Australia a startlingly realistic description of this "battle," describing gruesomely scenes of death and the screams and moans of the wounded. It was published in Australia, and caused much amusement in the Brigade when copies of the papers relating it reached Gallipoli.

So keenly did all hands take to this serious and extremely arduous training that on March 9th Monash proudly said that the 4th Brigade was fit to take its place with troops of much longer training; and Bean reports it as taking part in manoeuvres with the whole Division at a time when the 1st Division was still methodically pursuing its Brigade training. This was due, in addition to the keenness of all, to the ability and leadership qualities of Monash, who, even so early, became noted for "the methodical, painstaking thoroughness with which he worked out every detail of the activities of his brigade, and the extreme lucidity with which he could explain to his officers any plan of coming operations."

An interesting event took place on March 16th. For some reason the Battalion's pay was withheld from Thursday to Saturday, although the other battalions were paid. So keen was the C.O. on the training, in which he never spared himself, that he probably felt that it was better to pay on the Saturday, and give those whom the spending of the pay affected, Sunday to get over it, instead of having "after-pay slackness" on a week-day. Although training from 2 a.m. to 2 p.m. during which they marched 19 miles, 200 of the Battalion men fell in and marched in an orderly manner to Brigade Headquarters where its deputation, whose speaker was Corporal Boccard, laid the matter before the Brigadier. (Corporal Boccard later on received his commission for splendid service. He comes prominently into our history.)

On 22nd March our Division was inspected at Zeitoun by General Godley and Sir Henry McMahon, High Commissioner for Egypt, and General Maxwell, C.-in-C. of the Force in Egypt. Sir Henry wrote: "I desire to convey to General Godley my hearty congratulations on the splendid appearance, physique, equipment and efficiency of the N.Z. and A. Division under his command, whom I had the honor to inspect to-day. It was a source of both pleasure and pride to see so magnificent an addition to the Army of the Empire." General Maxwell added: "Personally I fully endorse Sir Henry's remarks and congratulate you and the Division under your command on the high state of efficiency they have attained. I feel confident that, when called on—as they shortly will be—they will maintain the fighting spirit of their race and worthily maintain the reputation of New Zealand and Australia." General Godley added: "I am indeed proud to have the honor of commanding a body of men of whom such a high opinion is formed by those most qualified to judge."

On March 29th Sir Ian Hamilton, accompanied by General Birdwood, reviewed the Division during one of those excruciating duststorms in which vigorous training was often carried out, and their congratulations were equally flattering. Egypt and the hardest of training had already left their marks on all. Bronzed and fit, and, as far as their knowledge of warfare went, trained to the minute. Route marches of over 20 miles, added to open warfare stunts or trench digging, were now common and were generally ended by 7 to 10 miles of whistling and singing until met by the band. Two landmarks will for ever remain in the memory of those trained at Heliopolis—No. 2 and No. 3 Towers on the Suez Road, about three miles apart.

The roughest trials experienced by our transport in the East were on that long route march through El Marg to Plantation of Princess Nemat Hanem. Lieut. Macarthur was never more worried, for he soon found that our travelling cookers would not stand such rough country. They were different from the cookers we had later. But although tea was scantier than it would otherwise have been, the whole unit gave itself up whole-heartedly to the enjoyment of a moonlight concert amid the palm trees. Then a short bivouac, an early substantial breakfast, and a long but cheery march back to camp. It was Good Friday, the day of the exaggerated "Wozzer Riot."

In this notorious incident only a few actually participated, there soon being, however, many interested spectators. It will probably never be known who actually started the riot, but it is thought that a few wild spirits—Australian, New Zealand or Imperial—in retaliation for injury, commenced to burn the furniture in one of the worst hells in that vile Wozzer area, near Shepheard's. The fire and excitement soon spread; the Egyptian Fire Brigade turned out, their hoses were cut or diverted, military police intervened, a few shots were fired and excitement became intense before the area was gradually cleared by the town piquet of East Lancs. and a troop of our own Light Horse.

Although the 13th took no part in this riot, a story was told of one well-known character who was enjoying the spraying of a cut hose. A fire officer came up in great anger and ordered the crowd back. "Don't you interfere with MY hoses!" he roared.

"Well, don't you interfere with OUR fire!" retorted our stalwart.

The idea that prevailed for a while in Australia that our troops lost their self-respect in Cairo was absolutely erroneous. It was only to be expected that some of the weakest or most riotous spirits should at times go too far, and that certain wasters should fulfil their destiny, but the vast majority showed themselves at all times the men their people at home desired they should be.

While trench digging near the Ostrich Farm at Helmieh on April 3rd, the 13th dug into a very ancient and forgotten cemetery and found bones and trinkets in any quantity, one man receiving £50 for a scarab.

We soon now began to get busy about our Color Patches, although there was a confusion for a while. Bde. Order No. 6, issued at Melbourne on November 17th, read: The Colors for the 4th Infantry Bde. will be Navy Blue. Flags for Battalions will therefore be: All Battalions:—Lower half, Navy Blue. 13th Battalion—Upper half Black; 14th Battalion—Upper half Yellow; 15th Battalion—Upper half Brown; 16th Battalion—Upper half White. These flags, 9 inches by 9 inches, are to be provided regimentally for identifying camp lines, transport, etc.

The black and navy blue of the 13th were so much alike after a little use that our flags were often mistaken for those of Brigade Headquarters; hence, in Egypt, Monash asked Burnage to suggest something more suitable. "Let us have light blue over the Navy, the New South Wales Sport color that has so often been victorious in hard-fought contests," suggested Durrant. It was agreed to, and the Two Blues quickly became endeared to the 13th. This change was one reason why the 4th Brigade color system was somewhat different from that of the others. There was another interesting reason. The second battalion in each Brigade should have had its upper half yellow like the 14th, the second battalion of the 4th Brigade, but when a sudden demand came in Egypt for colors for the whole of the A.I.F., Colonel Courtney, who never let the grass grow under his feet in matters of attention to the smart appearance of his battalion, sent immediately into Cairo for enough yellow not only for his men, but also for flags for lines, which soon put all in mind of masses of golden Australian wattle as they waved in the breeze. When the second battalions of other Brigades sent for their yellow there was none left in Cairo, and they had to take purple; black, purple, brown and white becoming the battalion colors of those Brigades instead of black, yellow, brown and white, as followed in 4th Bde. Orders of November 17th, 1914. Hence other Brigades differ from the 4th, not the 4th from them. Bde. Order No. 114, of 19/3/1915, contains:—

FLAGS.—Approval is given for the alteration of the 13th Bn. colors from black over navy blue to light blue over navy blue.

Bde. Order 134, of 31/3/1915, contains:—

HEADDRESS—PATCHES, NZA. 1860.—Approval has been given by Divisional Headquarters for the wearing of distinguishing "Patches" by units of this Brigade.

The patches will be rectangular in shape and of dimension 2½ inches by 1¼ over all, and, where two colors are involved, half the area of the patch will be allotted to each color. The patches will be worn on the left side of the capband or hatband."

This was altered in Bde. Order 145, which reads:—

DISTINGUISHING PATCHES.—(a) The wearing of same on caps or hats is suspended until further orders. (b) The G.O.C. Division has approved of shoulder badges being worn as per samples recently issued to officers commanding Brigade units.

Hence all soon had their soon-to-be-beloved-and-honored patches on their upper arms where they remained throughout our history, although, at first, they were slightly higher on the sleeve than later.

The Khamsin of the second week in April, which moved sand in great drifts and blew it into everything we possessed, made all wish more than ever to get out of Egypt with its heat, dirt and flies, to where something real was doing. Furphies had been frequent for weeks, but now came more definite rumors than previous ones until, on 8th April, 2 officers and 49 other ranks marched out en route for Alexandria to embark on the "Osmanieh." On the 10th "A" Coy. (6 officers and 218 other ranks) left to embark on the "Seeangbee," their send-off being marked by surges of cheering, which reflected the surges of pride and sentiment that arose in their thrown-out chests as the band struck up. Enthusiasm began to grow until it reached fever heat on Sunday, 11th, on the evening of which the Battalion marched out of camp to entrain at Pont de Koubbeh. The men had enlisted enthusiastically, had marched out of Liverpool even more enthusiastically; the embarkation at Melbourne, arrival in Egypt, each step had meant an extra wave of enthusiasm; but the happy satisfied smiles, the glowing cheeks and sparkling eyes, the springy swinging march and the quickening pulses that came with that final "Quick march!" at Heliopolis showed all to be filled with an intenser enthusiasm than ever. Not one slow on parade, not one but feared something might happen to postpone this march-out for an unknown destination. Some slipped out of hospital and risked a complete breakdown of their bodies so enfeebled with Egyptian illnesses, to go with their cobbers. The route was lined by cheering Australians, New Zealanders and Tommies, and volume on volume of cheering warned the German and Turk spies that abounded in Egypt of the spirit of the men their nations were so soon to meet.

The 12th was spent in the worst and dirtiest accommodation imaginable on a wharf at Alexandria. Clothes, packs and skin were blackened, and eyes irritated in that constant shower of coaldust in which the Battalion not only spent the day, but bivouacked all night. But "Who cares?" cheerfully questioned one after another. "It's nothing to the Big War." The clean Battalion of white men that had marched out from Heliopolis on the night of the 11th looked like a battalion of big coolies as daylight on the 13th enabled them to see one another. And the "Ascot," that night-marish old iron tramp on which the Battalion lived for the next 12 days, sleeping and living on an iron deck with two decks of horses above them, with undodgeable crevices through which filthy stable water poured; with Dago stokers too lazy, even at the commencement of the voyage, to get more than five knots out of her, and so indolent and insolent that the men unanimously volunteered to bundle them out and take their places, which was allowed when, six hours out, the engines ceased working. With these new stokers the speed was improved to over seven knots, and on the 15th Rhodes, with its Colossi was seen on the right, and Karpathos on the left. Some excitement and a change of route were caused the next day by rumors of a Turkish destroyer in the vicinity, and that the "Manitou" ahead of us had been attacked. We crossed towards Greece and sailed along the mainland, passing Skyro, with its famous Mt. Olympus on the right. In darkness the boat felt its way until, at daylight, a pilot from Lemnos came aboard and took us through the boom into Port Mudros. We were away from the dirt, flies and smells of Egypt.

"A" had been there since the 14th and living well, their food being so excellent that troops on adjoining ships used to present arms to their mess-orderlies carrying the steaming dinners along the deck. What a contrast to the food on the Ascot!

The troops had never seen so many warships of all kinds and transports as were in Mudros, for, in addition to those moving in and out, about 150 vessels were at anchor. Of the warships there were about a dozen British, several French, and one Russian, not counting the multitude of destroyers and submarines. The transports carried the 29th (Imperial) Division, the Australian Division, the N.Z. and A. Division and a French Division.

After landing for an enjoyable swimming parade on the 19th, the next four days were spent in boat-drill and practising descending rope ladders not only in full equipment, but with extra loads of iron-rations (Bully and hard biscuits), and small bundles of firewood. It was heavy and dizzy work but the spirit with which one and all entered into it made them wonderfully proficient within two days.

Then came Birdwood's letter to all:

"Officers and Men.—In conjunction with the Navy, we are about to undertake one of the most difficult tasks any soldier can be called on to perform, and a problem which has puzzled many soldiers for years past. That we will succeed, I have no doubt, simply because I know your full determination to do so. . . Before we start, there are one or two points which I must impress on all, and I most sincerely beg every single man to listen attentively and take these to heart.

"We are going to have a real hard and rough time of it until, at all events, we have turned the enemy out of our first objective. Hard, rough times none of us mind, but to get through them successfully we must always keep before us the following facts: Every possible endeavor will be made to bring up transport as often as possible; but the country whither we are bound is very difficult and we may not be able to get our wagons anywhere near us for days; so men must not think their wants have been neglected if they do not get all they want. On landing it will be necessary for every individual to carry with him all his requirements in food and clothing for three days. Remember then that it is essential for everyone to take the very greatest care, not only of food, but of ammunition, replenishment of which will be very difficult. Men are liable to throw away their food the first day out and to finish their water as soon as they start marching. If you do this we can hardly hope for success, as unfed men cannot fight, and you must make an effort to try and refrain from starting on your water until quite late in the day.—W. Birdwood."

Also a Special Force Order:—

"Soldiers of France and of the King.—Before us lies an adventure unprecedented in modern war. Together with our comrades of the Fleet we are about to force a landing upon an open beach in face of positions which have been vaunted by our enemies as impregnable. The landing will be made good by the help of God and the Navy; the position will be stormed and the war brought one step nearer to a glorious close.

" 'Remember,' said Lord Kitchener, when bidding adieu to your Commander; 'Remember once you set foot upon the Gallipoli Peninsula, you must fight the thing through to a finish. The whole world will be watching our progress. Let us prove ourselves worthy of the great feat of arms entrusted to us.—Ian Hamilton."

And Operation Order No. 1 by Col. John Monash:—

"H.M.T. Seangchoon, 22/4/1915:

1. Very Secret.—Information.—Enemy reported on Kilid Bahr Plateau and in neighbourhood of Anafarta and Maidos. British Division lands near Cape Helles; Australian Division lands between Kaba Tepe and Fisherman's hut.

2. Intention.—To land between Kaba Tepe and Fisherman's Hut immediately after the New Zealand Infantry Brigade, and to concentrate the Brigade.

3. The actual operation connected with the landing will be carried out by O. C. Troops on the several transports. This will be done under Naval control.

4. Preparations.—Each man armed with rifle, carries 200 rounds. All ranks carry food for three days. Each N.C.O. and man carries fuel. Water bottles filled are to strapped to back of pack. Caps to be worn. Machine guns and parts to be carried by hand or on biers. Three thousand five hundred rounds with each machine-gun. Picks and shovels to be distributed equally to platoons in handy bundles, points of picks to be protected. Warn each one to conserve food and water. Charge magazines, close cut-offs, and put safety-catches "on."

5. Passage from Ship.—An Officer or N.C.O. must be in charge of each boat. Perfect silence in boats. After personnel in boat is complete and seated, packs to be loosened and shoulder-straps unbuttoned. Rifles to be held loose in hands. Shoulder-straps to be rebuttoned, and packs made fast just prior to beaching of boats. All personnel in boat to remain seated until ordered to leave boat. Last two men in each boat to gather up and take ashore any ammunition dropped from pouches or bandoliers.

6. Action on Landing.—Distribute entrenching tools so that each platoon has fair share. Assemble by companies facing inland. If under fire lie down and wait. If under artillery fire form into small columns well dispersed in depth and laterlly and lie down."

On the 24th the First Division quietly sailed for the open sea again, while we finished the day with a band concert, after which the officers held a smoke concert.

Chapter IV.—Anzac.

DAWN, 25th April, 1915.—Ominous and thrilling sounds in the distance. All knew that their First Division mates were in it, and became impatient to join them. It seemed an age until 10.40 when the 13th steered for the open sea and the sound of guns. "A" Coy. had sailed on the "Seeanbee" at 6. Passing Cape Helles the battle in progress there was plainly visible, as also was the shelling of the village of Sedd-el-Bahr. At 4.30 p.m. anchor was cast off Anzac Cove and all strained eyes shorewards until nightfall. On all sides were battleships bombarding the distant hills; nearer in towards the shore were transports discharging their troops into destroyers, which then darted towards the shore to discharge the men into rowing-boats. Shells were bursting around and over the vessels and boats, while the crackling of machine-guns and rifles could be plainly heard.

At 9.30 p.m. destroyers came alongside to take off "B" and "C" Coys, "D" and "A" landing early next morning. In the dark loaded men climbed down the gangways and unsteady ladders, feeling uncomfortable in spite of their practice, until they felt their legs gripped by the strong and friendly hands of the sailors. As each destroyer received its complement it rushed shorewards and soon came within range of the enemy bullets. Nearer the beach the men climbed into the boats and were towed by launches or rowed to the shore, several being wounded and a few killed both on the destroyers and in the boats. The wonderfully cool and business-like way in which these youthful British sailors went to and fro between the destroyers and the beach instantly won the never-to-be-forgotten admiration of the Australians.

The rendezvous of the Battalion was on the slope of Ari Burnu, whence, at daybreak next morning, loaded up with extras, and wet with dismal rain that thad been falling since midnight, they moved in file on Monash Valley. Gen. MacLagan pointed out the position and asked Burnage to fill the gaps between him and Russell's Top. The 13th was now in the thick of the fight, passing scores of dead and wounded Australians and New Zealanders, and encountering plenty of shrapnel and bullets. Part of "B" was detailed early to go to the right to the assistance of a hard-pressed post—Sgt. G. Knox doing magnificent work—and Lt. Perry and a platoon to go as escort to a Mountain Battery out on the right, but the Battery had disappeared; so Perry reported back immediately. Perry's fine leadership qualities—especially his care for his men—had already marked him as one for rapid promotion, which his consistent gallantry and untiring energy hastened. Bn. Headquarters were established at Pope's Hill, that commanding bulwark at the head of Monash Valley, the defence and fortifying of which we shared with the 16th Battalion. Burnage himself placed the men in their firing positions here. Forsythe took his Company, as ordered by the Colonel, into what became Quinn's Post, scaling the cliffs and advancing as far as possible, which was, indeed, but a few yards after the top was reached. Herring was also sent there, but, not being urgently required at the time he was ordered on to Russell's Top, leaving Marks of his Coy. with part of his platoon with Forsythe. There was a serious gap in the line between the remnants of Col. Braund's troops on Walker's Ridge and Russell's Top, and the 16th Bn., under Col. Pope on Pope's Hill, and from this gap the enemy were shooting the troops at and on the right of Quinn's Post in the back. Herring was ordered to fill this gap by connecting Braund's right with Pope's left. "D" thereupon climbed the steep, exposed sides of Russell's opposite Pope's under a desultory fire, losing a dozen men, including the well-known and popular Sgt. Morrison (an ex-Major of the Imperial Army, who had enlisted as a private in our A.I.F., and a veteran of the South African war), who died of his wounds received while placing his men in greater safety. On the top of Russell's "D" found themselves in a thick, stunted prickly scrub, but could see no Turks, although under a heavy fire. They advanced under a lead shower from front and right, losing heavily but seeing no New Zealanders to connect up with. Herring's information was very vague, and his map, like all early Gallipoli maps, of little use. Spreading out and lying down in the scrub his men found bullets coming from all directions, and increasing in volume each minute, especially when machine guns from Baby 700 began to bark into their front as well, and others to enfilade them from the Chessboard. Bullets reached even those hugging the ground. "D" was well and truly in the air. Herring's gallant Signaller, Simpson, in spite of the tremendous fusillade he drew on himself waved his flags to send back their position, and read the orders repeated by a second Signaller, also under fire, to retire, which Herring did, after seeing his wounded safe, although there was no need to do so for every wounded man had mates who would never dream of leaving him behind.

After retiring over a furlong, "D" came in touch with Braund's troops at the junction of Russell's Top and Walker's Ridge, where they had had, and were soon again to have, a most desperate time, the Turks constantly sending reinforcements to their positions on the Nek and the Chessboard. It was a miracle that any of "D," who had advanced right on to the Nek, ever got back, especially as, when retiring, shrapnel showers were added to the bullets. They now began to dig in line with Braund's 2nd Bn. and New Zealanders, and dug and fought all day long without remembering that they had had nothing to eat. [Map next page.]

During the morning the swarms of Turks coming down Baby 700 were shelled by our warships, including "Queen Elizabeth" and "Queen," which caused them to break up into small parties of threes and fours at wide intervals, and to advance these driblets down in short rushes to minimise losses. In this way, in spite of heavy casualties they soon became overwhelming on the Nek and Chessboard. Then several of our own shells fell among "D," upon which being signalled to the "Queen" she ceased shelling altogether, in spite of repeated requests for aid, there being a misunderstanding about the signals. A few hours later the Turks commenced a tremendous rush down Baby 700. A single shell from one of "Big Lizzie's" 15in. guns broke the rush up into driblets as before, which delayed them somewhat, but soon they were so overwhelming in the scrub in "D" Coy's. front that Braund sent some of his tired 2nd. Bn. to support us. He was also sending a Coy. of New Zealanders, but, before they reached the position they met the thinned platoons of the 2nd retiring from the exposed Top where no one could live long in such a murderous fire as was then churning the ground. To conform with them the 13th were likewise retiring. When "D" reached Monash Valley it was a sadly-depleted company. Lt. F. G. Wilson, who, with part of "B," had accompanied Herring, had been killed while setting a glorious example. "B" and "C" had had as severe a time as "D," although not so strenuous perhaps. All day long men were losing cobbers they had learnt to love so much since those seemingly far-off days at Rosehill and Liverpool. Stretcher-bearers were kept busy, and, without exception, proved themselves magnificent. At times the noise was deafening. Orders of the most contradictory nature came along from both flanks, and worried officers and men alike. One officer of the First Brigade, utterly worn out and unnerved by thirty hours' close contact with the enemy, continually stood upon a conspicuous point near "C" Coy., and, waving two revolvers shouted, "Five rounds rapid, and charge!" For hours he led a charmed life. During the day Lt. Legge and his machine-gunners greatly distinguished themselves, especially from their position on the top of Pope's, Legge himself being the first to get there. This gallant young officer had as splendid a body of machine-gunners as ever possessed by the A.I.F.—N.C.Os. and men who were a constant source of admiration and inspiration to all near them. The stories of Legge's gunners on Gallipoli would make an inspiring volume in themselves. Lackenby, Eccles, Palin, A. and W. Walsh, Chapman, Maiden, Veness, Pontin, Clasper, Markillie, Wilson, Brinsmead, Lynch, Kirkland, James, Williams, Maher, Cox, Henwood, Olsen, Harris and J. Murray were all heroes. Many paid the full price, many gained high distinctions; all did their duty gallantly. Legge and Harry Murray were in their right place as officers of such a renowned section

Night brought no respite, for every now and again the digging was interrupted to "Stand-to!" Officers and men alike dug and used rifles. All preferred digging because of the intense cold—cold that was felt the more after the desert of Egypt, and in their scanty attire, for all packs and greatcoats had been left near the Beach. All through the night hosts of snipers crept close, and there was no moment when a bullet would not ping from some unexpected quarter. Turks were even captured in our trenches, fighting until overcome, expecting a brutal death if captured. Two brothers, E. and Hugo Cullen, were conspicuously splendid that day. Both are buried on Gallipoli.

The arrival of "A" Coy. on the right of Pope's next morning was a welcome strengthening to the wearied troops there. All the 13th were now face to face with the enemy and their strenuous training being tested.

During the night the firing became not only intenser, but closer, both sides striving to entrench within forty yards of one another on the same narrow ridge; and our positions were so precarious that the enemy needed only to drive our thin line back a few yards—"C" only five—in order to hurl us over into the valley. But our men were so solid, and our officers of the stamp of most of the Originals, so splendid, that every Turkish attempt was heavily repulsed.

So steep were the cliffs behind us that inplaces men had to use ropes to climb them and the Valley was so commanded by them that the loss of even one post would have been disaster to all the troops in it. Before daybreak Turks behind us, whither they had crept in the dark, sent messages to cease fire, as the British and French from Cape Helles were in our front. Then orders came that the troops on our left front were Indians and we were not to fire on them. Thus many a Turk from his picked position got his shot in first and fatally. Burnage, however, saw that they were Turks, and kept his men firing.

From dawn on the 27th until long after dark the Turks continued their heavy fire and their massing in the dead ground in our front, and, in addition to a few determined assaults, continually threatened attack. Early in the morning half of No. 3 Platoon reinforced the extreme left of Pope's, the now critical apex of the whole front line of Anzac, and an extremely unhealthy position; and here they acquitted themselves gloriously.

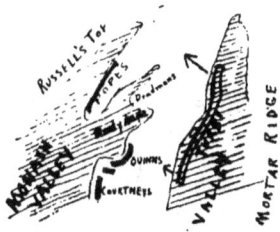

All day the 13th also, like the Turks, threatened and charged, most of our charges being organised and carried out on the spot by Company and Platoon Commanders, and even by Sergeants and Corporals, all ranks showing the greatest initiative and daring in clearing our front of the enemy with the bayonet. Our casualties were unfortunately again heavy. Lt. Watkins ("Poor Old Watkins," as he is popularly referred to by his surviving officer friends and men) was killed gallantly leading a glorious charge. His O.C. wrote: "I feel the loss of Watkins very keenly. He was a most reliable officer, loved by all and simply worshipped by his men." The Turks were driven back in confusion, but their machine-gunners from well-protected positions suddenly opened with terrible effect against the heroic Watkins and his gallant men, now close up to them. All through the afternoon charge after charge was made. Sgt. Shapley, just promised his commission for splendid work, would jump on his parapet, followed by his platoon, charge into the scrub with fixed bayonets, yelling "Imshi! Imshi!" and, after each successful charge, would stand and cheer regardless of the enemy.

Especially did the Turks worry us from Deadman's Ridge, and they got into the Valley behind Pope's, whence they sniped unceasingly. Their reinforcements must have come up, for swarms of them again appeared on every part of our front. Again the warships repeatedly smashed them up into driblets. We felt that this and the many charges we had made must have dampened their ardor; but several waves of them suddenly appeared, led by a gallant officer with his drawn sword flashing brightly. He was followed by other officers, revolvers in hand, coolly setting examples to their commands, and 300 men in ragged uniforms. The whole party was wiped out, and again Shapley rose on to the parapet and cheered. They were now quailed considerably, but further reinforcements and darkness increased their valor, and again they came on desperately determined to clear us off the Peninsula. After sounding our "Cease Fire!" they advanced to the weirdest accompaniment ever heard in battle. Bugles called eerily along the whole front, advancing and retiring, blaring suddenly close up and then in the dark distance, the echoes repeating in the gullies, while crashes of rifles and machine-guns occasionally drowned the efforts of the musicians. There was no tune about it; simply weird blasts, whistle-blowing and shouting, the blasts apparently being signals in Morse. If the lastnamed were orders to drive us into the sea, they were of little avail. Our bullets mowed down line after line. Newly-landed reinforcements were hurried up from the Beach and hurled straight into the fray anywhere required, several 13th officers finding themselves in charge of New Zealanders, men of the four Australian Bdes. on Gallipoli, and A.S.C. men —all splendid and all filled with the same spirit as their own men.

When morning of the 28th dawned men looked in vain for many comrades of the 25th. In some platoons less than a dozen were left without Officer or N.C.O. There were many of our dead along our front, surrounded by masses of enemy, but none of our wounded, for all had been gallantly carried in by heroes whose deeds became so common as to be almost unnoticed. A 16th Officer sent to ask an Officer of "B" Coy. the names of two of "B's" men who simply had to be noticed even among such heroes. He had seen them on the afternoon of the 27th carrying at least ten wounded comrades back between them, sometimes working together and sometimes independently, but always going out together. They no sooner placed the rescued in safety than they again ran out, one helping a cobber on to the other's back and then picking up his own man to stagger back with him to the trench, to reappear within a minute on a similar errand of heroic mercy. "You chaps have earned V.Cs. What are your names?" asked the 16th Officer; but the only reply he got was a smile from each and a "It's all right, sir." He tried to find out their names the next day by visiting our Coy., but he found that the Officers and N.C.Os. who could have given him the information had been either killed or wounded, and the men themselves, whom he felt he would recognise, had disappeared —probably killed in a charge, or themselves carried out wounded. Shapley died of his wounds.

Another example to illustrate the glorious spirit of our men is seen in the story of Cpl. A. E. Eccles. Eccles took a damaged gun down to the Beach to the "Triumph's" pinnace and exchanged it for one of theirs. As there was no water on Pope's, he filled it, thus making its weight 80lbs. Then, knowing the importance of a machine-gun on Pope's, he ran all the way back with it, arriving with it under his left arm, for a bone of his right arm had been broken in a fall. He continued his work uncomplainingly and did not report to the M.O. until three weeks later, when he had wasted away to a shadow. Foolish perhaps, but typical of the Dinkum's spirit. Decorations were not awarded for such conduct in those days. Eccles gave his life in Belgium in October, 1917. Sgts. C. F. Laseron, H. Hill, J. H. Holman, E. Davies, G. L. Foote and J. A. Lackenby, and men like R. A. Harvey, W. Parsonage, J. Hussey, A. E. Hughes, J. R. Hooper, H. Aslatt, W. Gocher, R. Coombes, J. Cook, W. Cross and H. C. Dickson were among the most distinguished in those early days, although such a list is unfortunately grievously incomplete.

All now remembered that they were hungry and thirsty. They were not fastidious now, for since they had left Heliopolis on the 11th they had had nothing but iron rations (excepting "A" at Lemnos). For many the haversacks of dead comrades provided their first meal on Gallipoli. The thirst that assailed the weary men on the afternoon of the 27th was so great that they would have risked any danger to assuage the pangs. Water for machineguns was also urgently required. "Water! God, I'm thirsty!" exclaimed a sergeant as he wiped a pebble to hold in his mouth. So intense was the thirst on the 29th that several crawled out to rattle the bottles that formed part of the equipment of their dead comrades and enemy in front; but these had mostly been emptied by the evening of the 27th. Then came a desire for a change from the iron rations, where even such were still obtainable; one section of 17 men shared during a stretch of 40 hours, seven biscuits and three tins of Bully.

Great joy was felt on the evening of the 28th, when "Lizzie" shelled the Chessboard and Deadman's Ridge. The joy was increased when rain commenced to fall, but when it lasted hour after hour, although light, and saturated all except a few with greatcoats, it made all rather miserable. The periscopes that arrived that day for the first time, were welcomed, and as their numbers increased later on, they saved many lives.

It was not until May 1st that "A," "B," and "D" Coys. on Pope's, and "C" on Quinn's with the 15th Bn., were properly reorganised, and the rolls checked. The sorting out of the various units that had become scattered on the first two days, took a considerable time.

The 13th was now able to obtain an idea of its heavy losses. As mentioned, Lt. F. G. Wilon was dead; Lts. F. G. Granger and G. G. Gardiner were severely wounded, and Capt. S. C. E. Herring was painfully wounded in the hand, but remained on duty, being assisted by a big Russian, P. Zenewich, who pulled him up the cliffs and followed him everywhere. Wilson was not only a very sterling character, but a splendid soldier and one whose work even thus early had made him noted. He was an officer of the greatest initiative, "full of buck and go," as a fellow officer wrote of him. The keen, intelligent, determined little Granger was unable to rejoin the Bn., but the lanky George Gardiner rejoined twice, his happy-go-lucky, cheery, apparently careless, yet sincere nature making each return a very welcome one.

In all these trying times the 13th were wonderfully inspired by the example of their "Game old Colonel." He was continually in the front line, accompanied generally by his Adjutant, Capt. Durrant, moving from post to post across the open. At an "A" post he wanted three to go out on a dangerous reconnaissance and the whole post immediately volunteered. "Some of you drop out," he ordered, but all remained offering themselves for almost certain death.

The Colonel waited. Still none would drop out.

"Come on; some one will have to drop out," he repeated.

"Well, we'll cut for it," suggested a Digger, as he pulled out a pack of cards. And so the patrol was chosen.

The men of "C" were proud of their Capt. Forsythe, whose organising work on Quinn's Post was such that to this day our men who were there call it "Forsythe's Post." When he arrived there on the 26th he found a few Australians and New Zealanders gallantly holding on to the ledge. He immediately commenced and organised a system of trenches, digging and fighting unceasingly until the 4th of May. His position was swept by the Turks from The Chessboard 70 yards away, and from German Officers' Trench 200 yards away on his other flank, both higher positions. They needed only to drive him back five yards to clear the ridge here, but his example was so splendid and his men so solid, that, on each of the many assaults, they were repulsed with frightful losses. Indeed, so offensive were "C" that the mere flashing of their bayonets over the parapet stampeded the Turks on several occasions. Sgt Sewell's repeated gallantry in this Post, cost him his life on the 28th.

It can therefore be easily imagined how exceedingly disappointed Forsythe's Coy. was and how unfair they regarded the Post's being called any name but Forsythe's Post. Capt. Quinn, of the 15th, although a splendid officer, did not arrive there until the 30th. On the 1st May Monash sent for both and asked who was the senior.

"I don't know, sir," replied Forsythe. "I believe Quinn is."

Monash then asked Quinn, "Who is senior, Quinn?"

"I think I am, sir," replied Quinn.

"Well, we'll call it 'Quinn's Post,'" replied the Brigadier.

Even thus early our stretcher-bearers, so conscientiously trained by Capt. Shellshear, made all ranks proud of them. Especially noticeable was the work of Corps. R. Pittendrigh and J. Sorrell, two clergymen, Ptes. R. Lingard and A. D. Turnbull, although these would be the first to urge that all their comrades were at least as worthy of mention as they. These bearers had often to lie down and act as a brake while their stretchers slid downhill, and their journeys to and from the ridges for the first fortnight were continually through swept areas. The men were simply superb. They were always splendid, but their conduct was the more noticeable that first tremendous week because even they themselves had wondered how they as individuals would stand the strain of active service—and such active service as modern troops had never before seen. Day after day they remained in the firing line without relief, and little groups in several places were to be found holding on without either officer or N.C.O. After a week their faces showed the terrible strain, not only of constant battle, but of hunger, thirst and exposure under the worst conditions. Not only were they wet, but the nights of that first week were generally bitterly cold, and for at least three days—a week in many cases—they had nothing warm, not even a warm drink, and sleep had been out of the question. A few got a drink of hot tea on the morning of the 29th by making fires in small recesses of the trench, and that was an absolute God-send to the fortunate ones. Still even when offered relief, many refused, urging that they knew their part of the front and its dangers better than any relief troops could. Sgt. Wardrop was one who so remained until carried back fatally wounded.

May 1st was a glorious day. Gallipoli was really a beautiful spot in Spring. The rugged hills and narrow winding gullies were covered with shrubs, many of which were flowering and perfumed; and stunted olive trees were scattered about, and there was the gloriously blue Aegean at our feet. But the perfect day didn't prevent the Turks attacking. They came in great waves against the right of Quinn's and Steele's. Lts. Lee and Perry and a platoon from a jutting-out portion of Quinn's did magnificent shooting at from 200 to 600 yards' range over the back of their trenches. They could not miss for they were firing along the waves and into huddled masses from which they could hear the cry of "Allah! Allah!" The next day the Turks attacked the Marines holding Steele's, and "C" Coy. had some equally excellent shooting.

Chapter V.—Bloody Angle and Chessboard, 2nd and 3rd May, 1915.

LIKE a bastion at the head of Monash Valley stood Pope's Hill. To the left was Baby 700, on the slopes of which, and overlooking our position, were the Turkish trenches of the Nek and the Chessboard, although the latter at this date were not the well-planned, bayed trenches that gave the system its name a little later. To the left was a gap between Pope's and Russell's Top, through which, as late as the 1st May, Turkish snipers crept into Monash Valley. To the right was another gap before our trenches on Quinn's were reached, and right in this gap were the Turkish trenches on Deadman's Ridge from which they could look point-blank down Monash Valley and Bloody Angle, the latter a small valley of which they could sweep every inch with bullets.

The trenches on Pope's were as a wedge driven from the apex of a sharp salient—a wedge like a sharp peninsula that could be sprayed by enemy bullets from three sides. Another bit of the wall of the head of Monash Valley on the edge of which we perched precariously contained Quinn's, Courtney's, and Steele's Posts. Even when May opened not only was there a constant danger of these posts being pushed back the few yards over the ledge, for the enemy could mass unseen in overwhelming numbers even in his front line so close to us, but, as they were, all communications to them and between them were under the eyes of the enemy stationed in the head of both arms of the Valley. Our Second-in-Command, that model soldier, Major Ellis, while returning from the Beach, was killed by a sniper. In his keenness for absolute military efficiency he had never spared either himself nor others, and his strong influence remained with the Battalion long after his death. Our R.S.M., H. MacDonald, in charge of our ammunition dump in the Valley, had his dump continually showered by bullets and shrapnel, but carried on issuing the ammunition and hurrying men away out of the danger zone, until he himself was severely wounded. Most other dumps and headquarters were similarly situated, so that our carriers and runners were constantly suffering.

The Turks truly held the keys of the Anzac position, and, even for defensive purposes, it was urgently necessary to secure these keys by an advance. Unfortunately this was impossible before 2nd May, and, before we were ready to make the attempt, we lost another extremely valuable officer in Lt. H. J. Salier, who was badly wounded through the cheeks at Quinn's. (He returned to the Bn. in August and did splendid work.)

The plan decided upon was an advance by the 16th, 13th and Otago Bn., the 16th on the right pivoting on Quinn's, the 13th in the centre, and the Otagos on the left. The left of the 13th was to be finally on the summit of Baby 700, where it was to join the Otago right.

In the dusk the 16th filed up past the foot of Quinn's to the end of Bloody Angle, The 13th followed to the opening of the Angle, also in file. Both Battalions were greatly weakened and extremely weary. The 16th had had two days' "rest" under heavy sniping fire; two Coys. of the 13th, "A" and "B," had just been relieved from Pope's, and "D" from Quinn's and Pope's to take part in the assault, the reliefs having taken place under short-range rifle fire.

Still all were aglow with keenness as they moved forward under the cover of the heaviest bombardment they had up to that time ever been under or heard. The shells from the eight warships and the few land batteries behind them roared viciously over them and gave even a more wonderful confidence than they in themselves possessed. It was the first time that they had been launched to an organised attack, and all were eager, especially Cpl. W. Muir, who, however, was killed before reaching the enemy. In the dusk our men on Pope's had seen some of the 16th going over the top at Quinn's, where they had been mown down by rifles and machine-guns, the wounded and dead tumbling down into the Valley. Then they had themselves dropped down into the Valley, and followed the rest of our Battalion up the Angle.

At 7.15 the gunfire slackened and lengthened, and the 16th turned like one man to the right, and with a cheer, scaled the steep sides of the Valley. During the bombardment they and the 13th had been singing "Tipperary" and "Australia Will be There," their hearty singing filling Bloody Angle and overflowing down the Valley until it was heard at the Beach three-quarters of a mile away. The head of the 13th took up the 16th's cheer, and sent it rolling along to the rear.

Darkness had now come on rapidly, and the 13th advanced with difficulty up the Angle, the narrow, steep valley being blocked by wounded, stretcher-bearers and ammunition-carriers of the 16th to such an extent that the 13th had to form single file. The Turks poured bullets blindly from their rifles, and showers from their machine-guns set on fixed platforms to sweep the Angle and the crest even in the darkness, but the singing of the advancing troops remained as firm and as hearty as ever. That singing and the thrills it inspired will never be forgotten by those who heard it from Monash Valley, the Beach and neighbouring boats.

Then came a more tremendous cheer from the 16th. They had reached their position, their right flank having been helped over Quinn's trenches by our "C" Coy.

The 13th were now also on the ridge advancing now silently, still in file up the slope towards Baby 700, led by their gallant Colonel and his Adjutant, Capt. Durrant, and six scouts. Those of the 16th who were still climbing the Valley side, as well as those on the top, received a hail of bullets from their rear, fired from the Nek, and many fell back dead or wounded on to our men following up the Angle.

Let me quote occasionally from Bean:

"About the foot of Deadman's Ridge Burnage wheeled to the left and led the file up the slope opposite to that which the 16th had climbed. Whereas the line of the 16th had turned simultaneously to the right and moved abreast up the hill, the manoeuvre of the 13th was a wheel, each man following the one in front, still in single file. At the top of the steep valley side Burnage reached the gentle slope of the Chessboard leading to Baby 700. There he stood with Durrant counting the men as they filed past."

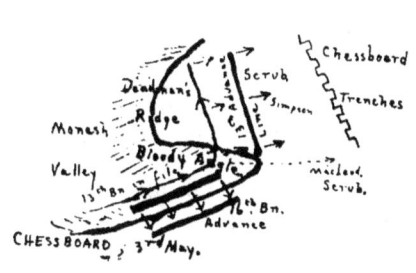

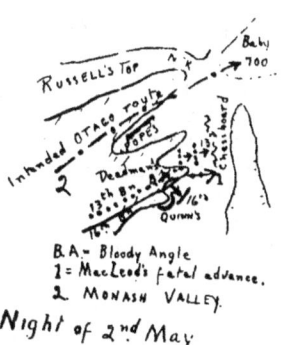

Burnage knew that there was a Turkish trench just ahead of him. When the 13th were holding Pope's Sgt. E. R. Cotterill and a few scouts had crawled out on to Deadman's and the Chessboard, cheerfully facing almost certain death. Two of these scouts—Cotterill and Pte. H. George—returned, their mates having been killed. They reported that the scrub was "crawling with Turks." But from further report from Lt. Marks, from Quinn's, Burnage knew the position of the trench. When 250 men had passed him he gave the order to turn to the right, and, with Capt. J. W. A. Simpson and Lt. Faddy with his compass leading, the line advanced upon it. Turks bolted from the scrub like startled game, Pte. W. Upton leading a charge after them. The trench was taken. Fire was coming from everywhere, and the enemy threw a few bombs, one of which wounded Faddy in the neck. He commenced to walk back, but was never heard of again. Meanwhile the rear platoons of the 13th were still filing on to the Chessboard. A heavy crossfire made them hesitate, but the Colonel himself steadied them by his calm, clear voice. A Digger, Knowles, wrote home: "As I reached the top and scrambled over the ridge, I heard a quiet voice say: 'It's all right, boys; we've got them moving. You are quite safe up here. Just work your way along there and spread yourselves out as far as you can to connect up with the New Zealanders; and then dig in before the moon rises or we'll meet trouble.'" Men were falling by the score around him, and bullets whizzing from two directions. Still he spoke as one who would say, "Pass the salt, please." Burnage was old enough to be the father of most of us; still age did not stop him from climbing that hill in front of us.

Since landing the 13th had learnt to know and to love their old Colonel, and would have gone to Hell with him had he said, "Come on, boys."

Presently the rear men ceased to arrive. The guide who had been standing at the bottom of the Valley directing the file up the hill had been killed. Our order of march had been Hqrs., "D," "B," "A." The leading platoon of A," under Lt. H. D. Pulling, followed the rest of the Battalion to the left. Lt. R. H. Crowe, not finding the guide, led straight on until the continual call for reinforcements from the 16th diverted him and his section to their help, his remaining three sections being directed by a new guide to the left at the proper place. Then came No. 4 Platoon, led by its big, gallant commander, Lt. K. MacLeod, who also found no guide at the turn-off point, the second guide having also been killed. He naturally kept straight on with his leading section, his remaining three sections, like those of Lt. Crowe, being guided correctly. Similarly Lt. Lee missed the guide, and similarly his remaining three sections were guided correctly. Lt. Crowe is known to have been wounded while fighting gallantly alongside the 16th. He continued fighting until the last, setting a splendid example of initiative, coolness and daring, in which he was as gallantly seconded by his Sgt., D. Williamson and Cpl. R. Harvey. The 16th Bn. always remembered the splendid heroism of this section of the 13th all of whom gave their lives that night.

Lt. MacLeod led his section straight on, followed, in the dark distance by Lt. Lee, who. through recognising the giant Scotsman of No. 4 Platoon, Pte. D. MacLeod, in the rear of his section, thought he was in touch with the rest of the Battalion. Lt. Lee, having been at Quinn's until half-an-hour before zero, had not been at the Officers' Conference on the attack Suddenly fire was opened on his party at about 20 yards' range wounding several. They threw themselves on the ground and returned the fire. They could see nothing of MacLeod's party, who must indeed have all been killed by this. Not one ever returned, and they were not captured; for it is the proud boast of the 13th that not one of the Battalion was ever captured by the Turks. The Turks continued heavy fire against Lee and threw bombs which set fire to the brush, making the extraction of his party the more difficult. However he got his wounded away; then his section, Cpl. F. Gilbert assisting him nobly in all this trying time. Almost 200 yards back Cpl. Gilbert met Cpl. Boccard, who had been sent by Durrant to locate the left of the 16th. Lee's section then moved across and joined the rest of the Battalion. It was only by magnificent coolness and gallantry on the part of all that Lee was able to save his party from the fate of MacLeod and his. His remaining three sections had been saved from following him by Durrant, who, seeing the break, had run down the hill and turned them to the left. In the absence of Lee and MacLeod the remainder of their platoons had been ably commanded by Sgts. G. Mitchell and J. Annoni, both later promoted to Commissions for splendid work. Mitchell was severely wounded next morning. All that night heavy fire continued against us, but the 13th, taking little notice of the incessant crackling and the humming and thudding of bullets, kept digging for dear life so that they would be in a tenable position by dawn. They completed a creditable front line with a support and a reserve, and commenced two communication trenches, so that now they were in a splendid position, ready to link with the 16th and the Otagos. But the latter were not there, their plans having miscarried terribly. They had been delayed by the encumbered Beach along which lay their track; in the Valley streams of bearers and wounded occupied the tracks; then crowds of snipers at the head of the Valley delayed them again; so that it was nearly two hours late when they debouched from the head of the Western Branch of Monash Valley for their objective.

Burnage had been repeatedly trying to get in touch with them, but of course they were not there until the 13th had dug in considerably. Then it was that Lt. F. M. Barton found them. Having missed the support of the barrage they had been almost annihiliated, were weary and disheartened, but still gallant and determined to reach their objective. But this was now impossible, for the Turks were aroused and reinforced. During the rest of the night and the early morning the Otagos attempted advance after advance, but each attempt only added to their previous losses. About midnight a Company of the 15th Bn. went forward to assist them by taking over their right where it joined the 13th. Still they were unable to advance.

It was the general opinion of the 13th that, had the Otagos not been so unfortunately delayed, the objective could have been reached and held with far fewer casualties than were already suffered. But with the flank so cut up and held up, further advance by the 13th was out of the question. So they dug in strenuously and, when morning came with its hellish tornado of death from right, front and left, they were able to hold on, and even to improve their position.

Otago crumbled under this morning hail and rushed back by twos and threes. The 15th Company, left in the air, and suffering frightfully, fell back likewise. The 13th alone still lay out on the Chessboard.

The 16th were suffering as severely as the New Zealanders had. Throughout the night and early morning line after line of swarming Turks withered under their fire, or ran from their bayonets. A scrub fire as they charged an enemy trench 80 yards away was responsible for one 16th failure, for it showed them up to the enemy. The fire on their left was so severe that they could not get in touch with the 13th, although their dead next morning showed how gallantly they had over and over again attempted to do so. Then at dawn they were shelled by our own guns. "After the strain of the night the apprehension that their friends did not know where they were and were about to bombard them from the rear was too much for the men. A part of the line of the 16th jumped back over the edge into the Valley." Some time later the few remaining 16th gradually fell back, rolling down the hill in twos and threes.

While the 13th were thus losing all flank support, the Nelson Bn. of the Naval Div. came up into our shallow support trench, and imagining they were in the front line, immediately opened fire on our men digging in the scrub in front. Durrant rushed back in the teeth of their fire and across a Turkish-swept zone, and stopped them, two officers falling as he was talking to them. Some of the Nelsons then advanced to the right of the 13th, but did not dig in, having no proper entrenching tools. With dawn came also the rat-a-tat of Turkish machine-guns from the right, front and left. To raise one's head meant certain death. It was bad enough for the 13th, but it was perfect hell for the sailors in the open. A dozen of them, maddened by being fired at without hope or retaliation, suddenly rose and rushed towards a hidden gun firing into them. In a few moments three of them returned each carrying a wounded comrade, the rest having been killed. Then some shells landed among them, on which they were ordered to retire, which message several of the 13th nearest them took to apply to them also. Finding, however, that their comrades were still in position, they separated themselves from the Nelsons and climbed the hill again to our trenches amid the cheers of their mates still there.

The Portsmouth Bn. of the Marines now tried to join the 13th, but, in spite of their bravery, they had no individual dash, looking to Officers and N.C.Os. for instructions, even while being mown down as they were, their dead lying so thickly on the rise as to give the name Deadman's Ridge to it. The 13th trenches were good and well-sited, but, owing to the failure of our flanks, were outflanked and overlooked, and without any possibility of being connected with the rear by a safe communication trench. Barton took the risk of crawling over the top to get information from his O.C., but was sniped. Sgt.-Major Foote raised his head to observe and got a bullet through it. (Fortunately he survived and received a Commission for splendid service.) We could get no word to or from our Brigade and knew not what was happening anywhere else, except that we had no flanks, and that Baby 700, the main objective, was still the enemy's. That terrible day was at last drawing to a close. It had been hot, and water and food scarce although our Q.M., Lt. Thompson, himself had gallantly visited us to learn how he could assist; and the trenches were filled with dead and wounded. Each man had several rifles, his own and his mate's, loaded on the parapet. The wounded were often unavoidably knocked in that narrow trench. They groaned, but thoughtfully added, in spite of their agony, "Its all right, cobber; I know you couldn't help it, but it's sore," or something similar.

At 3 p.m. Burnage had called a conference of Coy. Commanders, discussed the situation and decided that he or Durrant must make the journey to Bde. Hqrs. By the tossing of a coin it was decided that the Colonel should go. He made his way to Monash, and after a conference, it was decided that the 13th could not be usefully maintained in front of Pope's unsupported. The Colonel therefore returned to the trenches at dusk and dictated the order for withdrawal. The remaining wounded were evacuated first; L.-Cpl. W. C. Francis (in private life a Methodist clergyman), having with two volunteers, J. H. Sorrell and R. A. Coombes, done exceptionally splendid and gallant work all that afternoon as a voluntary stretcher-bearer, for which he was awarded the D.C.M., this and Upton's being the first D.C.Ms. gained by the Battalion. Francis carried back over 30, remarking when the danger was pointed out by his O.C., "I'm prepared to take the risk." All the dead comrades within sight were also carried back.

Then the 13th retired gradually, the Colonel remaining until he saw every man, with the exception of a few with Herring, and a section with Lt. Lee, Sgt. Annoni and Cpl. Boccard. safely away, these parties continuing to fire bursts every two minutes to give the enemy the idea that the trench was still strongly occupied.

By 10 p.m. the last of the Battalion had retired behind Pope's. We had had 80 killed, including other heroes like Sgt. Digby, J. Rogers, O. Rainbow, Dunkinson and L. Marks and Cpl. M. Hunt, and 200 wounded in the stunt.

On his way back, in the dim light, Burnage saw a man in a hole and called out, "Are you a marine?" "Oh! don't make it too hot, Colonel," was the reply, "I'm a New Zealander."

The trenches we had dug on the position so dearly won and held all night and day were incorporated into the Turkish Chessboard system, our Support line becoming their Front line.

On the 4th Pte. George Pappas, learning that a man, thought to be dead could be seen moving an arm as he lay out right under the enemy rifles, unhesitatingly went out, facing a veritable hail of lead leading a charmed life, and brought the helpless man in. (Received D.C.M.)

That same night a party from our "C" Coy. went out and filled in the trenches adjoining their's which had been dug by the 16th. Although not at Bloody Angle, "C" had had a strenuous time, assisting with covering fire wherever possible, and threatening and smashing attacks. Here Lt. G. Binnie was killed. He was one of the most loved and loveable officers the 13th ever possessed. His charming, happy, sunshiny disposition and earnest devotion to duty at all times won the hearts of all whose good fortune it was to know him. Lt. "Babe" Hopkins was in many ways a similar character, but "Little Mac.," Lt. G. S. McDowell, an O.P. of the Battalion, who became our Bombing Officer, was our nearest approach to Binnie in the combination of charm. loveableness and efficiency.

The Landing strength of the 13th was 25 officers and 934 other ranks; our strength on the evening of 3rd May was 9 officers and 500 other ranks, and the 15th and 16th had suffered even more severely.

Although not at Bloody Angle, Forsythe had lost his four officers and 112 other ranks out of his Company of 217 by 3rd May. The 4th Brigade had landed 105 officers and 3720 other ranks; its strength on the 3rd May was 41 officers and 1770 other ranks. Such was the bloody baptism of the 13th and its sister battalions. Bloody! Yet gloriously-ever-to-be-remembered while Australians remain the Australians of 1914.

It can safely be said that no men ever had a Colonel in whom they had more pride than the 13th now had of their "Grand Old Man." His example from beginning to end was inspiring indeed. At the meeting of officers prior to the attack, after he had explained, as he thought, everything, he was asked where the reports to him were to be sent. "To the head of the column," he replied, as if they ought to have known that without asking. The Head of a column going up Bloody Angle in file!

Chapter VI.—May, 1915.

MAY 4th was spent by the Battalion less "C," in Monash Valley reorganising, the men of "C" doing a splendid bit of work that day on their own account.

Some of the Marines occupying a trench in Quinn's System ran before showers of Turkish bombs and a threatened assault calling out "Help!" Without waiting orders the nearest 13th men rushed into the trenches evacuated, hurled back bombs, showed their bayonets and invited the Turks so enthusiastically that they stayed where they were.

On May 5th the 13th went back to the trenches on Pope's and there relieved the Chatham Marines, "C" however, still remaining on Quinn's.

Our attack against the Chessboard had made the Turks so apprehensive that during the succeeding nights they kept No Man's Land illuminated by flares and flare bombs. As a matter of fact our attack had upset his arrangements for an overwhelming attack on us. We, however, confined ourselves to making our disconnected trenches into continuous front lines, all, despite their strained feelings and loss of strength, preferring this work to remaining on guard in the cold night air in their scanty and torn clothes. During the days small parties were sent down to the Beach for a swim—a gloriously welcome, if a risky, luxury, the Beach being constantly under shrapnel.

Some of our men were enjoying the warm sunshine, a smoke and a yarn, while squatting in their most advanced post, when a German officer and two Turks hopped into the trench. "Now you hopping kangaroos, you've been looking for this," said the German as he held his revolver at our machine gunner's head. But he was rudely interrupted by a bayonet in his chest from a Digger who did not even rise to his feet; and the Turks were shot before they could move either way.

May 7th found the 13th in sectional reserve in Monash Valley, and enjoying tobacco and cigarettes sent them by the Navy, who were constantly sending presents to the Australians on Gallipoli. These cigarettes were addressed: "The Fighting Maniacs."

From the 8th to the 13th we were again in the front line on Pope's and Quinn's, and this period was a specially trying one, for not only did the enemy burst shrapnel right into our trenches, but it rained heavily, which rain was most tormenting to the troops on Pope's, preventing any cooking, and, during the first month on Gallipoli, each did his own cooking, most various being the dishes and the utensils devised, ground biscuit fried in bacon fat being the commonest, the grater being a jam-tin holed with a bayonet. And there was no sleep, for the Battalion was continually standing-to. Constant scouting was also necessary; one patrol, consisting of Sgt. E. Cotterill and Cpls. H. George, W. Sullivan, W. Currie and W. Clarke, crawling out on the 9th on to the Chessboard before the Turks saw them. Cotterill and Sullivan were killed, George died next day, and Currie and Clarke were severely wounded. Cotterill's Commission came out posthumously. Others recommended with him for specially distinguished work were H. S. Hill, B. Fletcher, D. Wilson, F. Leans and N. MacDonald.

Communication with Pope's remained risky for a considerable time, and the troops there used often to watch enviously the troops in the Valley and behind other posts cooking rations they could not get.

At 2 a.m. on the 10th a platoon from "D," in conjunction with parties from the 15th and 16th, made a glorious bayonet charge over the top at Quinn's. The Turks were alert, and opened a hellish fire. But our men pushed on unhesitatingly although only 12 out of 30 were now left. Into the Turkish trench they went, and along it to enemy Headquarters, bayoneting many, during which time part of the captured trench was being made part of ours by connecting it with a deep cut. Capt. Townsend, of the 16th Bn., well-known at Sydney University before going to Westralia, was wounded. Sgt. W. Cross rushed to him through a hail of bullets, picked him up, and was carrying him to safety when the Captain was instantly killed by another bullet through the head. Cross, although now in comparative safety, instead of remaining, crossed the swept zone to the Turkish trench where his six remaining comrades were, knowing that it was only a matter of a few minutes before they would all have to return across that zone again. (Received D.C.M.)

On 13th May the 1st A.L.H. relieved the 13th on Pope's, the horsemen joking heartily at their new role. They had to a man volunteered to take on "foot-slogging" in order to come to Gallipoli, and had already learnt all about heavy packs and blistered feet. The 13th went into Sectional Reserve in Monash Valley, had a good sleep and cleaned themselves up. Letters were soon being written by all, but "envelopes are like diamonds," wrote one officer.

But even "resting" was risky, for our killed and wounded averaged four a day until the 19th, when "C" and a part of "D" again went into Quinn's, while the remainder continued digging and carrying. The casualties among carriers caused Monash Valley to be called the "Valley of Death." On 1st May one of our signallers, whose duty it was to watch the Valley from Pope's had seen nine men killed within half-an-hour, all walking along in apparent safety. It was safer now, but still carriers with loads of 100 pounds ran when passing certain spots.

On the 14th Lts. Lee and H. Pulling were sent with 100 men to the Beach to unload stores—anything from a case of biscuits to a 6-inch howitzer. Their greatest trouble was to find room to camp on. The Beach itself was a narrow, sandy one, about 100 to 150 yards wide, and half-a-mile long. It was piled with stores of all kinds—food, clothing, guns, shells, S.A.A., iron, tools, etc. etc. Small piers were being built, and lighters laden with fresh stores constantly coming alongside, generally in charge of young middies filled with all the confidence of admirals and the courage of veterans. Our Beach party was called out at all hours, day or night. Among those conspicuous for cheerful and apparently untiring work on these duties was Cpl. J. Leddy. Specially fine was his work on the night of the 18th May, when the Turks launched their tremendous attack and the 13th had to carry extra supplies up to the line.

The remainder of the Battalion not on this work or on Quinn's had been improving the communications in Monash Valley, helping especially to make a deep and wide trench. "Wide enough for 'Paddy' McGlinn; deep enough for Godley," were the specifications generally quoted by the men. Col. McGlinn was our popular and well-conditioned Bde. Major, and Gen. Godley was very tall. Col. McGlinn came along often and encouraged, "Make them wide, boys; wide enough for a mule."

"Right, sir; and deep enough for Gen. Godley," was the cheery reply he received from a 13th Digger. And it was long after when he learnt why all laughed.

Gen. Bridges was fatally wounded in Monash Valley on the 15th near where some of the 13th were working, after being warned by them of the danger.

The 18th and 19th May were among the most strenuous Gallipoli days. On the 18th the Turks sent word by leaflets that we would all be in the sea or dead within 24 hours. Gen. Von Sanders was in charge of the 40,000 Turks taking part. The 13th were not in the front line, but a few details were, and our carrying parties and bearers were as much in the strafe as those more forward.

All day long they bombarded us from front line to Beach with shells of all sizes up to 8in., our guns remaining practically inactive until night, reserving their ammunition until the Turkish trenches were crowded with troops for assault. Then they pounded their trenches unmercifully. About midnight the terrific attack was launched, but assault after assault was beaten back. Then, just at daybreak, the greatest attack, in long thick lines was made. Their first line melted completely under our bullets; their second fell over them in the same way; their third line wavered, thinned, came on, wavered again, rushed rearwards, mixed with succeeding waves, and the whole confused mass not only gave a splendid target to the Anzacs, but was bombed by their own men, who thought we ourselves were attacking. They huddled in masses of from 100 to 150 crying "Allah! Allah!" the Anzacs sitting coolly on their parapets firing into them until their rifles were too hot to hold. By 10 a.m. all the attacks had dwindled to nothing, and Jacka, of the 14th Bn. had won the first Australian V.C. for the war.

Just at the conclusion of this attack our "C" Coy. and part of "D" took over Quinn's, coming in for plenty of work cleaning up and repairing. That night the Turks were extremely jumpy, and kept up a brisk fusillade interspersed with showers of bombs. It was then the custom of our men to throw their greatcoats or sandbags over the Turkish bombs, or to pick them up and throw them back. On the 20th one lobbed among a party of 13th. A man immediately threw his folded coat over it and sat on it. When he came to, after being pulled back into the trench, he dazedly remarked: "I wanted to save my mates. I'm a bit shook up, though."

That afternoon saw an unofficial armistice, a party of Turks appearing on our right with a white flag. All firing ceased, and Diggers and Turks showed themselves quite freely, joking across the 6 yards of No Man's Land at Quinn's, while Red Crescent flags appeared all along the Turkish trenches. However our powers that be refused the armistice, being suspicious as it was getting late. The Turks lowered their flags, and three minutes later, firing recommenced.

Our artillery on Walker's Ridge did some fine shooting that night, lobbing into the trenches 15 yards in our front. When "C" and "D" were relieved on the 21st by "A" they had had 20 casualties. Capt. Hunt, who had done consistently solid and conscientious work since the landing, especially on the Chessboard, had also been wounded on the 20th while in support with "B" near Courtney's. He was superintending the relief of his Coy. and guiding them past a dangerous spot when sniped. However he was back on duty soon enough to do excellent work at Quinn's on the 29th.

On the 22nd "A" used for the first time in their Sniper's Posts, periscope rifles, an Australian invention. Lt. R. G. Legge, M.C., had been chosen as O.C. of a 4th Bde. party of 25 picked men to act as a personal bodyguard to Sir Ian Hamilton at Mudros, and left Anzac on the 22nd for a fortnight. They had the distinction of preparing the camp site for G.H.Q. on Mudros. They also had a most enjoyable time on the tiny mules of the Greeks.

In and out, and in again, and those not in the line were digging or carrying in the Valley. Those in the line at Quinn's were fighting and digging, for the Turks were sapping under us, and we had to counter-sap. Sgt. J. Linn was killed.

The 24th was a day of uncanny quietness. The valleys were free from the pinging and crackling reverberations that had filled them for the past month. It was a most peculiar feeling indeed. From 7 a.m. to 4.30 p.m. there was an official armistice for the purpose of burying the dead in No Man's Land. The 13th supplied a burial party of 100, in charge of five officers as well as our M.O. and Chaplain. It was a terrible task; but necessary if any of either side were to occupy the front trenches. A line was marked out midway across No Man's Land, beyond which neither side crossed. Cigarettes, coins and other souvenirs were exchanged, as well as smiles and greetings. Turk and Digger seemed cobbers for the time. In addition to the burying our Battalion party carried back into our trenches a great deal of salvage, including over 100 rifles and 25,000 rounds of ammunition.

The thunderstorm of the next day was a most disastrous one to our dugouts and several trenches, and even during it we could hear the Turks digging under Quinn's, and expected to be blown skywards any minute. That night we waited four hours to be blown up standing to; but the expected explosion and attack did not eventuate.

The 27th found half the Battalion and 100 of the 10th A.L.H. on Quinn's. We counter-sapped for all we were worth to meet the Turk underground, and at 2.30 on the 28th we blew his sap in. It was right under us. We also threw proclamations in Turkish into their trenches.

On the 26th most of the 13th saw the pathetic sight of the "Triumph" sinking off Anzac. Fifteen minutes after being torpedoed it sank, but most of the crew were saved by destroyers that rushed to their rescue.

The sapping and counter-sapping still went on at Quinn's until 3.30 a.m. on the 29th May. It came where we didn't expect it—under No. 3 section of the post. A terrific explosion in between Forsythe's and Perry's positions. The men there—all 13th—were all killed or wounded. Hundreds of tons of earth and sandbags hurled into the air, whence it rained down violently. Then came showers of hundreds of bombs, and an enemy rush. One bomb —they were still superior to ours—burst against Burnage, and besides shaking him considerably, shattered his left elbow. He tried to carry on, but staggered from shock and loss of blood. Recovering, he stood upright as if nothing had happened. Bearers came along but he sent them away. "Prop me up against the side here, Durrant; I don't want the boys to know I'm hit," he said. Loss of blood, however, made him swoon. He recovered, but was so weak that he could not stand, and the bearers would now take no denial, although he protested that he could remain. As they moved off with him he called out: "Keep them together, Durrant, and they'll fight."

In the bright but dusty moonlight the fight went on with great severity, the 13th rallying quickly and rushing the trenches taken by the Turks in the first surprise. Our "D" Coy. in reserve, under Herring, and the 15th Battalion charged up unhesitatingly to help regain the position. Lt. C. W. L. Pulling, who had just landed on Gallipoli a few hours before, set a fine example of active leadership and self-careless devotion to duty, supported magnificently by Sgt. H. Scott, while Hunt and Edmonds, instantly grasping the seriousness of the position, personally reconnoitred the lost positions and led party after party into trenches occupied by the enemy. Capt. Forsyth, Lts. A. F. Smith, E. Wilson, and N. F. Vine-Hall were wounded doing their duty gallantly, Vine-Hall dying at sea shortly after. Cpl. Lenan and Pte Andrews fell after performing several deeds of the greatest valor. Cpl. E. Davis again set a splendid example, rushing the enemy positions without considering his own safety. In 25 minutes we had lost 13 killed and 81 wounded, while the enemy had lost over 300. We captured 19 and counted 35 dead in Quinn's—practically all who didn't clear out on our first charge. The situation was critical for several hours. It was probably more critical than any other we were ever in, for, had the Turks entered the Valley, there would almost certainly have been an irretrievable disaster. They not only continued attacking vigorously, but they shelled our rear heavily. Our own shelling was futile, but our wonderful rifle fire made up for that—specially wonderful, considering the terrifically demoralising explosion. Then, in face of lightning, scythe-like lines of screeching bullets our "D" Coy. and some 15th climbed up and charged unflinchingly. The 15th fell like corn, but fortunately for "D," by an extraordinary coincidence the Turks to our left attempted a charge at the same moment, and for a few seconds their fire ceased against our charging line, which short space enabled "D" to reach our original front line. Then, when the enemy opened again, the 15th retaliated magnificently by firing through the dust into their flashes and helped the 13th considerably. They then fought the Turks up the trenches to their final stronghold, where Major Quinn was shot.

Burnage had seen as much of the front line as any man, for he had never spared himself in the slightest. The Battalion had already earned the name of "The Fighting Thirteenth," and our Colonel that of "The G.O.M.," or "The Gamest Old Man." Before Gallipoli he had attracted the least attention of the four Commanding Officers of the Brigade, but, within 24 hours after landing, he was recognised as a gallant and able leader. It was as an Active Service leader more than as a trainer, that he proved himself. His constant thoughts were his men; still he never for an instant made the slightest endeavor to be regarded as a "good fellow." Indeed the 13th never possessed a Colonel who did. Burnage inspired his officers to regard constantly their men's comfort, physical condition and preservation of fighting spirit, and they backed him up loyally. The standard he set was of the highest, and fortunate we were to have had throughout our history Commanders who were able and keen to follow in his footsteps; Colonels who inspired their officers, as he did, to give cheery service on every occasion, although they were often more dog-tired than the men imagined. He was never heard complaining, and, following his example, it became a point of honor to 13th officers to act likewise.

Colonel Burnage's personality and courage on Gallipoli during those few tremendous weeks impressed not only his own men, but those of the other battalions of the 4th Brigade, so much so that, as he was being carried to the rear he was cheered throughout the journey by the whole Brigade and Light Horse. Our "Gamest Old Man" could not keep back his tears at these spontaneous bursts of recognition. Col. McGlinn wrote to him: "Your men are all immensely proud of you." A week after landing on Gallipoli he had expressed his pleasure that his faith in a certain few of his most troublesome men of Broadmeadows and Heliopolis had not been misplaced. Before leaving Egypt it was decided that all "undesirables" should be returned to Australia, and each battalion was asked for a list. Burnage would not recommend any, for which he received what some would call a "strafe." At the time we did have 20 out of our 1100 in guard or "clink" for short periods, mainly because of a surfeit of energy and the novel life; and the higher powers believed that some of these were undesirables; and rightly in a few cases in the A.I.F. But Burnage stuck to his guns, and he was justified within a week on Gallipoli, for these men, without exception, made good. "Bill Burnage's Circus," as we ourselves rather fondly called it at Broadmeadows and Heliopolis, became known throughout the A.I.F. within a fortnight as "The Fighting Thirteenth," and "Bill" Burnage as "The Gamest Old Man." Throughout our history his unwillingness to disgrace completely even his worst case was reflected in all the 13th Officers and N.C.Os.

To Burnage success in battle had been the object and ultimate end of all his training, to some picturesqueness and precision on parade were the essentials; not that the latter and correct habits do not help, as Burnage would be the first to admit they do considerably, but providing he thought a man was man enough to help to bring success in battle he would forgive a little casualness in the preparation.

Unfit for line duty, to his life-long regret, he was appointed, after some time in hospital, to command troopships between Australia and England. His last voyage in this position was on the ill-fated "Barunga," which left Plymouth on the 14th July, 1918, carrying 828 troops back to Australia. His organisation was so perfect and his influence so inspiring that, when the "Barunga" was torpedoed the next afternoon and commenced to sink rapidly, all without exception ran quickly and quietly to their stations and remained cheerful and steady, not one attempting to enter the boats conveying them to the destroyers until his allotted time came, although there was only boat accommodation for 254, and all showing a willingness to sacrifice themselves to save the crippled and sick.

The call to action was always a tonic to the 13th, and never more so than that morning of the 29th May. To have seen them on the 28th for the first time after the landing one would never have recognised them as the same men. Apart from the bearded faces, they were worn and wearied almost to exhaustion. All had aged years in that month, not only in experience, but in the sapping of strength and vitality. Still, to have seen them charging through showers of bullets, shells and bombs, into trenches filled with Turks that dawn, to have heard their cheery "Imshi, Johnno! Imshi, you blankard!" and to have seen their determined look as they started to recapture the position, and their brightening eyes and flashing faces as victory came nearer, one would immediately have overlooked the physical and the rough in recognition of the men of the some spirit as those of the long, long month before.

They poured showers of their own "home-made" bombs—jam-tins containing explosive, stones, bits of iron, barbed wire gramaphone needles and anything else they could get that was small and hard—along the trenches among the Turks with "Turkish delight coming over, Johnno!" "Another one for you, Johnno, you blankard!" and "Imshi, you blankard!" "Blankard" was often a term of endearment. One met his young brother, whom he believed to be at home, in the trenches with "You young blankard, Bill; how's Mum?" No wonder the Turks misunderstood its meaning.

"Why do you always call out 'Allah!' when you are fighting or running, Johnno?" a prisoner who understood a little English was asked.

"Allah same you Blankard. Allah our God; Blankard you God."

As the regained position was being cleared the body of a miner was recovered. He should have been in a safe position in the Valley, for he had been refused permission to return to Quinn's, having been there for a long period, but he had disobeyed, and so died among his Newcastle mining mates, underground.

Our old original Padre, Col. F. W. Wray, of Wangaratta, was, in 13th parlance, "one of the best," and a "dear old chap," and that meant something from the Diggers. He had, during that strenuous month never spared himself, going anywhere at any time, constantly on the move visiting sick and wounded, taking messages to send home, conducting burial services, and even setting an example of sharing the men's dangers and privations by constantly visiting the firing lines to chat with them. His eye was quick to detect the worst cases of fatigue, and a nip from his flask was a godsend to such, especially after standing-to in a drizzling rain all night. The second day after the landing he made soup for the wounded being the pioneer, probably of this idea which developed so in France.

On the 29th and 30th the 13th moved into Sectional Reserve, and on the 31st and 1st of June, back to Reserve Gully as Divisional Reserve. The M.G. Section, however, remained on Courtney's until the end of July, when weakened by dysentery, para-typhoid and constant strain, they were withdrawn for five days. The No Man's Land they left behind them was a different one to that of the first week, for bullets had mown down the prickly scrub and bushes, and left it as bare as a billiard table. And we had cured the Turks of their nasty habits of occupying No Man's Land. We were a little slow at the stalking and sniping game at first and the Turks had had rather a good innings. But that had quite altered, thanks to the sniping of men like J. Charnock, W. Armstrong and R. James, all of whom were killed in May. The rest of the Brigade was also withdrawn to Reserve Gully. Its losses during the five weeks had been:—Battalion Commanders, 2 out of 4; Seconds-in-Command, 2 out of 4; Adjutants, 2 out of 4; Company Commanders, 12 out of 16; Other Officers, 81 out of 104; N.C.Os., 377; Ranks 2303. Totals, 2779.

General Sir Ian Hamilton, who had seen many wars, including the Russo-Japanese, stated that the fighting on Gallipoli was the severest in his experience.

On June 3rd we had our first Battalion parade since leaving Egypt. The sad depletion in all ranks was heartbreaking. Then we had a Brigade parade and an address by Godley. He announced the following awards for the Brigade. Others, including Jacka's V.C., and our Colonel's C.B., came out later:—

Military Cross (2): Capt. J. W. A. Simpson, 13th Bn.; Lt. R. G. Legge, 13th Bn.

Distinguished Conduct Medals (7): 2 to the 13th; 2 to 15th; 1 to 16th and 2 to A.A.M.C. The two to the 13th went to Pte. W. Upton and Cpl. W. C. Francis. Many more names of heroes of those early days not already mentioned are mentioned later in this story. Many, owing to sickness, wounds or death, do not again come into our history. Sgts. Anderson (wounded 30/5/15), H. P. Ashburner (No. 1), H. B. Ashburner (1011), P. Donnelly and H. Knight, and Ptes. Dickson, Crooks, W. Morris and Knowles have been authoritatively mentioned by Originals as splendid men in those early days.

Address by Gen. Godley to 4th Brigade at Anzac, 2nd June, 1915: "I have come to-day to tell you all with what great pride and satisfaction I have watched your performances for the past five weeks, and to tell you also that not only your comrades of the Division, but also of the whole Australasian Army, have watched with the greatest admiration your doings from the moment you landed. You have been for 5 weeks continuously in the front line trenches, fighting particularly hard the whole of that time. Never have troops been subjected to such heavy shell and rifle fire, not to speak of bombs, and you have lived and fought in a sorely trying din and turmoil. You began your fighting immediately on landing, pitchforked, I might say, into the middle of the battle, with the whole Brigade scattered in fragments in different parts of the firing line. You were in the firing line continuously for several days with nothing but what you carried on you. During those days many deeds of heroism, many acts of gallantry, were performed which will remain unknown and unrewarded, and many of your comrades were killed or wounded. Again on the 2nd and 3rd of May the Bde. made a sortie from the lines which was very far-reaching in its results, shattering most effectively the enemy's plans for assault. Again on May 9th this Bde. made another highly-successful sortie, and only a few days ago, during the greater part of the 18th and 19th May, you bore the brunt of the very severe Turkish attack, by which they hoped to drive this Army Corps into the sea. Yours is a fine record, and one of which you yourselves and the whole of the people of Australia have the fullest reason to be proud. You have made history equal to that of any other Brigade or body of troops in the Empire, or in the world, and you have performed deeds and achieved successes of which the Commonwealth will surely be proud. Nor will be forgotten the gallant behaviour of the 13th Battalion, under Lt.-Col. Burnage, who, among many other fine performances, held on for a night and a day in a difficult advanced position which they had stormed and from which they did not withdraw until ordered to do so. . . . On behalf of the Imperial Government, because of the great services you have rendered to the Empire—greater services than you yourselves realise—I thank you, Colonel Monash, your Staff, your Commanding Officers, and all your personnel from the highest to the lowest for the work you have done during the past five weeks."

Major Durrant was now temporarily in charge of the 13th. On his appointment as Second-in-Command (3/5/15), Capt. Simpson became Adjutant. This very fine officer's constant thoughts were for the welfare of the Battalion, and his eagerness and exertions led him to overtax his strength. (He was invalided to Australia, where, however, he immediately joined the Third Div. Promoted to his Lt.-Colonelcy of the 33rd Bn., he was killed in the front line in France). Durrant had now to find another Adjutant, and his selection had a most important influence on the future of the 13th. He has recorded that, after considering each officer, he decided that the most promising for the position was D. G. Marks, for he had seen that this lad possessed courage, energy, character and ability. That he was right the future bore abundant proof. Tilney, on his appointment as C.O., heartily endorsed the choice.

Chapter VII.—Reserve Gully.

THROUGHOUT June and July the Brigade remained in Reserve Gully, the 14th and 16th, however, having a week's holiday on Imbros. The 13th were at the head of the Gully under the Sphinx, and nearest to Walker's Ridge. During this period we did not fire a shot although we had regular casualties from enemy bullets and shells, not only during our work, but in our bivouacs themselves. This was a monotonous period of digging trenches and tunnels in all directions, terracing gullies, unloading barges and carrying, but digging was the main work, and all only too well knew blistered hands and aching backs. The name "Diggers" didn't arrive as the name for the Australian fighting soldiers until we were on the Somme. Wonder it is indeed that they were not called "Diggers" on Gallipoli, for they dug and dug and dug there so much that one could walk mile after mile through trench and tunnel, and whole battalions could be hidden underground close up against the front line.

Our first big work was a huge communication trench to No. 2 Outpost. This was at least 6 feet deep and wide enough to allow two laden mules to pass. The work went on unceasingly, the men working two shifts of four hours each every day except one in four, when the Battalion was detailed for Inlying Piquet. Some humorously blamed the soil they had shifted for that truly remarkable duststorm of 24th June; an extraordinary thing considering we were only half-a-mile from the sea. Parties were often taken off digging to unload stores from barges, or to carry, which was regarded as a welcome change. On July 18th we commenced terracing Canterbury Gully, connnecting Monash and Rest Gullies, to provide accommodation for reinforcements of Kitchener's Army. Great rivers of perspiration must have poured from the Anzacs that Gallipoli summer, for the weather was steamy hot and most oppressive. And fresh water and soap were luxuries to be dreamt of.

The food was also monotonous. "Bully" or bacon, strong cheese, biscuits and marmalade day after day, week after week. One typical letter home reads: "Don't mention bacon. The next pig I see I am going to throw a stone at; and if you put bacon before me when I come home I will throw it at Babs, she being the smallest. And biscuits! Hell must be paved with them!" Fresh meat was absent, and fresh vegetables quite unknown during those months. Our water supply was also scanty, a pint a day often being the ration; and it was generally so treated with chemicals that the tea was nauseating, and, but for being liquid, would not have been drunk. The following yarns were common at the time and have probably appeared in print many times ere this; but they apply to the 13th as much as to any unit, the second especially being credited as a 13th original:—

A man took his dixie back to the cook and grumbled at the horrible taste his tea had. "It's worse than usual to-day, cook." The cook took the dixie, looked puzzlingly into it, frowned perplexedly, stirred it and finally tasted it. "Why, man," he explained, "that's not your tea; that's your SOUP!"

Another day a mess-orderly returned and complained: "This tea's funny, cook." "Oh! funny is it? Well, why don't you laugh?" roared the exasperated cook.

Towards the end of July an agreeable addition to our diet was issued in the form of dried fruit and rice; but the rice was continued so long that another typical letter contains: "Rice, rice, rice! Rice is now a perfect nightmare."

Reserve Gully was a frightfully cramped place, 4000 men being huddled up in an area about the size of Martin Place, in such a way that sanitary arrangements could not possibly be perfect, no matter how all strove to make them so. And the FLIES! Surely never had any Australian, even in our most fly-pested parts, ever nightmared such flies as those of Gallipoli. A tin of jam could not be opened except after dark without becoming immediately a dense mobile black, and biscuit and marmalade had to be held by one hand and guarded by the other until the teeth closed on it, and even then these plaguey tormentors would get into one's mouth. Lice—"chats" or "visitors," as they were generally called—were bad, but no pest on Gallipoli could equal those flies. Chats were kept down somewhat by constant changing of our scanty clothing (for all wore as little as possible), fumigating and swimming. Still they remained a worry. One fortunate man had got a monkey somewhere, and, whenever his shirt became chatty, he would throw it to his pet to clean up. "What are those chats?" a sweetheart asked in a letter to her Jim. "I can't describe them properly, so I'm putting one under here," was the reply; and a piece of stamp paper licked along its edges formed an effective prison for the monster.

No wonder there was so much illness. During July the general health was very poor, and we evacuated to hospital on the average 60 a week, although, on account of the scarcity of reinforcements, we evacuated none but serious cases. Mjr. Hunt went to hospital on 22nd June, and Capt. Shellshear on 24th, Capt. Beamish taking the later's place. Durrant, Acting C.O., also became too ill to remain, and Herring took his place as Temporary C.O. until the appointment, on 2nd July, of Lt.-Col. L. E. Tilney, V.D., late Major of the 16th Bn., as our new Commanding Officer. Tilney had already gained the admiration, not only of his old, but also of his new Battalion, for his splendid work and heroism on Quinn's and Pope's. At the formal "Taking Over" of the Battalion on the 6th July, General Monash spoke glowingly of the record of the 13th and of Tilney. But almost from the commencement of duty with the 13th Tilney was ill, too. He fought against it strenuously, as many of his Battalion were doing, for a fortnight, and then had to take a rest. He refused to evacuate, hoping each day to improve, but he was off color for many weeks, a good deal of the active management of the Battalion falling to Herring and young Marks.

But for our Army's efficient medical staff, conditions must certainly have been much more serious. As it was, fever and cholera werepractically unknown on Gallipoli, although, in July, owing to the danger of an outbreak of cholera, all were inoculated against it. Our evening swim helped greatly to keep us fit, and was the one enjoyable event we looked forward to each sultry day. Still, in spite of the monotony of food, work, flies, chats, heat and scenery; in spite, too, of the wearied bodies and thin, the morale of the Battalion remained splendid. Many of those evacuated sick or wounded to Egypt left hospital without leave to join in with the Light Horse units going to Gallipoli to get back with their cobbers. The spirit of mateship was the main call that took these men back, and that held others almost too ill to stand from parading sick; but the spirit of getting the job done was a close second.

As we were likely to be called upon at any moment to enter action we had repeated "stand-tos," all falling in and remaining ready to move anywhere at half-an-hour's notice. Sudden alarms were given, especially for the Battalion on Inlying Piquet, and tremendous rivalry was evinced between companies at falling in completely equipped. "C" Coy., now under Capt. Norton-Russell, became so famous at being unbeatable, that others began to wonder where, or if he had got the "dinkum oil" about the time for the alarm. Members of other companies still aver that "C" occasionally beat the whistle.

Enemy planes became active in July, one German plane dropping proclamations calling on us to surrender; and another, on 31st July, dropping bombs and showers of short steel arrows, almost harmlessly, however. Some of the darts failed to penetrate the waterproof sheets that formed the roofs of most of the "bivvies," but others went two feet into the ground, and were valued souvenirs when dug out.

We also heard, in July, that the Turks were preparing a tremendous attack during Ramadam, and that they had been supplied with the gas the Germans had used so brutally in April at Ypres. On 21st we were issued with gas helmets—clammy things chemically treated —which fitted right over the head like a sack, and which were tucked in under the tunic. They had eye-pieces, but no mouths. They were a big advance over the chemical cotton wool pads hurriedly issued after the first example of such Hunnish frightfulness, but by no means the perfect respirator issued later. By now we also had a fine lot of bombers, Lt. Hugh Pulling training them.

Although surrounded by mates, and with boats always in sight, there was on Gallipoli unforgettable loneliness. We seemed so isolated from the rest of the throbbing world. When off duty we visited friends in other units, even in the front line, although during those hot days the front trenches were almost uninhabitable on account of dead Turks lying in No Man's Land.

For a while in Reserve Gully the artistic had gained aesthetic enjoyment from the glorious sunsets behind Samothrace and the rugged outlines of Imbros, the blue Aegean Sea lapping the shore at their feet and its changing moods. Most of the Diggers were lovers of Nature and her works, but even the beauties of Aegean sunrises and sunsets became monotonous, and were forgotten in the stewing afternoons.

Concerts were frequently held and all joined in the choruses, which could be heard out on Pope's and Quinn's. The concert of 4th August was a memorable one. It went right from the beginning with a tremendous vim, for all not only felt that we had had a successful year, but all knew that tremendous changes would take place before the next concert, and desired to make the most of this one. We had, for the past few days, been preparing for a move somewhere. Ammunition supplies had been examined and made up not only individually, but Battalion and Brigade reserves had been built up, our Lt. H. McDonald being placed in charge of the latter. Our Brigade C.Os. and Co. Cmrs. had journeyed along the coast towards Suvla in a destroyer, and we rightly conjectured that our next move would be in that direction.

Chapter VIII.—A Wonderful Night March.

AS the day of our next big attack approached everyone became in the best of spirits, for all were "fed up" with the two months' so-called rest in Reserve Gully. The 6th Reinforcements, who had just arrived, were even keener for a fight. All believed that this attack would be a great success, for large forces were co-operating, and the Navy was to give considerable help with guns. The Australian Division was to attack at Lone Pine, and the Light Horse at Quinn's and Walker's Ridge. The New Zealanders were to assault Chunuk Bair from the direction of Chailak Dere.

The Left Assaulting Column was to include our 4th Bde. and an Indian Bde. under Gen. Cox. This column's objective was to be Koja Chemen Tepe and its Northern Spur, called Abdel Rahman Bair.

There was to be still another great assault by Imperial troops from Suvla Bay.

By this tremendous combined attack it was hoped to capture that great mass of Koja Chemen Tepe, with its highest point, Knoll 305 or "971," and all its spurs, which mass overtowered completely all the Peninsula between Anzac and the Narrows. How it failed, mainly through the Suvla Muddle, is a matter of general history. Had it succeeded the capture of the whole Peninsula was a foregone conclusion. The glorious, if small part, played by the 13th, is one to be proud of.

After a few days' preparation during which bayonets were sharpened and encased with hessian, except for the points, and battle rations issued, on the evening of 6th August, the Brigade fell in to bid farewell to Monash Valley Area. At 9 the 13th, as head of the column, marched out from Reserve Gully down towards the Beach, whence it turned Northwards to follow the Beach for about 2 miles to the mouth of Aghyl Dere Valley, up the three great, and many smaller, branches of which it was intended to advance.

Guided by Major Overton (a New Zealander) and a Turk, accompanied by our Staff Captain and three 13th Scouts, Col. Tilney, Herring, Marks and Padre Wray marched at the head of the Battalion, the Padre insisting on remaining there.

Like a long, dark caterpillar the column moved through the intense darkness, and, like a caterpillar, it was silent, and wriggling. No one who took part in it will ever forget that march. To many it was a nightmare, to others intensely interesting, to all uncanny. The Aegean Sea could be dimly seen, rising up to the horizon as if to fall on us, and on it were the shapeless blotches of warships; overhead were stars in a cloudy sky, and on our right were cliffs illumined by a searchlight from the "Colne" in order to blind the Turks who might be venturing to gaze beachwards in spite of the shells she was pouring into their lighted trenches. The gunboat had been playing this game on the Turks every night of late in order to get them used to the nightly stunt with the idea that they would retire to their dugouts until the strafe was over. Had those sailors accidentally slipped their light onto us just a few feet lower than its beam, there would have been a different story to tell, but no one felt uncomfortable about that light. The attack had already commenced on our Right and behind us, and we came in for a share of the "overs," bullets causing several casualties in the column, and many shells screaming overhead into the sea. It was an eerie feeling to be marching in column over ground where by day no one could safely show his head.

With the best of previous reconnaissance night-marches are generally nightmares. They must be more so when the line of march lies through enemy territory over which no previous observations can be made. This night became more intensely dark as the head of the column turned its back to the sea and our Scouts ran against an enemy post which was quickly rushed by them and the leading Platoon, giving us 20 prisoners. In the darkness we had turned up into Taylor's Gap instead of into Aghyl Dere, another 500 yards ahead, but, although the mistake was soon noticed, there was no turning back, for we guessed that this gap would lead into Aghyl Dere. It was perhaps a fortunate mistake, for we cut off a Turkish outpost on Walden Point, although such errors are likely to demoralise men who recognise that their guides are uncertain of the track. The Turks on Bauchop Hill on our Right were now aroused and fired heavily into and over us. The column halted while "A" Coy. went ahead to clear the way. No. 1 Platoon went up onto Bauchop, and No. 2 onto a spur of Damakjelik Bair, both Platoons, and the others later, making the enemy flashes their objectives. Still proceeding up the dry bed of the shallow Dere, "A" again ran into Turks. No. 3 Platoon, under Lee, gallantly charged this position and soon had the Turks running, following them closely up the valley until they were fired on from another bank at about 30 yards' range, the Platoon suffering severely. Dozens of shadowy figures could be seen moving about in the dim starlight. Lee ordered two of his sections to cover the advance of the other two with rifle fire—the only possible way to advance here. The Turks were soon routed, but Lee and many of his gallant men had become casualties, Lee being wounded in the arm and thigh. "A" Company of the 14th Bn. now relieved No. 3 Platoon, and Lee handed over his command to Lt. J. McLeod, who had just that evening received his commission. No. 4 Platoon was doing similar work on the North of the Dere, so "A" Coy. were soon all engaged. "B" and "C" were also soon drawn into these outposts fights, only one Company of the Battalion being left in the column. A Turkish colonel was captured in his pyjamas, but a gun near his Hqrs. escaped by a few seconds, being limbered up and dragged off at a gallop. Overton was shot dead at the head of the column at short range. The men nearest him rushed the enemy, a few more Turkish shots rang out above the crunching of the brushwood, a few agonised "Allahs!" and silence until more crunching told that our men were again advancing. Still the Turks challenged from both sides of the narrow valley through which the column was now advancing in twos. Lt. Perry who had been so consistent in his magnificent work ever since the landing, was badly wounded, his men feeling his loss as that of a dear friend, so self-sacrificing had he been in their interests. Lt. H. Ford led his Platoon over ridge after ridge, climbing up by hanging onto prickly shrubs, charging the enemy flashes before chasing the runaways into other inky valleys. It would take a book to describe the work of the various Platoons that night, all without exception being led and fighting gallantly.

Near the junction of Australia Valley and Aghyl Dere the remainder of the Battalion—"A", "B" and "C" having been detached—formed up in a wheatfield, when the Turks opened fire on them, but thanks to the darkness and the fact that they seemed rattled, their fire was not very serious. From here Tilney took charge of the 14th Bn. as well as the remnants of the 13th, and moved up Australia Valley to take up an outpost position facing North from Damakjelik Bair across to Abdel Rahman Bair. Australia Valley branched in all directions into so many black arms that soon no one had any idea of just where they were. Tilney halted and sent Hopkins out to locate a British Battalion supposed to be on the far side of Damakjelik Bair. Hopkins did a great bit of scout work, found the Wiltshires and returned and guided the column to its proper position in line with them on their right. It was now 3.20 a.m., which meant only an hour of semi-darkness in which to dig in, so all dug willingly although practically all the picks and shovels had been lost during the scraps along the route.

The other three companies guarded the line of march until the whole of the 4th and the Indian Bdes. had passed safely, and then came up to our new position, digging in like "D", only ceasing to capture a score of the hundred Turks rounded up by the 15th Bn. in the Dere and driven towards us.

Our Machine-Gun Section was given the task of guarding our left Brigade flank, facing towards Suvla. The 13th had always been proud of this section, so splendid had been its work and so gallant its personnel. During this march they had carried on the average 50lbs more than the others, and had arrived at their objective without losing a cartridge on the route, having carried even the load of one of their number wounded just after leaving Reserve Gully. Lt. Legge was rightly proud of them.

The wonderful night-march was over. It was indeed a magnificent penetration of the enemy's territory, and, although such a striking success, was likely to have been a tremendous disaster. It was only the gallantry of the platoons of the 13th in charging grimly up cliffs under the barrels of the enemy, and, with a very few necessary exceptions, without a word, cheer or shot, clearing the way at the point of the silent bayonet, that saved the march from being a disaster, and allowing it to rank as it does, with that night-march of Tel-el-Kebir in 1882. The night-march was over successfully, but the 13th had lost 11 killed and 59 wounded in and near Taylor's Gap, Aghyl Dere and Australia Valley.

With dawn enemy snipers got busy, but our shallow trenches protected us until they commenced shrapnelling. They had been so surprised, however, that it was not until many hours later that their firing and shelling became severe. By 8 o'clock the day was blazing hot and water was scarce. Men who had not conserved theirs soon began to be agonised. "I'll give ten bob for a mouthful", a thoughtless one called out, but there were no takers. We sat huddled in the sun until noon when "13th get ready to move!" came along, and soon we were making north again through a well-shrapnelled branch of Kaiajik Dere where dead Tommies and Gurkhas lay thick. We were now dead-beat, tired and thirsty and the mile seemed like five before we halted 50 yards behind the rest of the Brigade digging-in near Hill 60 and Kaiajik Dere. We were still under shrapnel and Lt. C. W. L. Pulling was killed. He was the makings of a fine officer and had done splendid work consistently since his famous stunt at Quinn's.

Some water which had been stored in tins for a long time was now issued. It was red with rust but was eagerly drunk. We also had a change of diet in the form of honey and mulberries obtained by parties fossicking near Susak Kuyu, gas-helmets being used to rob the hives, several making themselves sick with too much. It was not long before snipers sent the honey-seekers back into the Dere. During the remainder of the day we had 2 more killed, and 14 wounded, including Lt. Marks, our Adjutant Although we were now constantly under a hot fire from rifles, machine and field-guns from the Turks who had soon filled all the valleys and occupied all the spurs on our new front, all agreed that evening that the head of Australia Valley was a much more agreeable place to live in than Reserve Gully. All breathed deeper and enjoyed it for the air was purer and free from the dust that had constantly filled it back there. That night we took over the Front Line from the 14th Bn. to allow them to co-operate with the 15th and 16th Bns. in an attack on the remainder of Abdel Rahman Bair, which was unfortunately a failure and one of the bloodiest battles of the 4th Bde. It was a failure owing to the bungle of Suvla Bay. Hence it was that we had to spend the next month fighting stubbornly on the heights overlooking Australia Valley, and being overlooked by the enemy on Abdel Rahman Bair.

The SEAWARD VALLEYS of NORTH ANZAC

Chapter IX.—Australia Valley and Hill 60.

THE big attack by our sister Battalions commenced at dawn on the 8th August. The British divisions had landed at Suvla during the night. During the day the 13th held the whole of the Brigade Outpost Line and dug all day to the tune of crackling rifles and machine-guns, whistling bullets and bursting shrapnel, while the remnants of the broken 14th, 15th and 16th attackers worked their way back. During the day we had several casualties.

All night we stood-to, for the Turks had massed in overwhelming numbers all over Kaiajik Aghala on our immediate front. Finding no danger from Suvla, they turned their attention to our front. At dawn on the 9th the Dere in front of "C" was seen to be filled with them. They were rushing up the slope in small batches, but we withheld until 70 were right under us, when our hurricane fire wiped the whole of them out except half-a-dozen, who, escaping to shelter, worried us all the morning by sniping, hitting a dozen before the last was shot by Lt. Ford. Our losses for the day were 10 killed, including Lt. Hartnell-Sinclair, and 21 wounded. The war had been a great strain to one of Sinclair's temperament, but he had gallantly fought his inner self, and died while risking his life in the interests of his men. Another fine man to die here was Sgt. Iredale.

Again all day we dug under a blazing sun, with no water, a few at a time managing to get a few hours' sleep, most having had none for 80 hours. All night again fresh hordes of Turks massed in Kaiajik Dere and on Kaiajik Agahla, their patrols and ours scrapping among the bushes in the Dere. Just after midnight great masses of them assembled in battle formation within 50 yards of us. We watched into the gloom with our fingers on our triggers until 2 a.m., when we saw great hordes within a few yards creeping onto us. As we opened fire they rose and rushed, several reaching our trench, to die there, however. Within a moment a hundred hand-to-hand fights were taking place, those not using their bayonets pouring bullets into the second and third waves rushing up the slope. Men just fired without sighting in the gloom. It was a grim, voiceless struggle—no orders, invitations or callings on Allah from the combatants. Day dawned, and still the fight raged, but with the light the Turks had no chance of sending reinforcements. By 6 it was all over, and the 15th Bn. Bombers, who had hurried to our assistance, went back to their Support Line. Our losses were 13 killed, including Lt. J. H. McLeod, and 15 wounded. (The strength of our splendid brigade on the 6th was 3,333, on the 11th 1,250.)

After this strenuous period we were relieved by the 14th, and rested until evening, when the Turks attacked again and we went to the help of the 14th, remaining there all night on account of the threatening massing in the Dere. We were in and out 24 hours each way for the next ten days, the period out being employed in carrying, strengthening and burying parties, all under a harassing fire. There was always something doing with the Turks, and every day its casualty list, Capt. C. B. Hopkins being among the wounded on the 11th, and Capt. Legge on the 12th. Lt. H. W. Murray, D.C.M., now took charge of our machine-guns, Legge later becoming Bde. M.G.O., and winning the D.S.O. Murray, who had been a Cpl. in the 16th Bn., made a splendid reputation for himself in this area.

While in support some Diggers played cards with the Gurkhas, between whom there was strong mutual admiration, and, although understanding not a word of each other's language, they seemed to have interesting games.

The popular Pte. Horan was killed on the 17th.

The 20th August brought word that the Brigade was to capture Hill 60, the attack to be in charge of Herring, who was to have nine officers and 250 men from both the 13th and 14th Bns. Lt. Ford was informed that he was to lead the first line of 150, his task being to cross the Dere, clear the first ridge, take three lines of trenches and occupy a position beyond them.

The 13th quota consisted of Lts. G. G. Gardiner, just rejoined, and 60 of "B," Lts. H. Ford, E. Moseley, and D. E. Wilson (O.P.), and 94 of "C," and Lts. B. Fletcher (O.P.), Carter and W. Scobie, and 96 of "D," and Major Herring, Lt. F. Thompson and Lt. W. Sutherland (O.P.). The first wave consisted of 150 of the 13th under Ford; the second of the 13th and 14th Bns., under Major Dare, and the third of both battalions under Gardiner.

O.P.—Original Private or one at the Landing.

At 2.45 p.m. the warships commenced bombarding the objective; at 3.15 Ford led his party out of our trenches near the Pivot, and lay down in a gully where they were promptly enfiladed, quite a number of casualties happening here.

At 3.30 Ford called out to Herring, standing in the trench nearby, "It's 3.30!"

"Well go!" called out Herring.

"Come on!" yelled Ford, as he jumped up, and his men rose as one man and rushed forward, running, however, into a murderous fire of rifles and machine-guns as they topped the ridge, a fire which mowed down many. They raced down hill, breaking evens, the bullets falling like hail in a hurricane. Such speed could not last uphill. Still all that was left of Ford's party reached the objective ridge by 3.32—a 200 yards rush down and up hill, through prickly scrub and over rocks and holes, loaded with rifle, ammunition and battle rations. All that were left, indeed; for in that 200 yards' charge 110 had fallen leaving Ford with 40 men. He himself could see only 6, but Sgt. N. McDonald (afterwards Captain) reported 15 on the right, and Sgt. E. Fletcher 20 on the left. These gamely attempted to fire in order to assist the second wave, but more were killed, including gallant and popular Pte. C. Hatch (Orig.). It would have been madness to have continued with so weak a force of exhausted men, exhausted from 15 days' hard work, fighting and short rations, and that charge. Let an ordinary reader in good health rush 200 yards over rough country with a load of 50lbs.

As he ran up the ridge Ford had seen the Turks retiring from their first to their second trench 70 yards farther on, over open ground.

At 3.45 the second wave commenced its rush and suffered as severely as Ford's. Major Dare, however, got through and now took charge of the line. The firing was tremendous from the front and right flank; so Dare decided to dig-in and fill sandbags for protection.

The third wave, loaded with tools and wire, attempted to advance but suffered so heavily that they were unable to do so, although Gardiner's example was inspiring.

The Hampshire Coy., supporting us, then attempted the crossing, but failed completely in spite of the greatest gallantry, practically all falling. Those over the Dere worked feverishly at strengthening their position, especially when they saw there was no hope of help arriving during daylight. The wounded lying in the Dere were in a sad way, for the Turks cruelly fired on them every time they attempted to crawl or stagger back, and on every bearer who attempted to reach them. There was no doubt about it, and it was not isolated, but organised firing, not at a few, but at all the wounded and bearers. The dirt in the Turk came out that afternoon. One of their "Jack Johnsons," which blew the Hampshires to pieces, set fire to the scrub, and as the wounded crawled from the flames they became Turkish targets. The fire caught the clothes of those unable to move and exploded their ammunition and bombs. The splendid Padre Gillison, of the 14th, and our famous stretcher-bearer, Cpl. Pittendrigh, rushed out to pull these helpless men from the flames and were shot down, giving their lives as such heroes and dinkum followers of Christ would.

At dusk Herring and the third line, loaded with picks, shovels and sandbags, crossed, and the fire-pits were soon formed into a trench; our Scouts linked up with the New Zealanders on the right, and the 15th Bn. dug a communication trench across the Dere to Herring's Post, as the new position was to be called, after that gallant officer, who had done, and was still to do so splendidly on Gallipoli, before similar service in France.

Such was the Battle of the 21st August. The Turks counter-attacked during the night, but were easily driven off. We were here on the north or right of Kaiajik Dere for as long as we liked to stay. Still the gain had been far too dearly purchased. The remembrance of the glory of the day is the only recompense we now have for the loss of so many wonderful young Australians, the 13th losses alone being four officers and 108 other ranks. Lt. W. Sutherland was killed, and Lts. D. Wilson (second time), Thompson and Carter wounded, the latter losing his leg. Herring was personally congratulated by Godley, and Ford was mentioned in dispatches for the day. Carter's work had been particularly good here. Had the part of the valley to be crossed been screened by smoke our losses would certainly have been minimised, but that was a matter for Division. Our men did their part and did it magnificently.

Much amusement was caused the next morning by a centipede, which caused Major Dare to undress himself to get rid of it. The place was alive with them.

AUSTRALIA VALLEY AND HILL 60

On the 22nd the 18th Bn., just arrived, attempted Hill 60 from another front and failed after 800 casualties.

At 2 a.m. on the 23rd we were relieved by the 16th under Major Margolin. We spent the time until the 27th in and out of the Front Line. On the 26th Tilney, who had again been fighting illness for weeks, was sent to hospital, Herring commanding the 13th until the return of Durrant on the 28th.

The Battle of the 27th August was another attack on Hill 60 by 200 men of the 4th Brigade, supported by 100 from the 17th Bn. Major Adams, of the 14th Bn. was in charge of this attack, his first wave consisting of 100 of the 14th, and his second of 100 of the 13th, our officers being Capt. Salier, Lts. J. Annoni (O.P.), N. L. Clarke and A. N. Brierley.

At 4 p.m. our artillery bombardment commenced, and our machine-guns swept over the slopes of Kaiajik Aghala to prevent enemy movement. At 4.30 the bombardment ceased for five minutes, when a more intense barrage was hurled onto the objective and trenches commanding it. This lasted until 5 when the barrage was lengthened and the attack commenced. Our artillery did not seem to have affected the Turk, for immediately the 14th hopped out they manned their trenches and swept our comrades back, fully 30 per cent. falling, including gallant Sgt. R. Ward. Each attempt to leave our trench was similarly treated. Still, although for a time it seemed as though nothing but casualties would result, several parties did succeed in advancing up the slope of Kaiajik Aghala and capturing several trenches, but not the objective, Hill 60, the commanding knoll of the spur. Our casualties were again regretfully heavy, amounting to 65, including the three subalterns, all of whom did splendid work. Annoni, who gave his life, was undoubtedly one of the finest soldiers and personalities ever in the 13th, both as an N.C.O. and Officer.

The 13th, along with the rest of the 4th Brigade is rightly proud of its laurels won near Hill 60. Although the Battalion was never at any other time so weak physically, its members, by sheer will force fought, carried, dug, charged and appeared happy. Their will to do their job conquered their bodily weakness, and was perhaps the cause of their being kept in the line fighting when they should have been convalescing, the higher authorities believing from appearances, their reserve of strength higher than it was. On the 28th Capt. H. J. Salier, who had been fighting ill-health and doing his duty most splendidly at the same time, was taken to hospital ship. Lt. Harry Murray looked thin and ill, but he remained full of spirits, watching and sniping all day with his Maxim. He worried the Turks tremendously and they retaliated, but could never find his skilfully-hidden gun. How he enjoyed it!

On the 31st we were relieved by Essex and moved half-way back to Monash Valley to a post that was to be called after our gallant Acting-Commander, Durrant's Post.

During the month three of our Scouts, under Cpl. Kelly (O.P.), had been attached to the English troops near Suvla Bay, for special scouting work, and received much praise.

Others, who by consistent heroism, cheerful service and self-sacrifice had already made all ranks proud of them, were: G. Knox (after Major Knox, M.C.), C. Potts, W. Worner, A. Wright, J. Young, F. Pitt, E. Pennell, W. Rankin, G. Simpson, P. Lambert, J. Wise, A. W. Davis, R. Kell, C. Witcombe, J. Watson, A. Taylor, G. and H. Thompson, F. Wheal, K. Waugh, A. Nixon, J. and J. R. O'Donnell, H. Meehan, J. McCafferty, J. M'Kenzie, J. Middleton, W. Brown, L. Canning, J. Compton, W. Bailey, J. Holman, W. Schadel, A. Le Clerc, R. Wilson, R. Wells, H. B. Brown, N. J. Brown, R. Chapman, K. Elder, G. McDowell, E. Fathers, J. Prescott, J. Buckle, W. Edwards, H. Maiden, T. Mawer, W. Mallard, P. O'Reilly, R. Miles, E. Mozar, E. Lind, J. Lowick, W. Doig, A. Dowding, T. Downing, J. Edmonds, S. Gow, H. Gadsby, D. O'Leary, S. Watts, M. Wall, J. White, E. Upton, H. Paterson, W. Richardson, H. Gunderson, N. Tolmie, E. Stanford, F. Powell, W. Scott.

Chapter X.—Durrant's Post and Sarpi Camp.

AFTER a few hours' rest in Aghyl Dere behind Bauchop's Hill, we relieved the North Staffords on Durrant's Post and remained there until the 12th September, when we were relieved by the 25th Bn. A.I.F., to march to Anzac Beach to embark for Mudros for a month's rest. During this fortnight at Durrant's Post our main work had been digging a deep, wide trench from Chailak Dere right to the Post, in order that mules might carry supplies right up and so save man-handling, digging wells in search of water, some of them being 20 feet deep, deepening all trenches and tunnelling a new front line, the roof of which we afterwards burst to make it into a trench, improving accommodation, and patrolling.

Although the Post was a healthy position, being 700 yards above the sea, which seemed right under us, the weather was stifling, flies agonising and men weak. Hence there was a deal of sickness.

I would like to dwell upon the feelings of all as they boarded the barge climbed out of it onto the "Abbasieh" and sailed for Mudros for even a short rest, watching Anzac fading behind in the night, but the great things in our history which must be told will not permit more than a mention of sentiments, and one's feelings to open out must be curbed.

A joke cannot be omitted, however. As the 25th were coming in to relieve us, at a certain point they all fell flat on their stomachs and crawled thus for a chain, a couple of 13th Diggers urging them to "hug the bottom of the trench for nearly 50 yards." Platoon after platoon of the 25th crawled through here. When morning came they found that they had crawled through the deepest trench in the area, one over 12 feet deep, but their advisers had gone, luckily for them.

Durrant remained as Advising Officer to the new unit, and Murray in charge of the important machine-guns at the Apex until the new gunners became conversant with the position.

At 9 a.m. the next morning the Battalion arrived at Mudros and was met by Herring and guided to the tented camp at Sarpi, which that officer had made ready during the previous few days.

The relief of being away, right away, from the strain of constant battle, was intense. Men had forced their strength to such an extent to hang on that they had come to the end of their reserve, and many fell helpless to the ground on reaching the shore. About 250 remained of the Original 1,100 and six reinforcements of 800. It brings a lump in the throat to dwell on it. Apart from sickness the Battalion's casualties had already been:—

	Officers.	Other Ranks.	Total.
Killed	12	226	238
Wounded	28	625	653
Total	40	851	891

Still, after resting and building up, the Battalion went back to Anzac with its spirit as high as ever.

The rest at Mudros was not very eventful, and may be treated in the form of a few notes.

Stout or beer was issued each evening and was much appreciated.

16th September.—Brigade inspected by Admiral Geufratti (French Navy).

18th.—Lt. Marks left for duty at Alexandria, and Lt. A. G. Fox became Acting-Adjutant.

21st.—Inspection by Gen. Godley.

25th.—Cpl. H. Howden appointed 2nd-Lt. (He had done splendid work, and had still more to do before giving his life in Belgium (5/7/17.), as Major with M.C. and bar)

27.—Brigade Campfire Concert.

9th October.—Capt. G. Gardiner assumed command of the Battalion, vice Herring, in Egypt on duty with Monash.

Durrant in hospital, having been evacuated on his arrival at Sarpi at the beginning of the month.

13th.—Capt. Marks returned and assumed command of the Battalion.

DURRANT'S POST AND SARPI CAMP

20th.—Received farewell notice from Sir Ian Hamilton.

23rd.—Brigade Sports, 7th and 8th Reinforcements arrived. Moonlight Concert.

24th.—Inspection by Gen. Godley. Capt. Shellshear transferred and succeeded by Capt. J. C. Storey as R.M.O.

25th.—Reinforcements isolated on account of outbreak of mumps.

27th.—Inspection by C.-in-C., Gen. G. C. Munro.

In the afternoon the men paraded and sent a deputation to Marks for pay. They were told that the C.O. was doing all in his power to get it for them. They paraded to the Brigadier, who told them the same. The authorities were indeed doing all in their power to get the money from Egypt, but it seemed that their efforts were to be futile, for a few days at least. The 13th, however, struck it lucky, and in a peculiar way. A well-known two-up player came after dark to Marks and asked him to mind £300 for himself and £100 for his mate—their two-up winnings. They were afraid of having their wealth stolen. Marks was happy. He not only minded the money, but paid the Battalion with it the next morning to the envy of the other Bns. The men were indeed paid in their own coin, for the £400 they had lost gambling passed back to them as pay, all kinds and conditions of notes and coins being used. "I paid the 13th Battalion," was the proud boast of this fortunate gambler on several occasions later on.

28th.—Durrant returned.

31st.—Brigade moved from Lemnos back to Anzac. A busy and exciting day. 2 a.m., Reveille for Advanced Party. 3.30 a.m., Lt. Howden and 45 O.Rs. marched out to the Pier as baggage guard. 4 a.m., Reveille for remainder. 5.30, Battalion marched out to North Pier. 7.30 a.m., Battalion embarked on "Osmanieh" with 14th and 15th Battalions. Major Durrant O.C. Troops. 7.30 p.m., Arrived off Anzac, commenced to disembark at 8.50. A wind arose, and lighters containing Col. McGlinn, Capt. Twynam, Lts. Pulling, Fox, Henley, Henderson and 40 men had to cast off from the ship. So rough became the sea that the Landing Officer ordered a cessation of disembarking for the night. Stray bullets caused several casualties. The "Osmanieh" sailed away from Anzac to Imbros and remained there until 7 p.m. on the 1st November.

1st November.—Arrived at Anzac at 8.10 p.m., disembarked at Walker Pier, and marched to Watercourse Gully near Bauchop Hill. Lt. G. E. Knox evacuated with appendicitis.

3rd November.—Took over Durrant's Post from 28th Bn., The 13th took over Sections 1 and 2, the 14th Sections 3 to 6. The 13th also took over further frontage on the right from 27th Bn., the whole Post from the extreme right to Aghyl Dere being under command of Major Durrant. Our band broken up and instruments stored.

6th.—Epidemic of jaundice amongst "old hands." It had seemed strange coming back to the noise and bustle of Gallipoli after Lemnos, but all had settled down to it by the 6th. The rest now seemed like a dream, and it seemed that we had been on the Peninsula all our lives. Our battle casualties on Durrant's were light.

The following telegram was read in the front line: "Melbourne Cup first Patrobus second Westcourt third Carlita fourth Garlin 8/1, 50/1, 7/1 and 25/1 respectively. Half neck, length, length.—J. P. McGlinn, for G.O.C."

11th November.—Two have been killed during the past 10 days. Our greatest fight is against disease. Durrant has been ill with jaundice for a week, but is carrying on. The weather is now glorious—cold nights but warm, clear days. We have a fine M.O.—"Doc" Storey. He is full of go, and the men swear by him. He is determined to have the strictest sanitation everywhere in our area, and roundly strafes anyone guilty of the slightest neglect, even a high officer of another unit quailing before his plainly-expressed wrath. If every unit had a similar M.O. there would be no fear of disease. Capt. G. G. Gardiner has been doing good work as O.C., of No. 3 Post, containing men of the 13th and 14th Bns. We are now using telescopic rifles; also night sticks painted with phosphorus on our side for night firing.

13th.—Kitchener landed at Walker's Pier. All hands are at work building winter quarters.

16th.—"It's blowing like hell at present and our dugouts are full of dust, likewise our eyes, nose and ears. The sea is as rough as blazes. The Turks have been bombarding us lately. Our doctor is very energetic. He is short and thick-set and is called 'Tommy Burns.' He is living up to his reputation and has already had interviews with C.Os. of other units, and roused like blazes about their men fouling our area."

19th November.—Durrant evacuated with jaundice after a tough fight to remain. "We have been having mixed weather lately, tremendous wind-storms, thunder-storms and rain like 'cats and dogs.' Last night in the pelting rain the Turks got very jumpy and started a fusillade. So in the midst of the storm along came instructions to double all posts and have the supports in readiness. Everyone got wet. It is the sort of weather we get in midwinter in Goulburn. My hat, it is bitterly cold at night. Herring is in charge of the 13th.

24th November.—For 48 hours no guns, rifles or machine-guns are to be fired. Every available man is engaged on construction of underground winter quarters. We have completed the tunnel to the new firing line on the left of No. 1 Post.

25th.—Fierce gusts unroofed dugouts and rain poured in. The sea is stormy. All are wet and miserable and in the dark with sleet cutting into them. The thunder is terrific and the lightning blinding. The hillsides are slippery and the trenches scouring out with rushing waters. The rain is pouring into many of the dugouts. There will be a lot of work to do after this.

26th.—Ruse of silence extended another 24 hours. Turks are very jumpy and seem to expect something big from us. They have been exposing themselves and moving openly about.

27th.—Turks were seen massing on Chunuk Bair and dispersed by our artillery. Snow falling to-night. N.C.Os. like E. Cornish, J. Cooney and J. Coyle setting splendid examples.

28th.—A wonderful sight to most Australians who had never before seen snow. The hills and valleys this morning were all covered with a mantle of white. Most of us are still wet from the rain and the trenches are sloppy and muddy. The roofs of many of the shelters have collapsed with the weight of the snow. Our snipers to-day shot many Turks who evidently had thought we were going to remain silent again.

29th.—Still snowing. Ground is as hard as ice. Durrant and Herring have had a good deal of worry about the men's clothing, for they are not clothed as they should be. Both have sent in several requests for winter clothing. As soon as they were dry the men were cheerful. They are splendid, and doing their best to secure themselves against another "washing-out." Twynam is "setting us all an example of how to be cheerful when we ought to be miserable. He is well-liked by us all. Last time he was in Cairo he heard a row going on down a side street, and went to see what it was, when he heard R——, of "C," call out: "Are there any 13th in the crowd?" "I'm one," replied Twynam. "Well, hold my teeth while I stoush these cows," and R—— passed the Major his false teeth and returned to complete operations. Godley has complimented the Battalion on the general state of things. No stores have been landed for four days on account of the sea. Young Les Henley is brimming over with energy and bravery, his one aim in life lately being to capture a Turkish patrol." Ten men sent to hospital with frostbite. Lt. A. G. Fox is gallant, keen and humorous under all conditions.

30th.—Underground kitchen has been completed. Seven men sent to hospital with frostbites. Weather very rough and stores cannot land. "This cold weather has its good points, for the flies have gone and the lice are less lively."

"Lt. J. K. Henderson, one of the best, remains a source of amusement, never missing his daily bath in spite of snow and blizzards.

Each morning he is to be seen outside his dugout stripped naked bathing all over with a pint of water or rubbing all over with snow, never missing."

So ended the month of November, 1915. It had been about the most uncomfortable month on Gallipoli, with its myriads of flies for the first fortnight and its blizzards of dust, sleet and rain as well as the snow and cold of the last fortnight.

Chapter XI.—The Evacuation.

DESPITE the trials of the wintry weather, the health of all generally improved, so that on December 12th an official report reads: "Men in excellent health and spirits."

The 13th had dug so well in this area—they were past-masters now at digging—that, except when on duty they were well underground. They didn't expect, however the terrific rainstorms that came and flooded many out.

The first silent period had mystified both ourselves and Turks. The repetitions left no doubt in the minds of the Australians that they were evacuation stunts. Then rumors started, no one knowing how or on what authority but they were going strong by the 6th when Birdwood visited us and said: "I am hearing with astonishment rumors of evacuation." It was not until the 12th that Monash received his first intimation of evacuation and it then came to him "as a stupendous bolt from the blue."

In case the Turk should become aware of the removal of troops the bluff was broadcasted that units were being taken by turns to Imbros to winter quarters.

Despondent groups of Diggers gathered and they were unanimous in their desire to hang on through the winter and to continue their efforts to capture the Peninsula in 1916. They were willing to put up with winter discomforts, its storms, cold and short rations, and the loss of communication with the outside world in order to remain near where so many of their gallant comrades were lying. But the authorities felt that there was danger in attempting to remain with the certainty of weeks of stormy weather coming on.

On the 13th we bade a quiet farewell to the 15th Bn., who were taken off in barges. They packed and disappeared in two hours. The Brigade then extended its front, leaving the lines weakly held. Squads marched about in Aghyl and Chaijak Deres in order to keep up the appearance of continued strengthening.

On the 13th Monash wrote: "I have selected the pick of the 13th and 16th Bns. for our rearguard," and on the 14th: "Every man knows." Yes every man knew, and felt it more keenly than he had felt anything in his life; but Monash felt it even more keenly, his private journals indicating a feeling quite heartbreaking.

On the 16th he wrote: "The last 170, the 'Die-hards,' have been chosen from the most gallant and capable men in the Brigade."

Herring, in whom Monash had the greatest trust, was selected as O.C. of this Bde. Rear Party, and the 13th officers selected by him for the very final party were E. Twynam, H. C. Ford, G. G. Gardiner, and H. W. Murray, the lastnamed with his machine-guns.

The 16th had a similar party of "Die-hards," also under Herring.

On the 18th the enemy was exceptionally quiet, a fact that aroused suspicions. Each of the 170 "Die-hards" was given a card showing the exact timetable and map for his departure and route. Heavy weather begain to threaten and a strong wind to blow. The night air had become freezing, and the small band of watchers had neither overcoats nor blankets left to hamper, or to warm them. It seemed incredible to them that the evacuation was actually in progress behind them, so silent were all movements. During the last few days many had visited the graves of comrades for the last long look, a tear or a prayer.

Our four "Die-hard" officers had found great difficulty in selecting their men, so many volunteers having to be keenly disappointed. Practically every man volunteered on hearing the mere rumor of the fact that we were to provide one of the last parties. So acute was the disappointment that strong men brushed tears away. On their return from Headquarters to their Coys. the officers found that the news of their honor had preceded them, and they were greeted with "I'm with you, sir." Several pleaded hard over and over again. "I've been with you all along and I want to see the finish." Proud indeed were the men selected. Charlie Kaler fairly broke down when refusal met his repeated requests. The sole reason for the refusal of such a warrior was that he had been ill for weeks, refusing to report to the M.O., and Ford considered him not robust enough for a hard rearguard fight.

Several times Murray, Gardiner and Ford explained that they could only select a few, and that these must be the best and strongest and most active, in addition to their other proved gallant qualities. For the very final party Ford selected Sgt. G. T. Rogers and Ptes. G. S. McDowell, C. M. Potts and J. B. Kirkwood.

The 14th had left, along with several details, the night after the 15th. On the night of the 18th 125 of the 13th left, and the remainder spread out still more. From 8 that evening until 8 the next, all watches were synchronised every hour. All day Sunday the few paraded the Deres. At 5 p.m. 170 men, under Lt. Barton, left. At 9 the Turks were wiring. At 9.15 Marks took another 100 away, including the M.O. These parties moved off after quiet hand-clasps and whispered "Cheeros" and "Good Lucks." There were now less than 4000 men on the whole of Anzac against 170,000 Turks. Still the latter could be heard wiring—joyful sounds—against us. The night was clear, bright and icy.

Now commenced the most anxious time. For over four long hours about 50 men of the 13th and 16th held a front that should have been held by more than a brigade. The stillness could be felt. On other nights they had been able to walk through the trenches and yarn and smoke with mates, but now long stretches were deserted. The loneliness was a load. To pass the time the few not actually watching destroyed what little material was left in the shape of rifles, dixies, bully and spades, and burying bombs. Reports were sent to Twynam every hour. Pte. Butler remained in lonely charge of a signal lamp on Little Tabletop until midnight.

Shortly after midnight an enemy plane flew low over us, and "Beachy Bill" barked thrice. At 1.50 a.m. on the 20th Twynam left with 10 men. There was now no connection between the three small parties out there and the beach. At 2 Gardiner, with 10, left his lonely post out on our extreme left; at 2.5 Murray with his two heavy machine-guns and their crews. Ford and his four men climbed out over the parapet and occupied a hole commanding a wider view; each with two rifles and a heap of bombs, determined to go out dearly if attacked. Still the Turks could be heard strengthening their wire in the distance.

All the party had labels on, orders having been given to write on them, in case of casualties, the nature of the wounds. Two tablets of morphia were to be placed under the tongue of a casualty before leaving him, but things would have been serious indeed for any 13th party to have left a wounded mate behind.

The last 10 minutes seemed even longer than the others since midnight. They listened to hear if their watches were ticking. Five where a Brigade should have been.

At last—2.15. They crawled back to the trench. A last seemingly long and disappointed look into the darkness of No Man's Land. All had done the same. A Turk was hammering a stake into the hard ground, driving it home to make his wire a greater obstacle to the Anzacs. A few shots were crackling on their right in the distance. Stunted shrubs looked like enemies creeping towards them. They dropped down into the trench. The last of the 4th Brigade were on their way to the Beach. Round the bays in the deep trenches they filed and across narrow gullies with even steady tramp, not one thinking of hurrying, as not one had thought of leaving before his time, the three gallant leaders, Murray, Gardiner and Ford bringing up the rear of their parties. The lonely trenches and gullies were soon left behind and beach sand was underfoot and the ocean gleaming and rising up in front. On account of the varying distances the three parties reached the Beach about the same time, Ford reporting to the S.O.: "Last of the 4th Brigade." The last few, including Herring, who had received reports of the successful withdrawals of the various parties of the 13th and 16th, now boarded the lighter and were taken to a transport which took them, just before dawn, towards Lemnos.

On their arrival there the whole Brigade turned out to welcome the last "Die-hards," comrades carrying their equipment and all cheering to the echo. Our band and the Royal Scots pipers played them through a cheering lane of Diggers and Kiwis for a mile. "We were commencing to think we were heroes," wrote one, "but, on arriving at camp, Gen. Monash addressed and thanked us, and we became ordinary soldiers again."

Thus ended the 4th Brigade's part of the famous Evacuation. Parties of other units from posts nearer the Beach left a little later than our last parties, their routes being shorter.

The Evacuation was one of the greatest feats in military and naval history. In regarding the fame of the Anzacs we may forget the Navy, but there is no Digger who will not willingly and emphatically give the Navy its due. It was solely owing to its support that we were able to land and remain eight months on Gallipoli, and then get off without a single casualty.

In connection with one of the "Die-hards" a peculiar and interesting occurrence took place. Pte. Pollock, having been on duty for some time, was relieved and given permission to have a sleep. He told his mates that he was going "into the dugout," and asked them jokingly to be sure to wake him before leaving. He then went to his old dugout—the one he and his mates had occupied for a considerable time prior to the final day, and some distance away. The party believed he was in the dugout they—forgetting that he had been on duty—had been using that day. They searched it and every possible sleeping place in their area, even delaying their time of leaving, and then concluded that Pollock had gone to the Beach. There was no chance of making sure until reaching Lemnos.

When Pollock awoke he thought it was about time he was called, so he strolled along the trench. It came as a jolting shock to him to find he was alone. A Turk was still driving a stake in in the distance, but there might be others in the trench. He hastened. What would he find around the next bay? And the next? He was happy when he reached the final valley, happier when he saw the sea and felt the beach underfoot. But there was no lighter there. The last of the Bde. had gone. He ran along the shore, feeling hopeless, until he came to a few boarding a lighter. They were the final party of specialists. On rejoining the Bn. a few days later, he was completely exonerated.

Chapter XII.—Ismailia, Moascar, Tel-el-Kebir, Serapeum.

UNCANNY indeed seemed that quiet week on Lemnos—no booming or crackling even in the distance, no Suicide Corners, Jacko's Delights or Roads to Heaven; no rushing past or ducking in certain areas—all strolled about just to get used to it strolling extravagantly, merely for the swanky feeling of pleasure it gave them. No parades—just keeping our area clean, short marches and games to keep ourselves warm. Rainy hours were spent in writing, reading and gambling.

The Christmas Eve Campfire Concert went hilariously, all indulging in "Aussie" smokes from the much-appreciated billies received that day. Everything seemed the sweeter because of its origin—Australia. The Christmas dinner was another great success, for all received a parcel from Australia, 13 cases, containing Australian pudding among a hundred other luxuries, having that morning arrived from home. Our Comforts Committee ladies had been splendid, and remained so throughout our history. Many wives, mothers and sisters worked day after day for five years on the 13th, and later the 13th and 45th Bn. Comforts Committee, in order to make the lot of their beloved fighting men and their comrades a little happier and more comfortable, even after their own nearest and dearest had paid the full price. The 13th and 45th are indeed proud of and whole-heartedly grateful to these devoted women. It is our unanimous wish that they should share with us any honor the present or the future may accord our units. Had these women been present on various occasions to see how the "big children" enjoyed opening their parcels, they would have felt amply recompensed.

On the 26th a few left for Egypt, being followed during the next few days by the remainder of the Brigade, most of the 13th spending New Year's Day on the "Tunisian," Herring being C.O. Troops, and Marks Ship's Adjutant.

Before leaving Lemnos an English General—one of eight—boarded and sent for the Ship's S.M., who happened to be Sgt. Tuson, a 13th Original. The S.S.M. doubled along in shirt and slacks.

"Are you the Ship's Sergeant-Major?"

"Yes, sir."

"Well, Sar-Maj'r I've some cases of valuable souvenirs. Very valuable! Will you please get a party of really reliable men to place them on board and guard them for me? There's a crowd of Australians aboard, you know."

"Yes, sir. Very well, sir."

On our arrival in Egypt we were grieved to hear of the death of our most popular T.O., Lt. Macarthur, who had died on Christmas Day from typhoid. He was buried with full honors in Old Cairo Cemetery.

During the second week at Ismailia an outbreak of cerebro-spinal meningitis caused a scare, all precautions, including gargling parades, being taken. Here general routine parades were carried out until the 20th, when preparations were made to move to Moascar, which was reached the next day, and where the Brigade remained until the 26th February, when it entrained for Tel-el-Kebir, remaining there until 26th March.

At Moascar, on 16th February, Col. Tilney, who had received his D.S.O. for his own and his Battalion's splendid work on Gallipoli, resumed command.

The 2nd March was the birthday of the 12th Brigade as a daughter Brigade of the 4th, the 13th, 14th, 15th and 16th being the parents respectively of the 45th, 46th, 47th and 48th Battalions. The official handing-over ceremony took place at 11 a.m. It was a particularly sad moment for the troops and officers transferred. At 10.59 they were members of the now-famous 13th; at 11 of the new 45th. There was not the slightest culling-out, two splendid Companies—"B" and "D"—being handed over in their entirety with the exception of Coy. Commander, C.S.M. and C.Q.M.S., and Major Herring, the first C.O. of the 45th, being allowed by Tilney choice for choice of the other officers. The 45th are as justly proud of their birth as the 13th are of their daughter.

In forming these new battalions, two opposing considerations had to be taken into account. It was important that a new battalion should contain a nucleus of officers and men experienced in war, and yet it was felt that it would be hard on those transferred to leave the unit they had so much learnt to love. However, efficiency was studied first in war's stern school. To reconcile the members of the "13th's Baby" it was arranged that the 45th should be a New South Wales battalion and still carry the two blues of which they were so immensely proud, the 45th wearing them shaped to form a circle,

Throughout the war there remained a wonderful camaraderie between the two "Two-Blues" Battalions. Needless to say they upheld the glory of these colors throughout their history and are as proud of them as we. Herring had well earned his position as C.O. of the new 45th by his continuous gallant service on Gallipoli from the Landing to the Evacuation, not having been off duty during that strenuous period. Altogether he took with him 10 of our officers and 363 other ranks. For several weeks there remained heart-pangs and strongly-felt opposition among those transferred at their severance from their "Old Batt." Some on returning from hospital and finding themselves out of the 13th, begged for re-transfer. "It fairly broke me up," wrote one of our most distinguished Original officers so transferred.

But the class of men transferred could not fail to make a similar esprit de corps in their new unit.

It was now that the 13th Comforts Committee became the 13th and 45th Comforts Committee, the work, although more than doubled, being carried on even more efficiently if possible than before.

The distribution of officers on the strength on 2nd March was as follows:—Parent Battalion: Lt.-Col. L. E. Tilney, D.S.O., V.D., Major E. Twynam, Capts. H. C. Ford, F. M. Barton, D. G. Marks (Adjutant), H. D. Pulling, A. G. Fox; Lts. H. L. Henley, H. W. Murray, D.C.M., J. K. Henderson, A. W. Davis, H. F. Murray, P. A. A. Lambert, A. Lanagan, R. H. Kell. Wing Battalion: Major S. C. E. Herring, Capt. C. B. Hopkins, Lts. S. L. Perry, H. C. Howden, G. E. Knox, A. S. Allen J. H. Holman, J. B. Kirkwood, W. H. Schadel, W. T. Meggitt, W. L. Young.

Of the above Murray, D.C.M., Davis, Lambert, Kell, Knox, Holman and Schadel were Original Privates. Herring became Bde. Gen., with C.M.G., D.S.O., C. de G., L.d'H.; Hopkins was killed in France (20/7/16); Perry became Lt.-Col. with D.S.O. and M.C., Howden as Major, with M.C. and Bar, died of wounds 5/7/17; Knox became Major with M.C., Allen a Lt.-Col. with D.S.O. and C. de G., Holman a Capt. with M.C. and Bar; Kirkwood was awarded D.C.M. for the last days on Gallipoli, Schadel became Capt. with M.C., Meggitt was killed in France 21/2/17, Young became Capt. with M.C. and was killed 14/8/16.

Officers transferred on their return from hospital were Lee, who became Major with D.S.O. and M.C., and Scobie, who went to the 4th Pioneers, where he continued his good work, becoming Capt. before being killed 7/8/16.

A big reinforcement of 454 on the 4th built the 13th up to a strength greater than before the 2nd. Of these some were old men returning, some had left Australia as reinforcements to the 1st or 30th Bns., but most had come as 11th and 13th reinforcements to the 13th. Those originally destined for other battalions retained their original regimental numbers prefixed by their original battalion number—e.g., 30/2978 and 1/5476. The total strength on the 5th was 25 officers and 956 othe rranks.

Now came a fortnight of further reorganisation, 37 machine-gunners being sent to the new 4th Brigade Machine-gun Coy., 53 to the 4th Div. Artillery, 26 to Pioneers, and 5 to Div. Sigs.

On the 17th we held St. Patrick's Sports, and on the 23rd Brigade Sports, the 13th at the latter winning the Drill Competition, Tug-of-war, Bombing Teams' Race, and Officers' Flag Race, Twynam's fine horsemanship being responsible for the last named.

The 25th brought a new experience—that of loading camels in preparation for a march across the desert to Serapeum. Within half-an-hour the Diggers were quite able to take charge of the beasts and sent the Hindoos away. Great amusement was caused in making the animals kneel, the Diggers having been told to pull their heads down and hiss. "S-s-s-s!" could be heard on all sides, but Sgt. Warner's camel remained standing stubbornly in spite of 10 minutes' hissing, until he, completely aggravated broke out into what his mates called "good Australian," which was instantly effective.

The three days' march—45 miles—that commenced next day, 26th March, will never be anything but a nightmare to many who took part in it, although the 4th Bde. came through it better than any other Brigade owing to the well-thought-out plans of Monash and his Brigade Major, now Durrant.

26/3/16.—4 a.m., Reveille. 7 a.m., Commenced march to Serapeum, the strength of the Battalion being 18 officers and 662 other ranks, with 56 horses, 19 vehicles and 47 camels.

A camel carried a 300lb. load made up of 88 blankets, 4 cases of biscuits or 5 of meat. Tel-el-Kebir had been an interesting town, but none were sorry to leave it for a new environment. All swung merrily along, whistling and singing, and resting 10 minutes every hour until noon, when, near the dirty old village of Kassassim, we commenced a three-hour rest. At 4.30 we bivouaced for the night at Mahsama, all being in splendid condition and happy. The ground all day had been fairly good. Not one fell out in the 13th, although 14 did in the Brigade.

27/3/16.—6.10 a.m., march resumed through the Mahsama Oasis. A dense fog until 9 a.m. 11.30 to 2, rested at North end of oasis. 2 p.m., resumed march over heavy sand dunes. Excellent march discipline was maintained until 4 p.m., when six fell out to lie along the roadside complaining of severe chafing and blistered feet. The two miles of extremely heavy sand just passed through had been a sore trial. In the Brigade 132 fell out, but 118 rejoined their Battalions before dark, having come along at their own pace. A few others straggled in during the night, but several were unable even to drag themselves along. The temperature had been high all day and the march 17 miles. Hearing of our trials the New Zealanders from Moascar came out along the road to meet us and gave us a brotherly welcome, although at first they chiacked us for being dressed like "Chooms," for we were all wearing helmets and Tommy "slacks." As our leading troops approached them they were greeted with, "They're not the Aussies; they're Chooms!" One called out: "Zay, choom, Oi give 'ee sixpence for Aussie shillun' wi' kangaroo on." Another: "Where be 'ee from, chooms?" To which the nearest Digger replied: "Oi be Devon!" The roar that greeted this reply left no further doubt, the Kiwis calling out, "Hooray, they're Aussies!"

The officers and sergeants were made the guests of the New Zealand messes and their canteens opened to the Diggers. All remember that happy night when the Kiwi entertained the Kangaroo. They also lent their horses to assist ours through the sand.

During this trying day several empty trains had passed us going towards Serapeum, causing hasty criticism about the Staff, but these trains were no concern of anyone connected with the A.I.F.

Many feet were badly blistered before the third day's march commenced. The New Zealanders again lent their horses, the road now being heavier than before. Almost from the start we found weary and footsore men from units ahead lying or sitting on the roadside, or dragging themselves along. The high spirit of these men could not overcome bodily weakness and the agony of chafing and blisters. Thick clouds of dust choked us and millions of stinging flies and vicious mosquitos kept many cursing Egypt and everything connected with it. Then came a hot southerly wind. The old hands had conserved their water, but the inexperienced were soon suffering from thirst. Some of the stragglers were seen drinking from forbidden places, with serious results in many cases. The 3-hours' rest for lunch a mile north of Serapeum West was shortened to one hour's on account of the pestiferous insects that came in cloud on cloud. So far the 13th's march had been splendid, but now straggling commenced seriously. The whole Brigade in fact was a ragged column of lumps, the rear being composed of men of all battalions. At the end of a 10-minutes' rest the stragglers would in many cases have just managed to rejoin their platoons when the "Continue march" order would come along.

About 2 p.m. we went into camp at Serapeum, a mile east of the Canal. It had been the most fatiguing march in our history, and the Brigade had left behind during the day 480 men, most of these during the last three miles of the worst sand on the route. After a sanctioned swim in Suez Canal, the majority marched in in organised bodies, but 67 of the Brigade were still along the track after nightfall.

From the bottom of our hearts had we appreciated the spontaneous and active sympathy of the New Zealanders, but at the same time we felt ashamed that our "Heads" should allow such a march to take place and render the A.I.F. the objects of sympathy to any other troops. It was a test march with troops unfitted as a body to be so tested. Eighty per cent. of the Brigade could have repeated that march straight away, and had not felt the fatigue, although the heat, dust and insects had tormented them greatly; but there were others still ship-weak, or just returned from hospital after Gallipoli wounds or illness, men, who, following the example of most Gallipoli wounded heroes, had begged to be allowed to return to their units even before properly convalescent. "I'd do a dozen hop-overs before another march like this," a distinguished but weak Digger had told his officer at Serapeum West. Still it is recorded that "The 13th came through better than any Battalion."

The same evening we had to take on our strength 200 rejects from the 1st Brigade—very hard after losing our splendid men to the 45th and other units just before. We expected trouble and slackness from such a large body, but, whether it was the prestige of their new Battalion or the influence of the old hands, those we kept permanently—about 120—generally made good, and, later on, on the bloody, muddy fields of France and Belgium did work equal to that of any troops in the world, and died as gamely. Perhaps it was the fact that no Conduct sheets arrived with them all accordingly starting off in the 13th with "Clean Sheets," that helped. A "red" Conduct Sheet is a disheartening introduction. What a splendid thing it would be to destroy all soiled Conduct Sheets after, say, six months' dinkum service by their owners!

The physique and training of these rejects were far below the original 13th standard. Still those who remained with us turned out, on the whole, trumps. They perhaps troubled their officers, but they troubled the enemy more.

Another quota on 2nd April, including many returning Gallipoli veterans, brought our strength up to 1189, which, being too high, gave the opportunity of getting rid of 85 "least desirable"—practically all being from the "rejects" above mentioned. A few of these men were in eight units during their stay in Egypt, being rejected by each in turn. Four years after the war some of them were seen wearing the honorable badges of Returned Soldiers and the colors of Battalions of glorious history, rattling collection boxes as suffering Warriors! Had our nation treated all incapacitated Dinkums justly the public would know that there was no need for begging, and the charity they now dispense carelessly in the streets would perhaps go into more worthy channels. Thank heaven not 1 per cent. of the Diggers were such as even to desire charity. Thousands suffering cruelly are battling manfully to help themselves, trying even to forget that they were at the war. Of the others, too, one must make a great distinction between men whose minds, nerves and bodies were enfeebled by actual war service, and undesirable rejects.

Major Twynam was appointed Bde. Musketry Officer in April, and did splendid work, being highly complimented on his ingenious system of disappearing targets.

On the 10th April, 10 men were selected from each Coy. to be trained as special bombers, the first Bombing Officer being Lt. H. D. Pulling, who had had the training of our bombers on Gallipoli. Later B.Os. were Lts. R. Henderson, G. S. McDowell and T. A. White. In addition to special bombers, every man later on was trained in bombing.

At the Brigade aquatic sports in the Canal on the 12th, the 13th won the Brigade Cup and practically all the programme. Sir A. Murray and the Prince inspected us on the 20th, the latter especially being heartily and cordially cheered, as he had also been at Tel-el-Kebir.

After a Memorial Service at 6.45 a.m., Anzac Day was celebrated by Div. Aquatic Sports, the arrangements and programme leaving nothing to be desired. Those at the Landing wore red and blue ribbons during the day, others with Gallipoli service blue.

The remainder of April and May was spent training solidly in the desert, and other routine work and operations. The heat during May was fearful.

At Serapeum reinforcements that had taken part in the riot in Sydney arrived, and a few boasted of the part they had taken in the affair, until a well-known Original, Wilson, heard them. He asked the leading boaster: "Did you break any windows?"

"Yes, dozens."

Whack! Whack! "Now get up and tell what else you did," invited the indignant Wilson. "Get up!"

"I was only bragging," humbly replied the man on the ground.

"Did anyone else here break windows?" invited our warrior, but no one appeared to hear him.

On the evening of the 31st May the Battalion—32 officers and 992 other ranks—entrained at Serapeum for Alexandria, embarking the next day on the "Transylvania"—the transport on the "Haverford"—for Marseilles. We had finished with Egypt and were unanimously joyed to be proceeding to France where something was doing.

Chapter XIII.—Flanders, Bois Grenier.

AFTER an enjoyable and uneventful voyage the 13th reached Marseilles on the 7th, interested in everything in that busy port, especially the Chateu d'If. The voyage had been a soothing relief to the sand-tired eyes, but the scenery of the South and Centre of France was heavenly. What month is more glorious than June in France?

As the trains progressed northwards we were received with the greatest friendliness and enthusiasm. During the 8th, 9th, and 10th we passed through Orange, Lyon, Macon, Dijon, Montereau, Versailles, Amiens, Abbeville and Hazebrouck, ending our journey at Bailleul on the evening of the 10th and marching to its suburb Steent-Je, a mile to the south-west, the station being left behind by the whole Battalion within 33 minutes of arrival.

Along the route the French Red Cross ladies gave us refreshments. Especially at Dijon, where we passed crowds of French soldiers, the enthusiasm was intense. Our band played the "Marseillaise," stirring the populace as only it can stir, and they can be stirred. At Amiens we heard the big guns on the Somme, and from Bailleul could be heard the continuous rumble from Armentieres to Ypres, and the majority of the Battalion got their first views of shell bursts as a British plane circled over the German lines in a sky spotted with shell-puffs like measles.

Steent-Je was a delightful spot, not only for its green fields, orchards, hop-trellises and picturesque trees, but also for the warm-heartedness of its people. The change from Egypt and from anything in our lives before was novel and interesting, although later both these qualities disappeared from French and Belgian billets. It was a novelty for the French, too, for although already war-weary, they found the Australians so different to any other troops billeted among them. At least they said so. They turned out in a body to hear our band play the next afternoon—Sunday—in their square.

Much enjoyment, except to the owners of four roosters, was occasioned by the Battalion's bantam rooster, the mascot of the 13th reinforcements, on its arrival in its first farmyard since leaving Australia. In succession it defeated the four, the smallest being about eight times its size, the Diggers seeing fair play. That evening, listening to the rooster owners, the Diggers learnt practically all the French swear words in general use. Later this bantam and a wife picked up at a shattered farm, rode everywhere on our transport, and finally returned to Sydney, having been in the front line.

Another mascot—for a time—was a tiny mongrel that attached itself to the Bombers, marching everywhere with them, wearing its khaki tunic with becoming dignity. As time went on, it was promoted—one, two, three stripes and a M.M., and answered to the name of "Sgt. Toute de Suite, M.M."

13th July.—Memorial Service for Kitchener. Inspection of billets by Birdwood, who chatted freely with all.

15th.—Steel helmets issued. They were extremely valuable and meant the saving of many lives.

17th.—Moved to Erquinghem and the south-west outskirts of Armentieres preparatory to taking over part of the Line south of Bois Grenier. The 4th Bde. was transferred temporarily to the 2nd Australian Div. Here we commenced training raiding parties, the trenches for training being a model of those we would probably be called upon to attack.

Each day some officers went into the Front Line for a period to gain experience of Western Front conditions, Lt. D. P. Wells being wounded on this duty on the 26th, on which day our advanced parties went forward to arrange for the relief of the 18th Bn. Other of our parties moved into the Front Line on the 27th, and at midnight on the 28th we were in entire possession of our first Battalion area on the Western Front.

Three Coys. occupied the Front Line with seven Lewis and two Vickers guns, and one Coy. the Support Line on the southern outskirts of Bois Grenier, Bn. Hqrs. being at White City, between Queer Street and New Queer Street. The 13th was right in it on the Western Front, and in a most interesting, albeit quiet parded as a quiet area, being called "The Nur-art. Bois Grenier area was the scene of Ian Hay's first experiences. It had long been reg sery," because it was the breaking-in place for new troops. But it did not long remain "a home from home," when the Australians arrived, each day bringing its list of casualties.

The 14th Bn. made an unsuccessful but gallant raid on the 2nd July, and Fritz raided them on the 3rd, the 14th losing 73. Both sides were aroused and bursts of terrific cannonading crashed down every now and again. We had 4 killed and 10 wounded on the 2nd in Chord Line.

Each evening our scouts searched No Man's Land right to the German wire, Lt. C. Boccard repeating the magnificent patrolling that had made him and Howden so famous on Gallipoli.

On July 10th an enemy flag was seen flying in No Man's Land against the German wire. It was a challenge, and Boccard determined to accept it. With Pte. L. Ruhan (O.P.) he crept out that night. The enemy was particularly active, and determined to keep their flag, having stakes painted with phosphorus fixed in front of it in order to show up anyone moving between the stakes and them. The two gamely crept closer and closer under a hail of lead that told them that they were seen. They lay still for a few minutes, hugging the ground; then on again. A final rush and Boccard had the flag. Another fusillade poured towards them. They hugged the ground until the fury passed. They crawled cautiously, lying still as enemy flares were brightest over them or their hail heaviest. Then a few more yards towards home. A few more. A long crawl, and a rush, and they felt they were safe. But their luck was out. They had outwitted the Germans with all their preparations to fall to Australian bullets. The Lewis-gunners of the 29th Bn. fired on the figures rushing in the dimness towards our lines, and their firing was sadly accurate. Ruhan was killed and Boccard's leg smashed badly. As he, after dragging himself back, was being carried to our Aid Post, Tilney came to see him. "I've got the flag, Colonel"—he proudly drew it from his tunic— "but I'd sooner have my leg." He had only the previous month rejoined after his severe Gallipoli wound. With his artificial leg he was now ordered to return to Australia, but on his own request, was allowed to return to France, becoming Intelligence Officer to the 4th Div., and receiving the M.C. Later he became, on account of his fluent French, an Intelligence Officer at Amiens, and did magnificent work getting civilians away in 1918, receiving a Bar to M.C. and Croix de Guerre for what the French General de Laguiche called "glorious activity and unsurpassable devotion to duty in March and April, 1918. In spite of his infirmity, he went everywhere under shellfire, and continuously set a splendid example of coolness and sangfroid." He was always a welcome visitor to the 13th when we were in that area.

On the night of the 11th we were relieved by the 29th Bn., arriving back at Fort Rompu at 4 a.m., remaining there until after lunch, when we marched back to Steent-Je.

About noon on the 13th July we bade farewell to our dear friends and entrained at Bailleul for the Somme. Our "Nursery" training was over. It had been severe mainly owing to our own activity, but it had given all the greatest confidence that they could more than hold their own in the war as carried on in France.

Chapter XIV.—Pozieres

A PLEASANT train journey from Bailleul to Candas was followed by a tiring march to Domart where we went into billets about 11 p.m. (July 13th.) The late issues of boots were unsatisfactory, and many had worn-out boots, which caused sore feet generally. A route march on the 15th took us through Berneuil and Franqueville, and the next day we marched via Halloy and Pernoy to Naours, with its deep picturesque and historical valleys and its great Catacombs—Les Souterrains—the refuge for ages for all in distress—outlaws, Hugenots, Royalists. From here we route-marched through Waignies, Flesselles and Villers.

Our "French" had already generally improved, or rather the conversational conventions between Digger and French had become easier. Major Twynam distinguished himself by informing a demoiselle that one of her cows was leaving the yard. "Le lait promenades," he told her. A Digger entered a new billet with "Bongjou, madam. You needn't reply, for that's all I know." Another, after listening to an excited Frenchman for a long time, asked, "How does the chorus go?"

After a pleasant week we marched (25th) from Naours, via Talmas, to Rubempre, where the windows and doors repeatedly shook from the concussions of the guns down on the Somme and Ancre. Then, via Herissart, Toutencourt and Harponville to Warloy, where we prepared actively for our entry into the great Battle of the Somme.

The passing through of the wearied 1st Division, after their fortnight up near Pozieres was inspiring, if sad. Their platoons were pitifully weak, and their bronzed faces clearly reflected intense strain, which, however, struggled with pride for expression; but all lit up as our men cheered them wildly and our bands played them through the town. Soon they were being asked if they had seen a war knocking about, and much friendly banter was passed before they left Warloy behind.

August 4th took us to Brickfields, near Albert where we bivouacked while officers went forward to reconnoitre. At midnight on the 6th we got a foretaste of what was coming to us, for we were shelled out of bivouacs in Tara Valley, having to shelter in trenches. In Sausage Valley, our next home, where we spent the 7th, 8th and 9th, working strenuously carrying, digging and roadmaking, we were right among the biggest concentration of guns even seen up to this in any battle, giving us a better idea than we had had of the stupendousness of war organisation. They were massed row on row, wheel to wheel, for hundreds of yards. And the perpetual streams of vehicles of all kinds carrying forward food for men and guns, and protective material—thousands of tons—and bringing back nothing except broken men. Sausage Valley was half-a-mile long and 400 yards wide, with Contalmaison road running across the rise at the head of it. Here we had 36 casualties, especially among parties carrying rations forward, including Lts. W. Worner and G. Rogers.

Sgts. C. Kaler, R. Walter, G. S. McDowell and J. Cooney, all with records to be proud of, here received their first "pips."

On the 9th "A" went up to support the 16th, and on the 10th we relieved the 15th in Barton Trench. (Where trenches that played important parts in our Battalion history, that were important, perhaps for only a phase of a battle, have no generally recognised names, I have given them names to help the reader, and what better names than those of men who fought in or near them? Some such name is necessary, as map references in official papers would be tedious even to those there at the time.)

Casualties, especially to our patrols, quickly amounted to 25, including Lts. K. N. Pattrick, H. F. Murray, R. H. Kell and N. Wallach. "D"Coy., on the Left, had a bad time, being shelled from 6 to 11 p.m.

Before the account of the 13th's first assault in France the situation during the previous days should be understood. The beginning of August found the German Line on the Somme facing south from Thiepval to Flers, with a sharp salient at Thiepval, which was the gibraltaric tip of the salient, and so forbade direct assault. It was felt that a thrust through Pozieres and Mouquet Farm into the rear of Thiepval would be the most effective means of causing the enemy withdrawal.

On August 8th the 15th Battalion had gallantly captured Fifteenth and Barton Trenches from Point 85 on the Left to 95 on the Right. They had intended to capture from 77 on the Left, but the Suffolks on that flank were held up and German machine-gunners at 77 were strong. Then our guns shelled the new position so severely that the 15th had to retire to their original line, part of which I have called Henley Trench.

At 1 a.m. on the 10th the 16th Battalion, (our "A" Coy. supporting, and its bombers advancing with the 16th) under a tremendous barrage, advanced from Henley Trench between 85 and 69, recaptured what the 15th had captured and advanced still farther to Sixteenth and Barton Trenches between 77 and 95, the 14th Battalion also advancing their left from 12 in O.G. 2 to 24 in Fourteenth Trench.

During the advance of the 16th our "A"Coy., under heavy shelling, dug a deep C.T. —THIRTEENTH TRENCH—from Henley to Sixteenth Trench, Capt. Barton and Lt. Wells (Toby and Bomb) aligning, digging and moving about among the men in a cool and inspiring manner.

The 4th Brigade line therefore, at daybreak on August 10th ran along Sixteenth and Barton Trenches from 77 through 43, 53 and 95 to 24. The 16th also took over Ration Trench that morning, and that evening the 13th relieved the 15th in Barton Trench—43, 53, 95, 24 —with Battalion Headquarters near 91 in Henley Trench, and we immediately prepared for

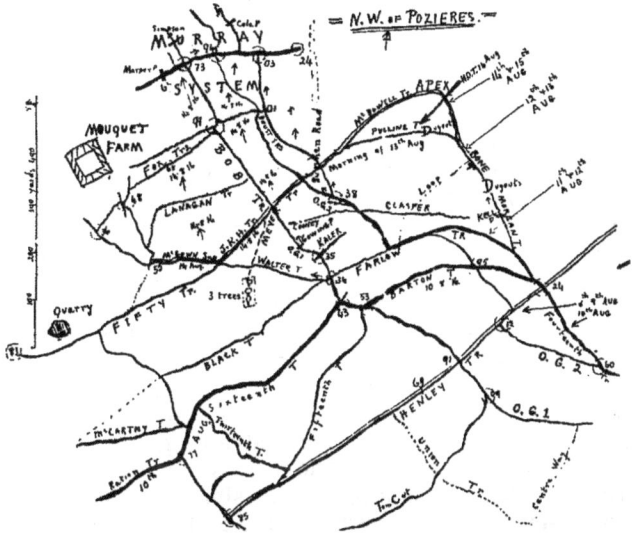

our first "hop-over" in France, and our first attack under a creeping barrage. This barrage, so the gunners told us, had to be uncertain, for, on account of the extinction of roads and landmarks, no one could say exactly where our H.O.T. was, or our objective. A sunken road nearby could not be found, the earth having been torn to pieces.

The night of the 10th was quiet for the Front Line, but cruel for supports, "B" suffering all night and next day, losing among so many their C.S.M. Nicholson.

At 1 a.m. on the 11th the barrage came down extremely heavily and closer to us than we had expected. For a while it remained stationary, "A" on the Right, and "D" on the Left, advancing almost up to it, many in their eagerness having to be held back. The night was not only very dark, but a heavy fog had descended, rendering observation even a yard in front a matter of difficulty. There was nothing to do but stumble forward behind the bursting shells amid the tornado of bullets from front and flanks, and even from the right rear.

Our objective was believed to be a trench 100 yards out, but we advanced 200 yards without meeting it or any enemy. When our barrage became stationary, all dug in. Barton moved about among his platoons supervising and inspiring. Leaving Wells to go farther left to see McGown, he disappeared, no one knowing just how, when or where but from that moment no trace of him has been found. As he was not captured he is placed K.I.A. Had he met the

D

enemy, "Toby" would certainly have sold his life dearly. Sgt. H. Jackson and Pte. J. Metcalfe, also well ahead fought several grim battles in the darkness, and continued advancing until severely wounded, when they were captured, both dying as wounded prisoners.

At 2 a.m. our runners arrived at Battalion Headquarters with the report that "A" and "D" were both digging a new trench—Farlow—beyond their objective, and consolidating. The 16th had also captured Black and McCarthy Trenches. Our bombers pushed up Morgan and O.G. Trenches and built blocks and our covering parties patrolled as far as Clasper and Kaler Trenches while the remainder dug in strenuously.

The Germans attempted to bomb us back. Massing around Point 35 and in Kaler Trench they made their attack. Their first efforts consisted of showers of bombs and bayonet rushes, but they more than met their match in a hundred grim duels fought in the darkness. Being repulsed, they retired for reinforcements and reorganisation. A terrific bombardment of our new line and of the rear lasted from 3.30 to 3.45 a.m. Then, under its increased fury, they came again, but were again repulsed. At 34 the fight was particularly severe, the Germans surrounding the post and rushing it from all directions. Three such rushes, however, abated their valor. Then "D" Coy. took the initiative and advanced again. And they did not stop at Kaler Trench, but pushed the Hun back another 40 yards—a good distance in that darkness, and there they built a block—Gowing Post. On the Right we also gained ground, building a block in Morgan Trench—Kell Post.

During the fighting an order was called out from somewhere for the 13th to retire, and several obeyed. Sgt. J. Riordan (O.P.), however, although out of touch in the fog with the rest of the Battalion, immediately rushed, countermanded the order, led the men back and placed them in position until he regained touch with the rest of the Battalion. He also patrolled well ahead to be able to give ample warning of any enemy movement. In a sap he found eight Huns around him calling on him to surrender, but, with his bayonet, he charged so suddenly into the nearest party and killed three that the others ran. (Awarded D.C.M.). He was killed that night. Lt. W. F. Shirtley ("Bluey"), Sgt. A. Perray ("Yank"), and Cpl. T. Morgan, all O.Ps., did magnificent work laying and repairing lines all that night, all deservedly receiving commissions soon after. Perray receiving his M.M. as well. "Gibraltar," the only structure left in Pozieres, having been built by the Germans of steel and concrete, of great thickness, was, among other things, the signallers' headquarters. The success of this night's attack is not to be judged merely by the area gained, but by its importance, for it held splendid observation points previously in enemy possession. Above all it proved the Battalion superior to Germans possessing every advantage of selected positions, and entrenched strongly. And the Germans here were the pick of their army. The inspiring influence of Capt. H. W. Murray, D.C.M., was one of the decisive factors in the successes of the following days. He seemed to sense the dangerous points and got there always in time to help save or regain them. He was already the 13th's hero, the one spontaneously regarded as the ideal leader in actions requiring coolness, thought, initiative, personality and gallantry. So quiet and unassuming, too, but always there. He had, to his chagrin, been kept out of the line, but, with the disappearance of Barton, had been sent to take "A."

When morning dawned, all were astonished to see our own shells falling in our rear, and the German shells falling along the same line. Reports were sent to the artillery, who replied that they were shelling along our front. Inquiries revealed the astonishing fact that we had attacked that morning from our objective, and that the barrage we had followed had been meant for the enemy supports and reserves. So much for the maps of that area.

That day, the 11th, was so warm that men discarded their tunics. All day the Hun bombardment continued, the object being the demoralisation of our men prior to their overwhelming attack again. From 2 p.m. our observers reported a continual stream of small columns leaving Mouquet, and spreading fanwise along Fifty and J.H.K. Trenches until almost 2,000 of them were ready to advance in assault lines. Black and McCarthy Trenches were their first objective. At 3 p.m. they rose and advanced most resolutely although falling in scores under the fire of the 16th and 13th rifles and Lewis guns. Especially destructive was the enfilade fire of our men from Points 34 and 35, line on line of Germans crumpling under it. The whole attack withered completely, the enemy losses being estimated at over 1,000.

The 11th was a trying day, as was all the night, too. The 12th was even more trying, for the enemy was still higher up the slope than we, and he was also sniping us from the rear, a sniper with a supply of food and ammunition being captured by a 13th Digger who threatened him with a brick, near Kell Post. During the nights, when not fighting, all were digging trenches.

On the 12th the 50th Battalion relieved the 16th on our Left, and plans were made for us to attack with them and the 12th British Divn. on their Left. According to our Bde. official records our objective was to be a line shown approximately by Clasper and Cooney Trenches; the objective of the 50th was the Quarry and a line through it from Point 81 to meet us. But, as already explained, the map references were unreliable. The 13th's objective was made the ridge in front—Pulling Trench—so named in recognition of the splendid organising work and example of Capt. H. D. Pulling, who was practically in charge of the front lines from the 10th to 15th August.

That night the 13th hopped over in one wave, Sgt. D. Strachan and Cpl. V. Dingle, gallant leaders, falling early. Our bombers dealt with the saps leading from 35 and 38, and Bone and Walter Trenches. In Bone and Pulling Trenches were found great dugouts, capable of holding hundreds of men, and containing stores of shells, many of them gas. These trenches were quickly consolidated, while Murray tried to find the 50th Battalion on his Left. The Left, however, was "in the air," for the 50th had not been able to capture the Quarry, their Left, the 12th Div., also being unable to advance. Our "C" Coy. quickly got to work, and, on a line selected and traversed by Murray, soon dug a trench back from our Left to the Three Trees—Meyer Trench. Our position was now a sharp salient containing Meyer, Pulling and Bone Trenches, which risky position we held when morning of the 13th dawned. On our Left, 300 yards away, was Mouquet Farm; on our front two broken waggons; and in our rear, a clear view for over a mile right into Tom's Cut and other trenches in which we had suffered so many losses during the past week.

It was expected that it would be difficult to hold such a position as this salient, but every man of the 13th was determined to die there rather than give back an inch. They were soon to prove this, for, in the dim light of the dawn of the 13th, hordes of Germans were seen creeping forward. They were 50 yards off when we first saw them—60 bombers. Uncertain who they were, we allowed them to come within 20 yards without opposing. A few of their shells were falling on us, but the acuteness of the salient saved us from their heavy barraging, their own trenches being close to us on three sides. At 20 yards we saw their officer wearing the Iron Cross ribbon, and behind the bombers we saw about 250 infantry advancing. The officer threw a bomb which blew off Sgt. Brown's leg and wounded four others, including three brothers named Partridge—all good soldiers—and he instantly fell with 18 bullets in him. The bombers wavered, threw more bombs, but within a second, less than half of them remained, for our Lewis guns and rifles were firing rapidly. Those not killed in our first burst fell flat on the ground. Not one bomber escaped. Their second wave simply toppled down under the hurricane of lead poured into it, but the ground gave but little cover for there were very few shellholes there at the time. When day came a party of 50 German bearers worked for two hours, our men speaking to them. In this victory Lewis-gunner McPhail was superb, climbing onto the parapet to fire, and capturing 11 Germans lucky enough to escape his bullets.

After such a strenuous time, including two advances and several defensive battles, all were weary and nauseated in all their senses. Still they had to remain. That Gallipoli hero, Sgt. Boyd, was killed during the day.

On the night of the 13th the 51st Bn. came in on our right, taking over part of our line, and we moved to the left and took over part of the 50th Bn.'s line—J.K.H. Trench and McGown Sap. We were between two battalions of the 13th Bde., having been handed over to General Glasgow that afternoon.

On the 14th the 13th was heavily shelled and lost heavily, especially in "C" and "A." Even our own guns shelled our position in the Sunken Road, although at first we thought they were enemy shells from Thiepval. During the day we lost 50.

For that night's attack we were to advance northwards from about 55 on our left, McGown Sap, J.K.H. Trench and part of Pulling Trench. Our objectives were Fox and Bob Trench and

Murray System, the last named being an intricate network of deep trenches and strongpoints. Our objectives included the Points 68, 91, 01, 63, 73, 94, 03, and to the right of 24. The 50th Bn. was to overrun Mouquet and join the 13th near 63 and the 51st was to conform on the right.

Murray himself had already patrolled a good deal of this area, having had many hand-to-hand encounters and narrow escapes, as he had been scouting even behind the enemy posts.

At 10 p.m. our barrage came down some distance ahead—rather too far in fact—and " A," "B" and "C" in the attack line ran out cheering to hug and follow it. The attack line consisted of two waves each of two platoons per Coy. In their training the men had been taught to yell when making bayonet charges, and, in this charge they followed out the instructions. "Ho, ho! I-yah! Halloo! Eat-em-alive! Imshi toute-suite! Wagga-Wagga! Into-em! Run, Fritz!" were some few of the understandable yells heard that night among a hundred other earsplitters. Within a few seconds the attackers encountered an unexpected trench Lanagan—75 yards out. The first wave instantly hopped into it, and after a few stiff fights, soon captured it. By 10.30 runners were back at Headquarters with news of its complete capture. A further 80 yards ahead Fox Trench was found to be full of Germans. Many were killed; most bolted when they came hand-to-hand with those yelling diggers; 12 men and a machine gun were captured. In one part of this trench the Germans climbed out and bolted when the Diggers were 15 yards off, but the latter fired from their sides as they ran, and most of the Germans fell back into the trench, there being practically a dead enemy to every yard of trench. Cpls. G. C. Smith and B. S. N. Pattrick threw a bomb onto a Hun machine gun and then rushed it, killing two and capturing 11. C.S.M. Hardy started with them, but got nine bullets in him. (He is still alive.) Four other machine guns were rushed near here and captured. Murray regarded Smith and Pattrick as worthy of the V.C.

German reinforcements seemed to pour out of the ground and these had to be dealt with before Murray was again ready to advance. Still, by 11.15 he was again advancing, nobly assisted by Lt. Bob Henderson. Plenty of opposition was overcome in Bob Trench and the systems between it and the Sunken road. All touch with the 50th and 51st Bns. had now been lost, neither battalion having been able to reach its objectives. At 73 showers of bombs came from all directions and bullets swept the surface. Still the 13th pushed on, capturing bay after bay, and charging strongposts over the top. No one will ever know the deeds of heroism done that night; but all who reached Murray System were certainly heroes. Some unfortunately went much further, forgetting distance and mates in the excitement of the fight, and thus it was we lost some of our first prisoners. In the network between 73 and 24 a dozen stubborn bomb and bayonet fights took place, but soon the main trench was ours. This, however, was not enough for such heroes; they pushed still further north up the trenches of the System, and down towards Mouquet, clearing out the enemy and then building blocks Marper, Simpson and Cole Posts. Murray now went across towards Mouquet, but could not find the 50th. He realised his dangerous position. Pulling got a message to him that the flanks had been held up; still he held on, knowing the sterling men he had with him.

By midnight hundreds of Germans were pressing in on three sides, and at 12.45 a.m. they attempted to rush our new positions. They could not be seen until within a few yards, but knowing the exact position of their lost trenches, they were able to shower their bombs very accurately. Beaten off in their first two attempts, they worked round to our rear on both flanks until Murray System was almost surrounded. Our retirement became a matter of urgency; so all the wounded were carried back as a preparatory measure. Bomber D. Muir, although painfully wounded four hours earlier, still refused to retire, but continued bombing here and in Bob Trench until day, and then carried several boxes of bombs forward to render the line safe before reporting to the M.O. (Received M.M.)

The main enemy attacks came in horseshoe fashion against 73 and 03. Time after time the Diggers hopped out and drove them back into the darkness, some unfortunately going too far and being captured or killed, several being wounded before surrendering.

But such an uneven fight must have but one end if persisted in. Therefore, the last wounded being safely on their way back, and as much damage as possible done to enemy material, the order was passed to retire. So severe had been the fighting that less than 20 bombs remained in Murray System. Guessing this, the enemy again attacked just as our men, except the rearguard, had left; but the remaining few bombers and Lewis gunners drove them back before retiring themselves.

The retirement was a masterpiece in defensive tactics, especially along Doust and Bob Trenches. Take, for example, Bob Trench, the most critically-contested one. Three bombers, throwing slowly and carefully, remained near 73 with two Lewis guns behind them, out in the open to sweep back Germans advancing over the top. Crowds of them could now be seen dimly in the thin moonlight, but our gunners could not fire without challenging even at 20 yards in case they might be our own men.

Now, when all behind these bombers and Lewis gunners were safe, and another bomb-post and Lewis position ready, this No. 1 party would retire and occupy No. 3 position to cover the later retirement of No. 2 party. Into one straight piece of trench, as we were short of bombs, we allowed the enemy to mass and then wiped them out with a Lewis gun in the trench, which shock gave us a breathing space before they came on again.

Still we had to retire, and were again soon closely pressed, and with only three bombs left. The position could not have been more critical when Bob Henderson and his bombers came across the top from the right. He had heard our retirement going on and had guessed we were hard pressed. He instantly took charge of the defence in the best possible way—by an offensive. His party had 30 bombs. A few were tossed over a traverse, and killed the three nearest Huns. Before others could take their places Bob's bombers were there. Two more bombs and a rush took them into the next bay, also filled with dead and dying Huns, victims of the second bombs. In the next bay they found many German bombs on the party wiped out by our Lewis gun, and used them. Again and again Henderson and his splendid men threw and rushed until they had driven the enemy back over 150 yards.

The rest of the Bn. having now consolidated their H.O.T. and dug another some distance ahead on the right—McDowell Trench—the bombers also retired. The six of them and their officer had accounted for at least 30 of the enemy and had driven back well over 100. Lt. C. Meyer had fought gallantly all night and had almost reached Mouquet. In our withdrawal, in order to prevent the Germans cutting him off, Murray sent Meyer to hold Lanagan Trench. Although attacked by crowds of Huns, he not only held his post, but by spirited charges, drove them back. After being wounded, he continued fighting. Murray sent him word to retire, but the enemy were attacking from three sides at the time and had to be repulsed first, after which Meyer sent his men back, remaining alone to keep the post until his men were safe. Three times again they rushed at him, but his accurate bombing quailed them. He then made a dash for our lines, but had his knee shattered, on which the close-following enemy captured him.

The first signs of dawn were showing. The night had brought into the 13th's history a glorious attack, a hundred heroic hand-to-hand struggles, and a wonderfully-organised and gallantly-conducted retirement.

"D" had been busy all night with picks and shovels, and carrying parties.

During the most strenuous part of the night the men in two positions carried on by themselves, their officers and n.c.o.'s having all fallen. Sgt. E. Kay (O.P.) had charge of the parties carrying back the wounded, and performed this duty most inspiringly. Sgt. R. Cole not only carried wounded comrades over the open, but throughout the whole night inspired his men by his calmness, daring and leadership qualities. (Received Commission). Lt. W.

Clasper, L.G. Officer, had throughout the night and previous week done magnificent work. Sgt. E. Fitzgerald (called by his mates "The cleanest-living man in the A.I.F.") did work similar to his splendid Gallipoli work before being fatally wounded. He and others were found by Murray and Henderson who fearlessly scouted No Man's Land before dawn to rescue wounded. On account of his wounds, it was impossible for them to move Fitzgerald. Lt. T. Wells crawled out to him—a most gallant action, for the light was improving, marked the spot with a spade and promised to bring a stretcher under the white flag. With the first available one he and Sgt. Kay, accompanied by Sgt. Lewis with a towel on a stick, rescued Fitzgerald from within a few yards of the enemy. Luckily they moved quickly, for the Huns only respected their flag until they themselves had carried in as prisoners Capt. Fox and three of his men lying helpless near them.

So fatiguing had been the night, after such a period in the line, including three battles and constant patrolling, beating off counter-attacks, digging and carrying, that most could barely hold themselves up that morning. They were utterly and painfully wearied. Still shells and aerial torpedoes crashed into them.

That evening we were relieved and passed through heavy barraging on the way out, Capt. H. L. Henley being killed. He had been left out of the line with the nucleus of the Battalion, but hearing of the strenuous times his comrades were having, and their losses, he had repeatedly written to Col. Tilney begging to be allowed up, and being repeatedly refused. However, being given charge of a ration party, he personally begged Tilney to allow him to remain, and this time his request was granted on account of the loss of so many other officers. His whole military life had made him extremely popular and admired by the whole Battalion, and he showed promise of a brilliant future.

Our losses for the period were 18 officers and 368 other ranks. "A" had gone in the week before with 5 officers and 180 other ranks; it came out one officer and 60 other ranks. Its first attack was made with 170 men, its third with 81; and "B" had suffered almost similarly.

On the way out one section of eight was wiped out in Tom's Cut by a 5.9, the only dazed survivor wandering into the German trench. Tom's Cut is surely the bloodiest trench in the history of the A.I.F.

Lt. McGown had, returning from Headquarters, also lost himself in the maze of trenches leading from Tom's Cut, and found himself surrounded by Huns.

At Albert we found 50 reinforcements and took them back to Warloy, where we arrived at 9.15 p.m., receiving a tremendous ovation from the rest of the Brigade. Diggers of the other battalions carried the rifles of our tired men and cheered them along the roads. There could never have been a more spontaneous outburst of appreciation towards any unit by its fellows.

All fatigues on the 16th were done by the new men; and on the 17th the Brigade, already cleaned and spruced, marched to La Vicogne via Contay, Herissart, Rubempre and Talmas, arriving there at sunset and bivouacking in an orchard.

The 18th took us via Naours to Halloy-le-Pernois, where we went into billets and received 94 "reinstouchments." It was here that our Div. Commander, Gen. H. Cox, presented our first "soup tickets"—congratulatory cards—to those recommended for distinguished conduct. During his term as our Div. Commander some received six such cards, a few prizing them highly at their true worth, but the majority treating them merely as "soup-tickets," carrying them in their pockets until crumpled up, or using them to score on at cards.

On 21st Tilney, who had been fighting illness for some considerable time and still doing splendid organisation and front line work, was ordered to hospital. It was our farewell to him—a most justly popular man throughout the Brigade, an able and thoughtful C.O., and the essence of a courteous gentleman.

Major J. M. A. Durrant, who had since Gallipoli been Bde. Major, came back to his original battalion as Lieut.-Colonel. As B.M. he had, in addition to doing his duty impartially towards the four Battalions, taken a specially personal interest in the 13th, which was, indeed, "the apple of his eye." He knew everybody in the Battalion—a big advantage for a C.O.

Col. Tilney's illness was rather unfortunate for several of the 13th's most splendid heroes, for fewer accounts of their deeds were written up, and consequently fewer decorations received for Pozieres by the 13th than by any other battalion of the Brigade, although the other battalions were unanimous in agreeing that the 13th's work for this period was outstanding. Our heroes certainly earned all they received and more, and official records prove conclusively that no other battalion did more or better work, or had more gallant deeds performed during this period than the 13th. Still the D.C.M. and M.M. figures for the Brigade for this period are: 13th, 6; 14th, 9; 15th, 22; 16th, 8. Our men were Cpl. H. Bartholomew (scout), Ptes. J. Butler and H. White (runners), A. Wild (bearer), and D. Muir (bomber), and Sig. Sgt. A. W. Perray. Capt. H. D. Pulling received his M.C. Capt. D. G. Marks also received his M.C. for splendid services as Adjutant during this and previous periods Cpl. T. Baxter, whom we had lent to the 4th L.T.M. Bty., made a glorious name for himself and his Battalion. He received his D.C.M. for splendid work with his mortar and rifle along Bob Trench, for stretcher-bearing, guiding, and general self-sacrificing conduct (killed 11/8/18). Sgt. R. Jones was wounded after proving himself one of our best. (Received Commission later.) Sgt. Le Clerc (O.P.) and Cpl. Tarling (O.P.) were among the heroes who gave their lives willingly. Our officer losses for this first Pozieres period were:—Killed, Capts. F. M. Barton, J. K. Henderson, and H. L. Henley. Wounded, Capt. A. G. Fox (captured), Lt. C. B. Meyer (captured), A. McGown (captured), W. Worner, G. Rogers (died), K. N. Pattrick, R. Kell, N. Wallach, H. F. Murray, E. Randall, G. S. McDowell, R. Walter, W. Clasper, C. Farlow (died), and A. Lanagan.

The officers who gave their lives were certainly among the most efficient and bravest ever in the Battalion, their loss being a heavy one indeed. Fox, Meyer and McGown had been too brave and eager. It can safely be said that they would not have been captured but for being wounded and hopelessly outnumbered.

The Brigade losses for the period were 49 officers and 1614 other ranks. Lts. A. W. Davis and E. Plucknett, of the Battalion Headquarters, were highly commended by all aware of their work for this period.

Chapter XV.—Mouquet Farm.

THE 22nd August found the 13th moving back for its second period in the north-west of Pozieres. On the 26th, after having marched through Naours, Talmas, Rubempre, Herissart and Vadencourt, we bivouacked at Brickfields again, this time in a heavy downpour.

On the 23rd eleven splendid N.c.o.'s all with records that made the 13th proud of them, were promoted to commissions. They were G. Marper, H. Simpson, C. D'Arcy-Irvine, N. J. Brown, F. Doust, J. Allen, T. Morgan (Originals), and R. Cole, B. S. N. Pattrick, G. Mills and C. G. Smith.

Tremendous firing was going on up the line, making us sorry for the 14th and 15th Battalions up there in the mud, rain and strafe.

While bivouacking in Crater Trench in Sausage Valley on the 27th and 28th, our officers and specialists went forward to reconnoitre the front lines, and at midnight on the 28th-29th we moved up and relieved the 15th, marching by companies in file at 10 minutes' interval, following the Tramline, Kay Trench and Tom's Cut. "B" remained behind until next morning in order to carry up rations, after which they went into Tom's Cut, Union and Joint Trenches to wait till night in order not to overcrowd the front line, Browning Trench, in daylight.

The trenches, crumbling under the constant soaking rain, were nowhere less than knee-deep in "sticky mud or soup." Crashing salvoes smashed them still more, and their occupants too; and the bearers were wearied even before the line was reached.

We found the right of the present line no further advanced than when we had left it on the 15th, and our left was less than 80 yards ahead. We relieved the 15th across our previous frontage, the Apex being our right, and Bob Trench our left. Here the 16th joined us, their line forming a salient near Mouquet Farm.

The task given the 13th and the 16th was the capture of Mouquet and the network of trenches and strong-points to its east, north and north-west.

As Mouquet was one of the hardest nuts in the war, it merits a brief description. Under it were dugouts so strongly reinforced with steel and cement as to be impervious to any of our shells, and into which hundreds of Germans could retire the instant our shelling started, ready to rush back the instant it ceased. There were well-lighted galleries with crowds of dry, fresh men, and stores of munitions and food, and even pulleys to haul machine-guns up and down.

Such a position should never have been attacked in "nibbles." It required a tremendous assault to overrun it; not a stunt in which a few exhausted men would arrive there to be met by overwhelming odds of fresh men.

From Mouquet the Hun could sweep along our present trenches, and into any line of assault even by night, for they had fixed gun-platforms which ensured the bullets sweeping the surface of the earth even if fired by blind men. And not only was there Mouquet, but there were scores of deep dugouts, constructed months before all along this front, many of them holding 100 men ready to rush when necessary to specially-prepared machine-gun nests. Our barrage would keep some of them occupied until our men got there, but there were so many that a few were always able to disgorge their gunners, and many just beyond the range of our attack could yet send their bullets sweeping back. For danger and trying conditions the Gallipoli Landing cannot be compared with the attack on Mouquet. The men who attacked Mouquet are even more to be admired in that they now knew what war was. For stubborn, strenuous, wearisome heroic and costly fighting Hougomont pales into insignificance compared with Mouquet. Our front line stretched irregularly from 91 on the left to 92 on the right, with bomb and observation posts in the saps running out into the trenches still held by the enemy at Massey, Marper, Turnbull and Brown Posts, and in shellholes in No Man's Land.

On the night of the 29th August the 16th was to capture and overrun Mouquet, and the 13th to capture the system stretching from 73 through 94, 03, and 36 to 95, called Murray System, Wells and Pattrick Trenches and Mills Sap.

Never has anyone seen a more miserable dawn than that of the 29th August, 1916. Those who have been at sea on a black day will remember the depressiveness of the dreary, black water-wastes. From our trenches the outlook was even more foreboding; nothing but twisted, heaped and churned mud, with jagged stumps and ragged wire that added, in their wasteful monotony, to the desolateness. The shelling all the 29th was fiendish, his shells lobbing on the 13th in dozens at a time—crashing, smashing salvoes. Yards of trench were blown up and down, and men with the mud. Other trenches were hastily dug, and destroyed ones rebuilt. Murray, T. Wells, Browning and Pulling did all in their power to save the men by scattering them; still 90 were killed or wounded during the day, including 32 in "A" (Murray), and 25 in "B" (Wells), although "B" was not in the front line.

Such conditions were not an ideal preparation for an assault. Even our own "Heavies" lobbed their shells short. If the 13th members have anything to do with our National Defence schemes they will insist on the training of artillerymen.

For this battle Durrant had moved his Headquarters and R.A.P. well forward to near the Loop, the R.A.P. moving out during the battle ahead of Browning Trench. He also created a splendid impression by personally reconnoitring No Man's Land and the front line.

During the most tremendous shelling of the day men crept out into shellholes and lay in the mud and water. In these holes many were killed or wounded, and Capt. Browning won the admiration of all by attending to them, walking about on the top quite upright and fearless. He also at dusk crept out into No Man's Land to examine the ground over which he was to lead his men that night. Murray also, although he knew the area thoroughly, did likewise.

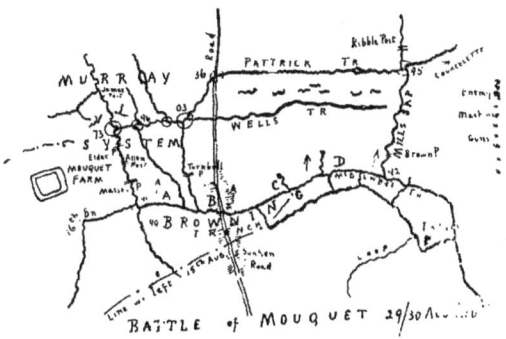

Bearers, like J. Banney, J. Watt, A. Lucock, A. Davis, C. Boyle and C. Casey were gallantly busy all day, night and the next day and night, attending wounded everywhere and carrying them steadily across patches of hell, many having sunk into the mud so far, or having been so covered by heaving clods, that they had to be dug out. It seemed that the bearers were leading a charmed life on their errands of mercy. On three occasions Sgt. W. Clark, a splendid man right through Gallipoli, finding the bearers unable to get to cases out near the enemy, crawled out and attended to them. Finding it impossible to carry them in that mud, he, after dressing their wounds, dragged them back to safety. Not only did he such work throughout the 29th and 30th, but he remained behind on the 31st after the relief to assure himself that no wounded were left. Bombers in Massey, Marper, Turnbull and Brown Posts were repeatedly wiped out. Still volunteers quickly took their places. One particularly dangerous post, the defenders of which had all been killed after a short while there, was for the third time left with only dead men. Cpl. H. B. Brown and A. Bently volunteered for it, and not only did their duty there effectively, but on several occasions attended wounded men in shellholes nearby. Three in succession were killed in an observation post. Then Pte. W. Galvin volunteered to remain out there, and, during the evening brought back several valuable reports. Pte. Davidge was splendid until killed. Pte. C. Dingle, whose brother had just been killed, was one of the best until he, too, was killed. Gallant F. Makinson (O.P.), Ptes. Edwards, Keen, Howes and Napper also died as brave men.

By midday of the 29th most of the rifles had become clogged with mud and refused to fire, to the annoyance of those with good targets. Every now and again newly-cleaned rifles and Lewis guns would be smothered in mud. Even bombs became so mudded that the pins became stuck, and even when drawn, slippery hands and bombs made accurate throwing impossible.

After dark "A" closed into the left to make room for "B," and soon the four Coys. were ready for battle, the order from left to right being "A," "B," "C," "D." Although painfully wounded in the hand early that morning, Capt. T. Wells had remained in order to lead his Coy. in that night's battle, and immediately he arrived in the front line he went ahead almost to the German trenches to reconnoitre the area.

About 10 p.m. Mills and his scouts again crept across our front to arrange guiding lights for the different companies. These, after being necessarily dimmed with rags—red, white, blue—were banked up well with mud on the enemy side and then switched on. With this idea to direct attackers Durrant was anticipating the use of tapes. This night, however, owing to displacement and burying by shells, these lights were of no use. Despite the terrible weather conditions, Mills traversed No Man's Land from one of our flanks to the other several times.

Just before zero (11 p.m.), as Coys. were making final arrangements and massing, the 5.9 shelling from Courcelette became frightful, one shell killing nine men in "A" before they got into No Man's Land. At 11 Murray had but three officers and 60 men left for the attack —so weak a company that he had to weaken it still more by leaving Lewis guns behind in Browning Trench as rallying points in case of his being driven back, with orders to wait for instructions. "D" Coy. of the 15th were our reserves in Tom's Cut.

At 11 the attack was launched. Another perfectly arranged bombing stunt took place along Bob Trench, this time to capture instead of to defend it. Two mortars were placed near Point 90 to shell along the trench ahead of Bob Henderson's bombers. His first section moved out to Massey Post, whence they hurled their first shower and made their first rush, if "rush" it could be called, in that gluey mud. They soon captured the enemy Allen Post, strengthened considerably since the last battle, and were dealing with Elder Post when Murray's men, having followed our barrage closely, delivered their assault between 94 and 03. "A" captured this trench after a stubborn but quick fight, but there remained the trenches between 73 and 94, and Murray had only 40 men left. He was pleased to hear Henderson's bombers progressing towards 73, which progress could be told by the sound of the Mills bombs. Murray sent a patrol across to establish touch with Henderson.

At 73 the bombers were assailed, as Murray had been earlier that month, by showers of bombs from a horseshoe system. No. 1 Section continued to deal with the German main trench straight ahead, Cpl. C. James fighting magnificently. The mortars increased their range 15 yards every three shots, and the bombers rushed after their bursts. James Post was soon captured and overrun by another 20 yards, where Henderson built a block.

Meanwhile No. 2 Section had been cleaning up Murray System on the left and right of 73, and soon we were in possession of considerably more than our objective on this flank.

How long we could remain was the problem, for Murray now had only 28 men for 150 yards of frontage, which included 300 yards of trenches. He rapidly organised seven posts of three men each, and five bombers with a roving commission to reinforce wherever required. They had not long to wait before two attacks were hurled against their right near 03, but both were beaten off with heavy enemy loss.

Murray now led a patrol of two men across to look for the 16th on the north of Mouquet. He recognised points he had seen on the night of the 14th. About 80 yards from 73, almost against the north of Mouquet, he was searching about when two German bombs lobbed from out of the darkness, blowing one man's foot off and blinding an eye of the other. No previous sign had come from the enemy. Murray instantly sprang ahead and jumped on top of a party of five lying on the ground. They attacked him with knobkerries, one blow dinting his helmet and another bruising his chest, before they seized him in a bear-hug. While being hugged he shot both the huggers, on which the others cleared. He and the half-blind man then carried the footless man back.

Murray now knew that the 13th was again out on its own without flank protection, for the 16th had failed to reach their objective.

On his return Murray found the enemy attacking 94, Lt. Marper, now "A's" only unwounded officer, setting a splendid example of cheerful and gallant leadership. Again an enemy repulse. Still again came another attack, this time against 73. Murray's men now were only 16 and were consequently scattered in ones and twos, each fighting grimly in the mud and darkness without knowing what was happening five yards from him; knowing only that he was going to fight to the last. Murray moved rapidly from man to man, fighting alongside one after another, or encouraging the lonely man. Not one but would gladly have died there for such a leader. Nine men at 73 climbed out and charged into almost a hundred, each man choosing his own direction. The enemy fled in confusion before such men, who again calmly took their places in the trench to wait. The enemy now held back for some time, and the men began to feel how weary they really were.

Weary and nerve-racked with 30 hours' shelling, rain and mud, and continual loss of mates, and their Captain twice wounded, these few men fought on and repelled four more great assaults.

The 16th had reached their objective, but had been compelled to retire with heavy losses, the enemy having come up in scores from underground behind them. Murray, still unable to get in touch with the 16th, now felt that a retirement was inevitable, and sent back his wounded in preparation.

The other Companies!

After reaching their first objective, Wells Trench, also a battered and sloppy ditch, patrols from "B" pushed ahead to Pattrick Trench and found it unoccupied and much damaged. The enemy had retired from our shelling to dugouts, except his machine-gunners, and his artillery crashed down even more frightfully onto "B" and "C". All night shells poured over from Courcelette, and bullets swept from front, flanks and right rear. "B's" exceedingly heavy losses were nearly all from machine guns on their right.

Browning's "C" Coy., after capturing their first objective, found the enemy in strength in holes and saps between Wells and Pattrick Trenches, and cleared them out, the Germans carrying their guns away as the Diggers approached. And not a rifle could be fired at them. Each man cursed and chased them with bomb and bayonet into the darkness, many running into nests of their dugouts and never returning. Browning was leading one of these bomb-fights when he fell severely wounded in the thigh. Suffering agony, he made a tourniquet from his whistle lanyard to stop the bleeding, and remained in charge of his Coy. all night, taking an active interest in the battle and his men. When retirement became necessary he refused to allow the bearers to carry him, ordering them to attend to his men first. He then crawled back 250 yards before collapsing.

"D" crushed strong enemy resistance all along Mills Sap, and established a block at Kibble Post beyond their objective. This chanced to be surrounded by several big dugouts, and few of our men got back from there. On this flank Sgt. A. Turnbull and L. Gillett did magnificent bombing. Cpl. Ratcliffe fought and rescued the wounded from amongst the enemy until he himself, surrounded by the enemy, was fatally wounded, dying as a prisoner. Sgt. F. Powell, too eager, went too far ahead, and was captured.

The 13th was now surrounded on three sides—a handful of men hanging on, and even advancing, against at least 3,000 Germans. From O3 Lt. B. S. N. Pattrick, hero of the last battle, went out against a horde and was killed. Cpl. Craig and Pte. Charlesworth established themselves in a German trench, drove back two attacks and held the enemy back for over an hour. Pte. Olling was as solid as usual.

Had the 16th been strong enough to mop-up Mouquet, the 13th would, even in its weakness, have held Murray and Pattrick Trenches. As it was, beyond gaining valuable information for future action and again proving the stuff Diggers are made of, we gained nothing, and the morning of the 30th found our weary, disappointed and heart-broken men back in Browning Trench.

Whether the High Command was justified in making such attacks on Mouquet, whether they made miscalculations concerning its vulnerability, whether they were unable to adapt themselves quickly to circumstances or whether they were ignorant of how such rain and mud affected men and weapons, I am not prepared to say. Like many similar attacks in the Ypres Salient, these advances did not aim at overrunning the enemy guns which simply shortened their range onto their lost trenches, whose distance their gunners knew exactly, and shelled our gallant victors out again. So many of these small advances were attempted that one is compelled to think that our "Heads" were nervous about their ability to manage big affairs. However, beyond the scope of this! Mouquet, like Bullecourt later, smashed some of the finest fighting battalions ever known in history without anything like commensurate gain in land or enemy losses. Luckily the Australian spirit could not be smashed.

Dawn showed that some wounded men had been missed in the darkness. We hoisted a small red-cross flag, and the Germans did likewise, and together Diggers and Germans searched No Man's Land, each handing over to the other their own cases. Fritz was a gentleman that day.

The keeping-up of supplies of bombs and ammunition across that knee-deep mud had been a tremendous task, but men like Sgts. Goodlad and H. Simpson, Cpl. Gillman and Pte. Watters set such a splendid example to their parties that munitions were plentiful in all parts throughout this period. True the weary men grumbled at the absence of any food other than wet biscuit and rhubarb jam for two days, but that was not the carriers' fault. Goodlad, Simpson and Gillman were O.P.'s. Unfortunately Gillman, who had been wounded three times on Gallipoli, and his party of five were all killed that night.

In this carrying the runners helped considerably, not only guiding parties with unerring accuracy, but also carrying loads. These runners without exception distinguished themselves, among the most distinguished being W. Chaseling, who, after being severely wounded in three places, struggled on until he had delivered his message, G. Gregory, A. Cormack (also a splendid scout), W. O'Shea (O.P.), T. Ryan, H. Rollings, J. McLennan, G. Goldsmith, R. Dunn, O. Selig and L. Brown.

Scouting and guiding near Mouquet were naturally difficult and dangerous, but, in addition to Lt. G. Mills, men like F. Forbes, A. Pawley, G. Andrews and F. Massey specially distinguished themselves.

Even more difficult was the work of the linesmen, who were continually laying and repairing lines under heavy fire. Our signallers were always regarded as men of the highest type possessed by the A.I.F., and at Mouquet they again proved the fact. G. Falkiner (O.P.), A. Long, C. Monday, J. Dawe and A. Wright repeated their previous splendid work, not only laying and repairing lines, but lying out for hours along them listening in, in order to ascertain immediately a break and its position. Sgt. Robeson and Cpls. Weedon and H. Whyte, M.M.—three untiring and devoted leaders—fought, carried, and organised heroically until killed.

Others who are known to have done most distinguished acts of heroism during those two terrible days and nights were Sgts. B. Rose, B. Marlin and P. Kibble (O.P.'s), Sgt. K. Elder, C.S.M., C. Brown, Cpl. T. Marshall (bomber), Cpls. G. Cross, R. Groves and H. Meeham, and Ptes. H. Walker, E. James, W. Kerr, C. Morris, J. Kevans, H. Townsend, and A. Davies. Marlin, right ahead by himself, on one occasion, found nine Germans rushing him from all sides. He parried their bayonets for a few seconds, but would certainly have been killed had not Murray rushed into the fight. Four Germans immediately fell, the others vanished into the darkness. Still Marlin again pushed ahead to reconnoitre.

Space will not permit accounts of their deeds or of other heroisms near Mouquet—books could be filled with the narratives—but, in addition to those officers already mentioned Lts. R. Cole, C. D'Arcy Irvine, J. Allen (O.P., killed), T. Morgan (O.P.), and A. W. Davies (O.P.) proved themselves heroes and leaders worthy of their men. Col. Durrant and Adj. D. Marks again made their Battalion proud of them, as also did our M.O., Capt. Shierlaw.

Like Browning and Wells, Murray only consented to evacuate on the 30th after fainting from loss of blood.

On the night of the 30th the 48th relieved us, being guided in in the darkness, mud and rain by Mills. In the 40 hours we had lost 10 officers and 231 O.R., the Bde.'s losses for the 5 days being 704.

A very wet, cold, muddy and weary lot were the 13th as they trudged out in the consistent rain, for they had been saturated for a week. None will ever forget that awful journey back. The saps were full of sloppy, yet tenacious, smelly mud. It took the last ounce of the remaining strength to haul each foot up. Most were often bogged, too weary to budge until a panting rest gave them enough strength to recommence the struggle. The 3 miles from Battalion Headquarters took over 5 hours.

Still, within a few days, they were clean, active and cheerful, as if they had never seen hell, and were never likely to see it again. Nevertheless they kept room in their minds and hearts for the memories of their cobbers gone west up there in the mud.

While our nation possesses such men as fought and died at Pozieres and Mouquet, it will be a nation to be as proud of as the 13th is of its heroes.

For their outstanding brilliant work Murray received the D.S.O., Browning, Wells and Mills M.C.'s.

Chapter XVI.—Second Period up North.—Voormezeele.

SO slow were all movements in that thigh-deep mud and blinding rain that it was 8 a.m. on the 1st September before the relief was complete. During the morning the 13th rendezvoused in Sausage Valley, moved to Brickfields and thence to Warloy where they arrived at 7 p.m. It had rained all day.

At Rubempre, where the 1st, 2nd and 3rd were spent, General Birdwood presented M.M.'s., and we had a splendid concert at which Canadians and Tommies helped.

From Rubempre on the 4th we marched to Montrelet, and, on the 6th, via Candas to Gezaincourt, where Gen. Cox visited our billets and found all engaged washing clothes or swimming, the day being so fine. Cox expressed delight at the splendidly fit appearance of all ranks after "their excessive physical exertions."

The morning of the 8th found us at Doullens entraining for the north again; detraining that evening at Poperinghe and marching into Ontario Camp at Reninghelst.

At 9 a.m. on the 8th a gas alarm was sent back from the Front. All put on their helmets and remained perfectly calm. Fortunately no gas reached our area. A few days later all received the small-box-respirators, the best of all gas protectives.

The 9th found W. Parsonage, B. Rose, D.C.M., A. Turnbull, M.M., J. Gallagher, A. Perray, M.M., A. Wild, M.M., (originals) and R. Swinbourne, K. Elder, S. Owen and L. Cleland wearing their first "pip," proud at being officially informed that the whole Battalion regarded them as specially worthy of the honor. Wild lost an eye that week.

That the work of the 13th at Mouquet was officially recognised was proved on the 13th, when Cox presented 54 Congratulatory Cards to our members. Later (October 11th) he presented 32 Military Medals for the same period out of 64 to the Brigade. September 16th found several Officers, Lewis-gunners, Bombers and Scouts in the line below Voormezeele with the 75th Canadians, who held a successful raid next evening, on completiion of which they were relieved by the 13th, our line running from the S.-west of St. Eloi still farther S.-west for 800 yards, our right being opposite Piccadilly Farm, and our rear towards Voormezeele, about 1200 yards away.

Going in, we passed Dickiebusch and Lake, Ridge Wood and the Brasserie, where our R.A.P. established itself. Bn. Hqrs. were at Dead Fog Farm, and "A" Coy. nearby. "B" was in Reserve, "C" in Support, and "D" in the Front Line. During the period in, the Companies changed over in these positions. It was rather a quiet time, although Platoon and Company Commanders were greatly worried by the danger of trench-feet, having received the strictest orders that every man had to have three pairs of socks, had to change them daily and have his feet rubbed and whale-oiled regularly. The area was low and badly drained even in peace-time by almost stagnant ditches. Trenches had continually to be pumped out, and even then thigh boots were necessary in several places where the water remained knee-deep. The German position slightly overlooked ours. The trenches were about 160 yards apart, but both sides had posts forward in No-Man's Land. Our patrols nightly aimed at capturing these enemy posts, but they were too well protected by wire. Lts. G. Mills and F. B. Fitzpatrick spent night after night crawling about with their patrols in No Man's Land, an eerie task, as the Germans had search-lights to sweep the area as well as flares. Their well-protected machine guns also swept practically every yard. Still Mills, Fitzpatrick and their gallant men minutely examined the enemy wire every night for a week in order to find a way through it into their trenches with a view of capturing prisoners for identification purposes. Fitzpatrick, who was given charge of the raid was an ideal leader, and Gen. Brand, Col. Durrant and his own men had the greatest confidence in him.

After the minutest examination possible a decision was made to make the raid into the German trenches west of Piccadilly Farm on the morning of the 28th, between 1 and 3 o'clock. The preceding nights the sanguine raiders crawled almost up to their objective in spite of flares, searchlights and bullets. Col. Durrant talked the matter over with Fitzpatrick and his men individually, being rightly convinced that each thoroughly understood his part of the adventure. A novel feature was to be the opening of our barrage on the signal "Go" by telephone from Fitzpatrick himself when he was ready to hop into the enemy. It was felt that such a procedure would not arouse the enemy as the bombardments prior to previous raids had. The artillery, on receipt of "Go" were to fire heavily on known enemy guns and to form a three-sided box of shells around the point of entry of the raid to keep enemy reinforcements back.

From 1 to 2 the gunners back in and beyond Vermozeele waited with guns loaded and ranged to hurl their showers of death onto the doomed spots. Fitzpatrick and his 13 blackened men rested awhile in a ditch they knew so well in No Man's Land, and made final arrangements. "Keep close behind me", was the leader's last order as he climbed out of the ditch and crept through the first gap in the wire. He wound to the right and then back to the left on account of various obstacles, and they followed. He had never appeared cooler or more confident, and such a leader they wouldfollow unquestioningly although they knew that he should have left that ragged stump ten yards on his left instead of a chain on his right. "Fitz's going too far to his left," whispered one to his mate. Still they had the greatest confidence, believing that he was looking for a better track through the belt, and that he would soon be heading towards the proper spot. The ragged stump was now out of sight. There were many similar ones, but theyknew that one. They were almost on the enemy parapet.. For a while they lay still. The enemy was unsuspecting. They would probably now crawl to the left along the front of his trench, the signal would be sent along to the artillery, and in they would jump for their exciting two minutes, grab their prisoners, search for maps and papers, destroy dugouts and retire, lying in shellholes near the enemy until their retaliation had died down. But all in a fraction of a second there came hundreds of hellish hisses and blinding crashes, and myriads of pinging balls and hurtling lumps of jagged metal, and their leader called out "Scatter for your lives!"

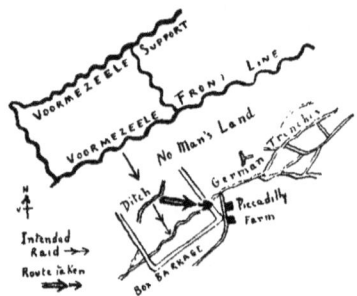

The gunners, at 2-45, anxious and still keen, poured in their shells as fast as they could. Their Signaller had received along his waiting wire Fitzpatrick's "Go", and he had called it out to them, all hearing and pulling lanyards simultaneously.

"Go!" Crouched ready to rush in on the enemy Fitzpatrick had sent it along. But, instead of the "Come on, Boys!" they had expected to hear with the opening of our guns, they heard, amid the hissing and crashing, "Scatter for your lives." His thoughts had flown to his men as he had recognised his awful mistake. He had led them into the area of our own barrage and had, in a supremely happy moment at the thought of immediately leading his men into the astonished enemy, called down upon himself and them our barrage.

When the shelling ceased his men returned to search for his body and that of the gallant Cpl. D. Muir, M.M., but the enemy was now thoroughly aroused, and dawn was approaching. The fortunate 8 men helped 4 wounded comrades back, but Fitzpatrick and Muir remained where they fell on the enemy parapet near Piccadilly Farm. Muir recovered however, to find himself a prisoner.

Such was one of the war's unfortunate and unavoidable incidents. No raid was ever more carefully organised and rehearsed, or had a more trustworthy leader and men. Still No Man's Land with its monotony of holes, iron stakes, jagged stumps and old trenches, was a treacherous place for direction even in daylight. Fifty yards more to the right would have made all the difference, and would have brought high distinctions to all taking part. Similar raids later on were guided by a gun lobbing an occasional shell along a flank as advised by Col. Durrant to Corps.

In this area, as in several later, rations were carried forward on trucks pushed along narrow lines, and many were the risks taken by adventurous men in switchbacking on return journeys. By the 7th October when we were relieved by the 49th Bn., we had, notwithstanding the enjoyment and the deception of Colonels, Generals and Officers and men of other units, created by the "Voormezeele Switch Girl," become tired of the area. We were met by our Band at La Clytte, and marched to the Regimental Tune into Quebec Camp near Reninghelst.

Three days later our officers went forward to reconnoitre a new position in Zillebeke Area, called Bluff Sector, where on the 12th we relieved the 1st Bn., Hqrs. and "A" taking over Swan Chateau, and "B", "C" and "D", Bluff Tunnels, being commanded there by Capt. D. P. Wells. Marks was now for a week in charge of the 13th, and, although only 21, proved himself an able and experienced administrator. Lt. A W. Davis took Marks' place as Adjutant, and it soon became recognised that the 4th Bde. had never possessed a better one, "Son" having had long Orderly Room experience as a clerk and Sgt. with such worthy instructors as Marks and Durrant, and having been the aptest andkeenest of understudies.

In this area as Reserve Bn., we tunnelledand carried for a week before being relieved by the Londoners on the 19th, when we returnd to Quebec Camp.

Dirty farms near quaint old Flemish Steenvoorde were our billets from the 21st to 26th, when we marched to Caestre before daybreak and again entrained for the Somme, travelling via Calais, Boulogne and Abbeville to Pont Remy where we detrained to march to Vauchelles Les Quesnoy. Here we spent such a pleasant time that we were sorry to leave, although it chanced that our next home for a week was beautiful Belloy Sur Somme, in the famous old Chateau of which village,—the Chatean d'en Haut,—Hqrs. were established.

At Vauchelles an interesting table, eloquent of the sacrifices paid by only one Australian Battalion, was compiled. The 13th was again up to full strength, 1028, but of the Original 1100 who left Melbourne in 1914, there were only 144 left with the Bn.
The figures were:—

    Officers who left Australia as such .. .. ..   4 out of 32
    Officers who left Australia in the ranks.. ..   18
    Other ranks 122

Of those who served on Gallipoli at any time the numbers still with the 13th were 24 officers and 264 others. Of those who landed on Gallipoli during April the numbers still with the Battalion were 20 officers and 137 others.

Chapter XVII.—Flers and Gueudecourt.
"The Cruellest Winter for Fifty Years, Monsieur."

AN exceptionally cold winter was heralded not only by chilly mornings and nights during October, but by early snow in November. The inhabitants predicted a severe winter, but they did not expect it to be what it was, "the cruellest winter for fifty years, Monsieur,"—Thus it was that the Maire of La Chausee expressed it to us in the presence of a crowd of old people who all agreed with him. We bade the kind people of Belloy farewell on Nov. 8th, and marched along the causeway, over the Canal and railway to Picquigny where we climbed into French 'buses to be carried to Ribemont-Sur-Ancre, the home of "Incinerator Kate" and her wheel-barrow. Here Capt. W. J. M. Locke, M.C., who had rejoined the Battalion after a long period of distinguished service with Brigade, commanded the 13th for a week, Col. Durrant being on conferences.

On the 12th "A" and "B" marched along slippery roads to Willow Siding the rest of the Bn. the next day to Dernancourt. Reconnaissances were made ahead and on the 14th, the Bn. marched along the most fearfully sloppy and congested roads imaginable to bivouacs at Bernafay and Quarry Siding near Montauban. Here all were engaged on road—and railway-making, pushing and unloading trucks cleaning out old German dugouts, draining camps, scraping mud, rubbing and oiling feet, chopping frozen bread with bayonets, and huddling round small braziers burning wood salvaged from shattered trees, and coal 'souvenired'. Feet were continually wet, snow fell, sleet cut and rain drizzled, guns roared and shells screeched, and men and animals slipped heavily on the frozen surface when not deep in churned slush. Along any mile of road between Albert and Montauban could always be seen animals killed and dragged aside on account of broken legs. However, many books have been written about this winter. To the 13th it was a winter of hard work. Amid the traffic streams that were in continual flood, "A", "B" and "D" marched to Carlton Camp near Bazentin, on the 23rd, "C" remaining at Quarry Siding.

Reconnaissances of Flers and Gueudecourt areas were soon made and on the 27th, the 13th moved into the Front Line. Bn. Hqrs. were in Possum Reserve just south of Gueudecourt, "A" in Grease Trench and Goodwin's Post, and "B" on its right. "A" was in a specially dangerous position, its Goodwin's Post being closely surrounded on three sides by enemy trenches and strongpoints. Here the Germans held a sharp and strong salient where Bayonet and Lard Trenches formed an apex. Being so dangerous it was naturally given to Capt. Harry Murray, and within two days most splendid work was done in strengthening it from the enemy, and improving it for the accommodation of our men. "B" Coy., facing the junction of Lard and Stormy Trenches, also did splendid work strengthening, improving, patrolling, and worrying the enemy. The part of Grease Trench they took over was in an appalling state, being simply a slushy ditch. "C" bivouacked in Pilgrim's Way, and "D" in Pioneer Trench, had a busy time digging strongposts, Communication and Support Trenches, the ground often being too hard for the picks, and carrying wire, iron, bombs, rations, etc.

At Goodwin's Post Lt. N. J. Brown, a distinguished O.P., again shone out and won the M.C. Inspired by "John" his platoon dug so well that its trench was soon not only comparatively safe but practically impregnable. Goodwin's was an ideal post for such a man. He not only patrolled it on its three sides, but crawled over one night and looked into the German Trench, leaving his men fifteen yards back. On another occasion a bomb lever flew off; the smoke from the fuse caught John's eye, and several men were near it. It might explode any second, at the outside but five seconds after the release of the lever. John rushed, jumped over men, grabbed the fizzing death and hurled it over the top, his hand receiving a splinter of it, for it burst the instant he threw it. Heremained on duty however, as calm as if such were everyday occurrences. His men accounted for several snipers; still one remained persistently annoying. John took a rifle and bomb, told his men he would be back within an hour, disappeared into the mist, found the aggressive one, shot him and was back within ten minutes. Later he sprained his ankle but remained on duty in great pain all next day until ordered to leave. John, who had many other heroic deeds to perform, wore his ribbon proudly, although unostentatiously, until someone he knew received the same decoration "buckshee," after which he cut his off and refused to wear it again until threatened with arrest. Another splendid man on Goodwin's was Cpl. A. Read, Lewis Gunner. For 80 hours Read remained at the gun vigilant and assertive. Sniper after sniper challenged him from three sides, but he silenced them all. In addition he swept away six parties of the enemy that came within his range. Cpl. A. Ahradsen also distinguished himself as a fighting Lewis Gunner. Among those who helped to protect these advanced guns was Cpl. C. Trick—"Bluey"—who, with his Bombers, had charge of our most advanced bombing post. Although so close to the enemy, Trick and his men occupied a hole still nearer and dug a trench back to the main trench. Night after night the enemy endeavored to get near enough to hurl showers of bombs into Goodwin's, but our bombers were never unprepared. In returning to Goodwin's on the 3rd December. Trick was wounded, but led his men almost a mile and placed them in position, remaining with them until ordered to leave. After having an iron splinter extracted from his side he begged permission to return to his post. So keen was he that, after dressing the wound, the M.O. gave him permission to do so. Goodwin's remained ours only through the constant work of such men. Cpl. J. Ellery, Ptes. N. Chapman, H. Rollings were conspicuous among our splendid Scouts patrolling No Man's Land nightly. Ellery captured a German runner with important messages; Chapman volunteered to carry messages across an area swept by bullets and shrapnel, in addition to his constant scouting; and Rollings, constantly on dangerous missions, became noted for his unfailing cheerfulness. He remained out under heavy fire with a wounded man until the opportunity came to carry him in. Sgt. T. Gilday, although quite ill, remained on duty and proved an invaluable help to his officers in the Front Line, scouting, bombing and attending assiduously to the welfare of his men. "Tommy's" personality inspired bigger men (he was small) and made him one of the most efficient of the Battalion's N.c.o.'s. Cpl. H. Gunderson (O.P.) showed a wonderful example of doggedness as a Telephonist in the Front Line, remaining there for 9 days without relief. For the first 3 days and nights he and his mate sat in the open trench in the cold, and exposed to regular shelling. When the companies changed over he remained as a volunteer. Although not a linesman he went out on three occasions under heavy shelling and repaired his line. Night after night Cpl. J. Hawken led his laden mules up to Gueudecourt. The ground was treacherous and his mules were continually bogged through breaking through the ice covering of deep holes; shells and bullets regularly swept over the areas he had to pass through, but he never failed. Hawken, an original, had long proved a stolid and trustworthy man. Lt. W. Stones, new to the Battalion, quickly proved himself to be an active, inspiring and conscientious leader, and won his way into the esteem of men and fellow-officers. Col. Wray, "Padre," remained during these trying days the strong, inspiring influence he had constantly been throughout our history. Capts. Bone and T. Wells were inspiring leaders, as usual, under such awful trench and weather conditions.

On the 29th November, "C" and "D" changed over with "A" and "B". That day the Germans heavily shelled their own Lard Trench, intended the strafe for Goodwin's. The trench occupants sent up hundreds of red rockets but the shelling remained on them for some time. Later, when their guns shortened on to us, they sent up green cluster rockets and a white one,—altogether a most brilliant display, amusing our men greatly.

On the 3rd "A" and "C" again changed over, and on the 6th we were relieved by the 5th Bn. and moved back to Quarry Siding. Our losses for the 10 days had been:— K.I.A. 5; D.O.W. 2; W. 14; Total 21.

The next morning (7th) we entrained at the Siding, detrained at Meaulte and marched to Ribemont again.

We were finished with Front Line work for 1916.

In addition to those mentioned for splendid service on the Somme, there were many who did not get the chance to be conspicuous, but who were constantly solid, cheerful and keen in the most uncomfortable and dangerous periods. Sgts. A. Makins, F. Brandt and H. Curtis, and Cpls. Wearne, Tidey, Sparrow, State, R. Sinclair, J. H. O'Neill, M'Leenan, Hensby, C. Ford and R.S.M. C. Brown come readily to one's mind as examples of many more such men.

Concerning Gueudecourt, Murray, after noting the regular hours during which the enemy shelled it with "heavies," carefully explored the village in between the periods and furnished Hqrs. with valuable reports and sketches concerning water and gun-positions. He was accompanied by that bright brave boy, Runner Rollings. Rollings wrote to him from hospital later: "The bullet is still in my side; they've had two tries to set my leg, and are going to take the shrapnel out of my arm and the splinters out of my head soon. Otherwise I am quite all right." And the boy had no idea of attempting an effect. His Anzac spirit simply could not be quenched.

E

Chapter XVIII.—Christmas, 1916.

EXCEPT on the main roads, kept clean by German prisoners, and the billet yards, looked after by the Diggers, Ribemont was a vile quagmire, several huts standing in seas of knee-deep mud. "Incinerator Kate," the most untidy and unkempt young lady imaginable, collected whatever she could find anywhere about billets in her wheelbarrow, the incinerator being her special delight, for there she salvaged delightedly much about to be cast into the fire. Her bare legs were generally shod in Digger boots about six sizes too large, and occasionally she wore an old Tommy tunic. At a sports meeting later a 13th Digger appeared in fancy costume as "Incinerator Kate," having "borrowed" her barrow when she wasn't looking. Very perturbed, she sought her vehicle everywhere before at last visiting the sports, where her arrival became the event of the day. Disconsolately she bewailed her loss to Digger after Digger until she suddenly discovered "herself" and barrow across the field. A wild scream, excited exclamations and a whirlwind rush brought her alongside her beloved barrow and the "Beaucoup Brigand." Imitator and Dinkum Kate then entered into a loud argument, Kate losing her voice with rage. When she finally got her barrow she retired in hysterical indignation, and never after forgave the 4th Bde., although its members sent her 100 francs for the worry she had suffered.

The most joyful moments in this area, apart from leave to Amiens, were the visits to the hot showers at Heilly. At Heilly also were Anzac Headquarters, on which our guard, after a 10-days' tour, was highly complimented by Birdwood. Prevailing cold winds and driving rains were most uncomfortable during this month. On the 16th we marched to Coisy—12 miles—the last mile uphill being especially trying.

Of the five Christmases away from home that spent at Coisy was the central one. It marks the halfway between the formation of the 13th and its disbandment. It was, indeed, a delightful Christmas, mainly perhaps on account of the foil of that winter and the war. But all from Colonel to Digger did their best to make everyone else happy. Each Company had a common fund to which the men subscribed from 5 to 10 francs, N.C.Os. 10 to 25, and Officers from 30 to 60. Regimental funds and comforts provided money also in addition to goods. From our own 13th Committee of Sydney ladies, we received, as at every Christmas, most liberal supplies of the best of good things—puddings, nuts, sweets, tobacco, cigars and cigarettes, socks, gloves, scarves, etc. Although other battalions were wonderfully helped by their committees the 13th stood out as the "Lucky Battalion" in this respect, the General himself remarking it. And solely because of our dear women's work. We had tobacco, socks, scarves, balaclavas, and many other good things whenever required. We had only to want to receive.

Company committees visited Amiens to purchase wines, ales, poultry, mutton, paper plates and decorations, and to hire glasses and crockery. One Company had goose at 3/- a pound live weight, another mutton at 2/- a pound. The hams from the bacon issues had been saved for some time to be issued for Christmas. Cooks, assisted by volunteers who prepared the poultry and vegetables, willingly worked overtime. It was impossible to get a room large enough, but the schoolroom with its accommodation for 35 children was made to hold 60 men and a hatroom 40. Fortunately it was a bitterly cold day and so nobody minded the crowding. The officers acted as waiters before joining their men in eating and drinking. The King, Battalion, Australia, Absent Comrades, Wives and Sweethearts, our Comforts Committees, and Allies were the toasts honored. A few in each Company were able to recall the first Christmas on the "Ulysses," and the second on Lemnos.

Those little schoolrooms at Coisy had never before held and are not again likely to hold such a body of happy men. One Company ate there from 12 to 2, and other from 3 to 5 and the evening found the rooms still festive.

The Diggers were intensely sentimental, despite their efforts at carelessness and nonchalance regarding this feeling. For some reason they felt a certain shame at being found sentimental; still they could not camouflage it entirely from keen observers. Visitors to Westminster Abbey, watching the Digger stroll about in an apparently unconcerned, unobservant and unreverential manner, felt that he was an absolutely unsentimental being, and occasionally felt generously-enough disposed towards him to put this sacrilegious indifference down to his lack of historical knowledge instead to lack of reverence. For how could one be indifferent if he only knew? But the Digger had probably read more of the stories of these monuments than the average Englishman, and loved with a deeper love these glories of our Nation's part, his casual manner simply camouflaging, as they did in battle, hidden thoughts, glowing hearts and thrilling minds. He felt these monuments were as much to him as to anyone, but he hated demonstrativeness over such things although he could be the most demonstrative person in the world over less sacred things. From the Abbey he would go away and write the most accurate descriptions in a letter emitting sentiment in every line to his wife, sweetheart or mother. So it was in action. But over Christmas the Australian didn't mind how sentimental even his cobbers thought him. He loved its celebration in all its joy and good fellowship, and would willingly do two periods in the Line before or after to one over Christmas. For weeks before he looked forward to being where he could spend the day as it should be spent. His people at home knew his feelings in this matter and catered magnificently to satisfy them. Many have the impression that the Diggers were a happy-go-lucky crowd of jokers. They were certainly witty, enjoyed a joke, and would joke even with death hovering close—probably to camouflage deep feelings—but the same Diggers were the most serious lot of men in the world. They knew full well the seriousness of leaving home for unknown destinations for unlimited time, and the seriousness of everything connected with the war and its management. They were serious even in their salvaging of scraps of paper for munitions, and therefore they were so extraordinarily efficient. And for their tremendous seriousness they were the greater heroes, because they were not fools who did not know.

In addition to their dinner with their men the officers held a second dinner at night, "B" Coy. for example, inviting visitors to make up a party of 13 who sat down to 13 wonderful courses prepared by Madame, who had been given a free hand and unlimited cash, and 13 toasts were honored. "Monsieur" had never before tasted "Ooeeskee," and declared his first one very strong and very good. He was afraid two would make him "zig-zag," but the party wished him to have 13. He had completed seven when Madame sent him to bed in a most ecstatic condition. Next morning, in Madame's presence, he told us we were "no bon," and that "ooeeskee" was also "no bon"; but when she was out he came to our room and thought that another "leetle one" would help him. He had four before he heard Madame returning, and departed, remarking so that Madame would hear, "Officier no bon; ooeeskee no bon."

During our stay at Coisy, Company, Battalion and Brigade sports were held, the last-named at Rainneville being of the high standard of all 4th Brigade sports.

A sad occurrence befell four of our men who were away from the Battalion on special duty during December. So cold was it that they closed off all ventilation and went to sleep around a brazier, with the result that they were asphyxiated. One was Sgt. H. Meehan (O.P.), who had distinguished himself in practically every battle in our history to that time.

On 2nd January we returned to Ribemont, being most cordially welcomed by the inhabitants.

On the 7th we marched to Melbourne Camp, Mametz, miles of the march being in single file on account of the congestion, which could not have been worse. The next morning "A" and "D" moved to Quarry Siding, where Capt. Murray was in charge. Heavy snow fell frequently and snow fights were indulged in in addition to the heavy work each day, the duties being similar to those mentioned for the previous period.

To celebrate his new decoration, Gen. Brand, the popular "Old Brig," who had come to the 4th Brigade in August, was entertained at a Mess Dinner in a Mametz hut, Cpl. Tait receiving unstinted praise for his menu designs and penmanship. Tait's cartoons were always popular in the 13th.

Reconnaissances of Flers and Gueudecourt areas were again made on the 22nd, and on the 24th the 13th relieved the 45th in Gap and Switch Trenches, near Flers. Being under the eyes of the Germans here most of the Battalion lived like 'possums, sleeping in narrow little holes by day and working all night. Digger sang-froid was never shown better than here. A direct hit by a shell smashed some duckboards two men were carrying. When they recovered their senses after lying half-an-hour in the snow, they picked up the pieces and took them to their dugout for firewood to the envy of their mates. Others were playing cards when their roof was blown off. Their stakes worried them more than the shell and snow. On account of the awful roads our rations were often delayed, and on several occasions one loaf was the issue for 16 men, a little more than an ounce each; and the fatigues were especially heavy.

At the end of January the Brigade was given the task of capturing Stormy Trench, the position that not only overlooked our area for miles, but was of tremendous tactical importance. On the night of the 1st February the 15th Battalion attacked the two known strong points in this trench under a barrage. Their Left quickly captured their post, but their Right encountered heavy wire, had to move to the left and bomb down the trench. They captured 52 prisoners, the stunt being regarded as a great success until 2 a.m., when overwhelming masses poured in on them from three sides, our artillery being inadequate. The 15th had to retire, their losses for the night being 52 killed or missing and 87 wounded. That night we relieved them, taking over parts of Shine and Grease Trenches, orders soon arriving to prepare to reattack the position, the night of the 4th being the time decided on. We were fortunate in having the experience of the 15th to help us, their officers willingly passing on their dearly-bought experience.

[The general purpose of the British Army at this time, on this front, was to improve our line, left ragged at the end of the Somme Battle, in order to prepare for the next advance. A commanding feature like Stormy Trench was most important.]

Chapter XIX.—Stormy Trench, February, 1917
Murray's V.C.

IMMEDIATELY on the relief of the 15th Bn. and the posting of his men Murray and some of his scouts crawled out into No Man's Land to examine the enemy wire and the area over which he was soon to lead his men. He was never the man to leave anything undone that would help to save his men and make victory surer. Before dawn on the 3rd he was familiar with every shell-hole and strand of wire in No Man's Land, and every possible route back to Battalion Headquarters, and several of his officers, scouts and n.c.o.'s were almost as familiar. Eight men who were to go on "Blighty" leave on the 3rd refused to go, preferring to remain for the "hop-over." Such examples were common throughout our history, although "Blighty" was always looked forward to most longingly. On the 3rd Col. Durrant received definite orders to attack Stormy Trench on the night of the 4th, the objective to be the same as that attacked by the 15th Battalion. He immediately assembled his Coy. Commanders and explained their work, confirming their orders in writing later. All Coy. Commanders became familiar with No Man's Land that night. They were D. P. Wells, N. McDonald and W. S. Bone, in addition to Murray. Capt. McDonald (O.P.) had just rejoined the 13th after a year's service with the Camel Corps in Egypt.

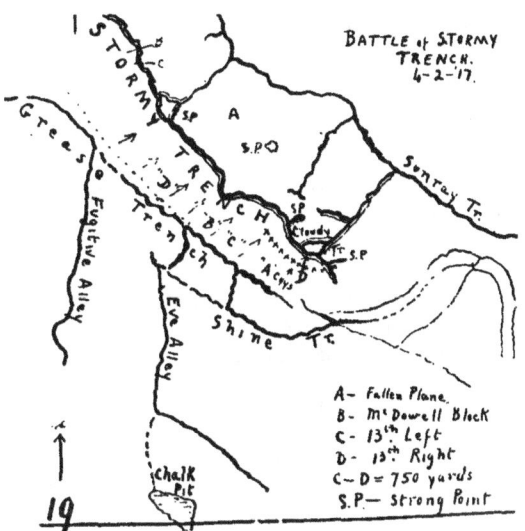

Realising that his greatest difficulty would be to hold the position against counter-attacks, the enemy having many well-garrisoned strong-points nearby, the Colonel asked for 20,000 Mills bombs, 1,000 rifle grenades, and strong artillery support. During daylight on the 4th 12,000 bombs were carried up into Shine and Grease Trenches, and 8,000 to Chalk Pit, the average weight of the bombs, including cases, being 2lbs. Each Coy. was ordered to detail 20 carriers to carry their bombs across immediately the position was captured.

At 4 p.m. on the 4th Durrant again assembled his Coy. Commanders, and went over every detail with them. As at Pozieres and Mouquet, Murray was given the most dangerous and critical point, this time the Right. On their return the Captains called their Subs. together, explained the whole and individual parts, and gave orders that the men should be taken into full confidence.

To Murray, Durrant specially stressed the certainty of heavy counter-attacks. The former replied grimly: "If the enemy ever get my trenches back, they will only find a cemetery."

In order to prevent German airmen seeing our Front Line full of men, the Battalion did not mass there until after dark, only two platoons of "A" and "B" being there until late in the day, when the other two platoons went up in twos and threes, all carrying bombs. After dark "A" closed to its Right to its jumping off place, "C" went up from Pilgrims' Way through Eve Alley to its place, "B" closed to its Right, and "D" went up from Bull's Trench through Fugitive Alley to Grease Trench, all going in wrapping sandbags around their boots to muffle the sounds of tramping on the hard frosty ground, such sounds travelling far. The Colonel had thought of many similar details. Each carried 6 bombs in his pockets, the Coy. bombers 20 each in addition, and the carriers 24 to 30 each making a total of over 2,000 bombs in each Coy. During the day all the watches had been synchronised twice.

At 8 p.m. the Colonel moved his Headquarters forward to Chalk Pit, where "Doc" Shierlaw also established his R.A.P. With Durrant remained Major Marks, and Lts. A. W. Davis (Adjt.), Mills (I.O.), and Perray (S.P.), all having important duties although not actually in the assault.

At 9.50 Durrant received word that we were in position for the assault, and that everything was quiet. By this time every officer had crawled across No Man's Land, close up to the enemy. The enemy wire on the whole was satisfactorily cut, but on "A's" front there was strong wire for 75 yards, for which, however, Murray was prepared, having decided, if it were still uncut by our artillery, to lead his men around the left of it and to bomb down the trench to the right.

It was frightfully cold lying in No Man's Land, as many did for 40 minutes, before zero. Fortunately a rum issue arrived and the jars were passed along quietly. Our Scouts, who had been watching out further now returned and took their places in the wave. On both flanks guns were roaring, but we were unconscious of them, feeling instead the deep silence of our front, the silence of the enemy appearing ominous. Sudden hisses, crashes and flashes startled us for a second at 9.57, and many prepared to advance; but the gunners were only warming their icy guns which soon would be too hot to touch. "Two minutes," was whispered. . . "One minute." What a profound silence! How those guns over near Warlencourt were flashing. And those machine guns over beyond Goodwin's! "Get ready!"

Hiss-s-s-s! Crash-ash-ash! Boomoomoom! Hundreds of guns spoke as one on the tick of 10, and the air above and before the rising line of Diggers was spiked by millions of sharp flashes, and raked ahead by a hail of shrapnel. So keen were the men that they had to be held back, for the line had to take two minutes to cross the narrowest part—about 100 yards. Our own shells were bursting right over the heads of the unbroken line, but not a man was hit, so excellent was the shooting, and the shrapnel being hurled forward on explosion. The 13th will always gratefully remember Colonel W. Waite, M.C., and his gunners, not only for that wonderful barrage, but also for their instant response to S.O.S.'s. later on. Waite controlled the fire of his guns from Durrant's advanced Headquarters—quite a new idea —and readily met every suggestion of our Colonel. "D" was not in position when the barrage opened, having been delayed by blocked trenches, but Bone led them over the top and got them into line under the barrage. Wonderful discipline.

More than half-way across a machine-gun was captured and its remaining crew quickly accounted for. They had evidently rushed it out the instant they became aware that an attack was coming.

At 10.2 the barrage lifted and all rushed into the trench. Most of the Germans were coming up from their dugouts, and, had we been slower, they would have manned the trench. At such a time a second means a lot. As it was, they surrendered freely on the Left and Centre, but on the right they fought hand to hand with Murray and "A," being speedily overcome, however, until "A" commenced moving along to the Right still further. Then the enemy bombers offered not only a stiff resistance, but even attempted to drive "A" out, their small egg-bombs, weighing 9ozs., outranging our Mills, weighing 22ozs. Murray, Cpls R. Withers and M. D. Robertson and their bombers charged over the top to get at them, but they fought until 12 were killed. Then their machine-guns swept along the parapet, while others bombed along the trench. Showers of hundreds of "eggs" and "potato-mashers" were hurled against the determined Diggers. Withers, a big strong lad, who could hurl our bombs 60 yards, stood on top and threw bomb after bomb, exposing himself recklessly. Murray again charged over the top to get at the enemy in bomb-posts on three side of him. He jumped into six Germans, shot three within a second and captured the other three. This made one side safe. Returning to the trench he found three wounded Diggers who had followed him, and carried them to safety one after the other. His uniform was torn by bullets in several places. Meanwhile Capts. McDonald, of "C", D. P. Wells, of "B," and Bone, of "D" in that order from Right to Left, had examined their portions of the captured trench, sent their prisoners back, and fired their green flares as a signal of success. It was McDonald's last act. He had gallantly organised and led his company to victory and had just seen success attend his work when he fell. Another Gallipoli hero. About 40 Germans were already dead, and 70 running back as prisoners, with a few Diggers as escorts, and we had lost very few. Our second wave of men, loaded with bombs, picks and spades, had arrived and consolidation had commenced. The trench was so deep that firesteps were needed, except on the right. But the ground was so frozen that pickhandles broke and picks made no impression. Then a fierce and frightful concentration of enemy shells fell on the captured trench, especially on "A," and on Grease and Shine Trenches, and all communication trenches. Within a few minutes hundreds of yards of these trenches were smashed beyond recognition, their occupants likewise. The Company of the 14th Bn. that had occupied our J.O.T. as a support, Germans running back, stretcher-bearers and bomb-carriers, all caught the fury of this strafe as heavily as the new line. It was "the severest shelling the 13th had yet encountered." Under it the enemy was expected to counter-attack, and so men remained watching resolutely over the top, as one fell back another taking his place. Pte F. Finlayson heard someone groaning 10 yards out, climbed over the top and carried him in. It was a German officer, badly wounded. Lt. Shirtley (O.P.) saw two Germans in the light of a bursting shell, rushed out and captured them. He had recently been promoted for "extraordinary good work right throughout his career." It being dangerous to keep prisoners in the trench in case of a counter-attack Pte. W. Coady volunteered to conduct a party of them back through the barrage, being severely wounded, but continuing until he had handed them safely over.

By 10.15 identification of prisoners was made at Battalion Headquarters, and a message despatched to General Headquarters, reaching Haig before 11—a record on which the Bn. was highly complimented. In fact Haig received the news of our success two minutes after Murray wrote that he was "Set." Perray's signallers were in fine form. Additional bombs were being called for. Sgt. A. Gove, in charge of "C's" supply made three trips with his party within half-an-hour, carrying 1,000 bombs. With his first load, instead of waiting with the second wave, he had been one of the first to jump into the objective and had captured single-handed five prisoners. Pte. F. McQueen, in charge of five men carrying to "A," made six trips during the first two hours. Two of his party were killed, but McQueen carried their loads. To him can be given a big share of the credit for "A's" victory. L-Cpl. J. Rankin was making his seventh trip with a load when he was severely wounded These illustrate the spirit of the 80 bomb-carriers, not one of whom failed to be a hero that night, although the tornado they faced was so severe that at daybreak only two remained of "A's" party of 20 carriers.

At 10.35 the bombardment was at its worst, and Germans could be heard shouting apparently giving orders, out near a trench running into ours. Cpl. G. Johnson immediately ran out into this trench, calling on his bomb section to follow him, which they did, clearing out the enemy speedily. Cpl. Hurley (O.P.) fell fighting gallantly.

At 10.40 the strafe died down; but within a few minutes Murray was fiercely attacked by swarms of bombers who had massed on three sides again during the barrage. Their first shower killed seven out of his nine men in one post. The rest nearby gave way for 20 yards, but Murray again led the nearest over the top and at the point of the bayonet they cleared one side, Murray again carrying back two wounded men. Cpl. Withers heard the fight, seized a bag of bombs, called out, "Who'll come over the top with me?" and climbed out of the trench into a hail of bullets, being wounded in the knee while doing so, but still continuing running along the top bombing the attackers until they gave way, leaving many dead. He was ordered to the R.A.P. to have his wound dressed and he carried back a wounded mate. Insisting on returning to his Company, he carried back a load of flares. The trench now being crowded with wounded he carried back the four severest cases he could find, each time returning with a load of bombs. Returning from his second trip he found another terrific attack in progress. This attack, commencing at 11.50, was accompanied by even heavier shelling than before, the whole trench suffering, Lt. G. Bentley, who had been setting a fine example all the night, being killed. From 11.50 to 12.10 our men fell fast, and five separate attacks were made against "A." Cpl. Robertson, in charge of Murray's flank post, had his section annihilated twice, excepting Bomber F. Bray but he reorganised new sections from other men, inspired them, and with them held fast. In this midnight struggle our Lewis gunners behaved magnificently, climbing out and firing into the enemy machine-gun flashes. Sgt. H. Thompson, a Gallipoli veteran, placed "A's" guns and moved about from gun to gun, taking charge of one after another, and repairing two under fire. Pte. A. Bushell, another Gallipoli hero, the only man of five left on his gun, carried it out and fired into holes full of enemy bombers. Cpl. J. Whitbread, in charge of three guns, walked coolly about from gun to gun, helping where necessary with loading and repairs. L.-Cpl. A. McKenzie had established his gun well forward and now continued working it in face of enemy machine guns aimed at him. H. Luff did similarly gallant work. Headquarters L.G. Sgt., E. Wallbank was supervising all Lewis guns that night, and did it splendidly, on one occasion running back to Chalk Pit to get another gun to replace one destroyed.

From 1 to 3 a.m. there was a comparative calm, and Murray completed two bomb-stops and trench-blocks, made from timber and frozen earth, on the Right, and McDowell and Bone one of each on the Left, while Scouts and Patrols went well forward reconnoitring, bearers cleared the trenches somewhat, and others began to dig a communication trench back. Lt. G. S. McDowell (O.P.) had already made a glorious name for himself by clearing the enemy out of strong-posts and 100 yards of trench on Bone's left and holding it against three counter-attacks, which, if not as severe as those against Murray, were nevertheless determined. Bomber J. Bice was one of his most excellent men that night, coolly standing high up to observe and direct the throwing of his mates. Sgt. E. Harradine was again, as at Mouquet, conspicuous for fearlessness and gallantry.

During this spell Sgts. G. Cross and C. McElroy, Runner C. Morris, Ptes. A. Lord and T. Stevens, and Lts. W. H. (Bill) Turner and J. Cooney, made valuable reconnaissances, taking big risks to get information. Morris was one of the most daring runners and scouts the Battalion ever possessed, and on this occasion crawled to within 6 yards of a German working party to see what they were doing.

About 2.40 Murray guessed that he was in for another attack, for the enemy began ranging with "rum-jars" and "pineapples"—great bombs that were fired from any range up to 1,000 yards. He was right, and at 2.55 he saw them as thick as ants approaching by short rushes from hole to hole, and his scouts reported them in great number. He new their trenches were full of them also. He hurried from man to man advising and inspiring.

At 3 the attack came. Showers of bombs of all sizes, and crowds of yelling Huns. A few minutes' lightning strafe preceded the main rush, which, however, Murray did not wait for. Immediately they advanced he, with a lacerated hand, Withers with his painful knee, and Robertson with a wounded face—all with bullet-torn clothes—led charges in three different directions from the extreme Right, and Lt. Marper one towards the front. There was fierce hand-to-hand fighting, the enemy slowly but surely giving way. They were fresh men and determined, but no troops could withstand those leaders and those Stormy Trench Diggers. Their first wave being beaten their second was rushing on when Cpl. H. B. Brown led a party over the top and charged with bayonets right into them, Murray joining in the fight and chase. The Germans had had enough for that night. Bomber Bray had again distinguished himself.

Dawn came at last, after a seemingly week-long night, and Stormy Trench was ours for keeps. But "A" had suffered cruelly, and their trench was a shambles, 60 weary, bruised and bleeding men remaining out of 149 who had hopped over seven hours earlier. In addition to Lt. Bentley, "A" had lost Lts. R. H. Kell (O.P.),, and G. H. Pulling, both of whom had done splendid work before being wounded, the former having got out of bed after five days of dysentery to go into the battle.

After their defeat between 3 and 4 a.m. the Germans concentrated more guns even than before onto their lost position, and men fell rapidly. Stretcher-bearers worked most gallantly, and officers and N.c.o's. moved about among their men endeavoring to place them more safely. Murray again went out all over the area of his Coy's. attacks looking for wounded men and carrying two more back. S.B. V. Corby made nine trips back with wounded, his helpers becoming exhausted one after another. S.Bs. J. Harris F. Gibson, E. Leahy, J. Foster and J. Watt also attended wounded under fire hour after hour, Watt being greatly worried when he himself was wounded, not at the wound, but at the thought of men still lying out there unattended. Space will not permit details of the glorious deeds and examples set by Capts. Bone and D. P. Wells, Lts. Mills, Morgan, Lanagan, Swinburne and Trim, in addition to the others already mentioned, or of the fine work of Lt. A. Perray and his Sigs. R. S. M. Kay (O.P.), Sgts. F. Bourne, W. Fitzpatrick (O.P.), and W. Grierson (O.P.), must be mentioned as most inspiring leaders. Others specially mentioned are runners A. Winsor, F. Jackson and C. Stewart —the last named also doing splendid bomb work with "A," L.-Cpl. W. Purssell and Ptes. T. Cullen and J. S. Marsh, for leadership and ration-carrying, and Pte R. Walton for general heroism, and the popular Sgt. J. Grady (O.P.) for ration-carrying. Sgt. Sykes died of wounds and Cpl H. Walker, M.M., was killed on the 5th. Both heroes,

"A" having suffered so, the Colonel asked the General for relief. Immediately the 16th Battalion heard that a Company was wanted to relieve Murray every man vounteered. Capt. Ahearn and his Company changed over with "A" that night. The 16th also sent the following wire: "Heartiest congratulations. Tell Murray we are all delighted he got throuh safely."

If only that magnificent spirit of cheerful spontaneity leavened our industrial lives as it did throughout our army! Motor drivers would go to great personal inconvenience to make the infantrymen's walk shorter, infantrymen would crank up the lorries and help load, artillerymen would hop down into the mud to help a bogged transport driver—all cheerfully and spontaneously. The fact that death was rushing about made no difference. The following was a recent personal experience at Newcastle Dyke: A sailor high up dropped a short rope onto the wharf at the feet of a trucker warming himself at a brazier. "Chuck it aboard, mate!" called out Jack. "Three bob!" was the trucker's reply, as he held up three fingers to signify that work in connection with ship's ropes was not his job unless he received the wages due for an hour's such work. "Strike me pink; be 'uman!" growled the astonished sailor, as he climbed down thirty feet and over the side. "Three bob! Three bob!" was all the "mate" would shamefacedly and apologetically repeat. "You're a 'do nothin' for nothin' sort!" was the sailor's final retort. "Yes, the 16th of Westralia to a man wanted to face death where a hundred had died within an hour, and to face it for an indefinite number of freezing nights in a series of smashed frozen holes to help the 13th of New South Wales. Three bob, indeed!"

Each day and night until the 9th "B," "C," and "D" were shelled and bombed by "pineapples" and "rum-jars," casualties amounting up steadily. The cold became intenser, too, the water becoming frozen in water-bottles although men slept with them against their bodies to prevent it. The greatest efforts were required to prevent frostbite and trench-feet, but all were keen. The grit displayed in remaining cheerfully in the Front Line from the 2nd to the 9th in that weather, not to mention the shelling, was admirable, and would make a fine epic but for being overshadowed by that of Murray and "A."

On the 9th a shell set a heap of German bombs alight to the great danger of "C's" men. Several exploded and the flames were spreading until Sgt. Gove smothered them with bags of earth pulled from the parapet, risking his life to save others.

Dr. Shierlaw had a trying time, but remained determinedly at duty. For the first 30 hours the wounded came in in streams, but he attended to the last as to the first, and continued doing so until the Battalion's relief. He had already been twice recommended for gallantry.

Official records state: "The devotion to duty, the keenness, fighting spirit and courage displayed by officers, n.c.o's and men are beyond all praise." Also: "The bravery and devotion to duty of "C" Coy., 14th Battalion, in support was most commendable, for they helped our bomb-carriers and bearers untiringly." All the friction between the 13th and 14th had disappeared before this.

Our losses in Stormy Trench were 61 killed and 172 wounded, many of the latter dying. The trench captured was 700 yards long and was an excellent trench in most places, containing deep accommodation for 150 men. It afforded observation to the front and rear for miles. Its capture was one of the most important minor operations of the war, having, on account of its position, a great influence on the almost immediate retirement of the enemy from the Warlencourt Salient. The 13th are as rightly proud of Stormy Trench (so named long before) as of any other battle in their history. Prisoners (77 captured here) were always questioned. These believed the 13th to be a specially picked body of storm-toops, one saying that they knew we were Australians because we were in their trench so soon after the barrage. They made repeated reference to their astonishment at the extraordinarily efficient way in which the attack was carried out, the noiseless and rapid consolidation, and the sportsmanlike manner of the Australians.

Durrant not only visited the new trench immediately after its capture, but went backwards and forwards constantly, siting and aligning new communication and support trenches and strong-posts, and looking into every detail likely to add to the comfort and well-being of his men. All loved him to come along with his cheery words and kindly advice.

Stormy Trench was remarkable for the number of men taking part in battle there for their first time in action, great numbers having arrived to make up for the losses at Pozieres and Mouquet. They had a stiffening of veteran officers, n.c.os. and men whom they quickly imitated. Both Durrant and Murray expressed unbounded admiration at the manner in which these new men—mostly young—upheld the traditions of the Originals.

Murray, Withers and Robertson were strongly recommended for V.Cs., but such were sparingly awarded. Murray, whose work throughout the war was that of a superman—a superman in heroism, energy, spirit and self-sacrifice, resourcefulness and devotion to duty —was the one to receive it. Not only was the 13th proud of him, but the whole Brigade was, from General to Digger. And his unconscious modesty won him still greater admiration. He told the deeds of his men, but would give no information about his own doings. Durrant had to piece the story of his doings together from accounts given him by those with him at the time, although all of these asserted that they were unable to do him justice. It had been the same on previous occasions and had not so many men died that night more deeds proving his heroism would certainly have been related. No V.C. was ever more truly merited.

Murray's courage was not a reckless exposure to danger like that of Jacka and Sexton, who didn't know fear. His courage was a deliberately formed quality derived from a fervent loyalty, an earnest sense of duty, a thorough confidence in himself and his men, and a firm belief in the justice of his cause.

Some V.C. winners aimed at death; Murray always at victory. The knowledge that death was the probability never deterred nor held him from his main aim.

We cannot claim Murray as a New South Welshman. He is the essence of an Australian.

Born at "Clairville," near Evandale, in Northern Tasmania, enlisting in Westralia, where he was working at the outbreak of the war, he served and won his honors with the 13th of N.S.W. (after a few months on Gallipoli with the 16th Battalion), and ended the war as the C.O. of a Machine Gun Battalion, representing every State in Australia. And on discharge he made his home in Queensland, marrying shortly after. It was Col. Tilney who brought him from the 16th to take charge of our machine guns in Australia Valley after the promotion of Legge as Bde. M.G. Officer.

That parochialism had no place in the A.I.F. is also shown in the fact that our second V.C. (Sexton) was a Victorian.

Referring officially to the counter-attacks and Murray's work, Durrant wrote:—"Then followed the severest fighting in the history of the 13th, and I am sure that the position could not have been held and our efforts crowned with victory but for the wonderful work of this officer. His Company beat off one counter-attack after another—three big attacks in all —although one consisted of no less than five separate bombing attacks. All through the night the enemy concentrated the fire of many 4.2's and 5.9's on the sector held by this Coy., and in 24 hours the fighting strength dwindled from 140 to 48—92 casualties, including one officer killed and two wounded. On one occasion the men gave ground for 20 yards, but Murray rushed to the front and rallied them by sheer valor, his revolver in one hand and a bomb in the other. He shot three Germans and took three others prisoners single-handed. From one end of the line to the other he was ubiquitous, cheering his men, heading bombing parties, leading bayonet charges, or carrying wounded from the dangerously-shelled zones. So great was his power of inspiration, so great his example, that not a single man in his company reported shell-shocked, although the shelling was frightful and the trench at times a shambles that beggars description."

The decorations awarded the 13th for Stormy Trench were V.C. (1); D.C.M. (3), Cpls Withers and Robertson and Sgt. Gove; M.C. (3), Capt. Shierlaw, R.M.O., Capt. Bone and Lt. McDowell; M.M. (14).

On the night of the 9th we were relieved by the 46th Bn., having a hot meal on the way out and a rum issue on arrival at Mametz huts after a weary march. Troops we passed along the tracks back freely expressed their envy of the reputation the 13th had won at Stormy Trench, and those who had fought there felt that it had been worth while. Col. Durrant received messages of congratulation from far and wide on what was generally recognised as a masterpiece of organisation.

So splendid had Rosenthal's 4th Div. Artillery been that Durrant had a special order sent to them expressing the 13th's heartfelt appreciation for their magnificent support. The gunners had been delighted at having an extra supply of shells delivered to them, for the quick eye of Marks had discovered a snow-covered dump of old shells near Flers, and we had carried them across to the artillery to "thicken the barrage." Very little of value to his Battalion escaped Marks' notice at any time.

Chapter XX.—Bullecourt.

AFTER another period of hard work on roads, camps and railways near Mametz the Bde. moved back to Ribemont on the 22nd February. During most of our time here snow lay deep on the fields, and the roads become even more sloppy as the warmer sun thawed the ground. Col. Durant acted as Brigadier until the 7th March when Brand returned.

The beginning of March was even colder than February, "very cold, more snow and rain" being typical weather entries in Bde. journals for this period. However, open warfare training was carried out, the idea being that, as the Hun was supposed to be about to leave his final Somme systems to retire to his Hindenburg Line, we should be trained to follow such a retreat rapidly. Some of these exercises were made in conjunction with planes.

There was great joy throughout the Bde. on the 12th March when word of the award of Murray's V.C. was received.

The 22nd March found the Bde. moving to the Forward Area again, the enemy having commenced his big retirement. That evening we camped at Fricourt, "D" remaining at Meaulte. On the 26th we marched to Bazentin, "D" moving by rail. On the 27th to Warlencourt in rain and wind, and the next day to dug-outs between Favreuil and Biefvillers, where we strenuously improved the accommodation by using old material from German dug-outs and villages nearby. A clockwork mine blew up the 14th Hqrs. this day at Beugnatre. What a contrast this area presented to that behind us! The only evidences of war were a few trench systems and plenty of wire belts, and the absence of civilians.

April came in very cold with sleet and snow. On the 3rd we moved to Favreuil in a strong sleety wind, and here we worked solidly for a week roadmaking, cable-burying and carrying. On the 5th and following days officers reconnoitred the Hindenburg Line and Riencourt with glasses from the high ground near Noreuil. On the 8th Durrant conferred with the General re the proposed attack, after which the latter and his four Colonels again reconnoitred the ground in front of Reincourt.

The Bde. was now better trained for fighting Germans than at any other period in its history. After its success in 1916 Gen. C. B.B. White wrote:— "The recent successes of the 4th Bde. are due as much to sound training as to careful preparation and gallantry. Prior to going into the Line this Bde. carried out, both by day and night a series of exercises in the attack." And such opinions were now even more appropriate for Brand had spared neither himself nor his Colonels in practice stunts under all likely conditions. Certainly the 13th were never in their history in a higher state of efficiency.

Trench life tends to kill the offensive spirit by creating a horror of the open. The fact that the enemy in the open is such a target from a trench creates a terror of the enemy trenches. But the General had aimed at showing his Bns. how harmless enemy trenches were to men of a well-trained Bde., attacking in a well-planned scheme. He had contrived to build up in each Bn. a faith in the other Bns., as each Coy. of a Bn. possessed regarding its sister Coys. The "Old Brig." was firm and expected the utmost of all, but, as he was impartial and just, and did not spare himself, he was highly respected and got such excellent results from his Bde. He was a worthy successor to Monash.

At 8 p.m. on the 9th we received word that the impending attack was to take place at dawn on the 10th, and that the 13th was to move up to Noreuil and join the rest of the Bde. The Hindenburg Line was to be broken completely through without artillery, but by Infantry with tanks. That night Jacka (14th) and Wadge and Bradley (16th) examined the enemy first wire-belt, and reported that the Hun was strong and had strong patrols out, and advised that it was useless to attack the Hindenburg Line without artillery support, and until the wire was thoroughly cut. However, it was to be gone on with, and the following plans were sent to Bns.—

4-30 a.m.—Artillery will put down a flank barrage on Queant and Bullecourt. The 12 tanks will move forward.

4.45 a.m.—Infantry will advance.

5 a.m.—All Artillery fire on Bullecourt will cease in order to allow 4 tanks and a Battalion to enter the village.

5-15 a.m.—Heavy artillery fire on Riencourt ceases and creeps back. Barrage on Queant ceases to allow 2 tanks to go along.

The attack to be made on the south side of a salient of which Arras was the north. Up there the Germans had been getting a bad time. It was intended that our push and another at Arras would cut off all the enemy between Bullecourt and Arras. (See sketch)

We were to have 12 tanks, 6 each to the 4th and 12th Bdes. Diagrams were issued explaining what they would do. According to Fig. 1 the tanks were to go into the H.L. first, and the Infantry to follow. That was fine. Notice how beautifully and successfully they were to come up and advance; it could not have been better in a sham fight. The First Line captured so easily, 4 Tanks (V. Fig. 2) would lumber over into Bullecourt, from where the artillery had ceased, followed by a smiling Battalion; 2 would go to the right beyond Queant to prevent the bewildered Hun from escaping, and 6 would appropriate the Second Hindenburg Line. More splendid still. The Infantry were mere adjuncts to occupy places captured by the Tanks and to round-up and souvenir the prisoners. The instructions were so simple:—

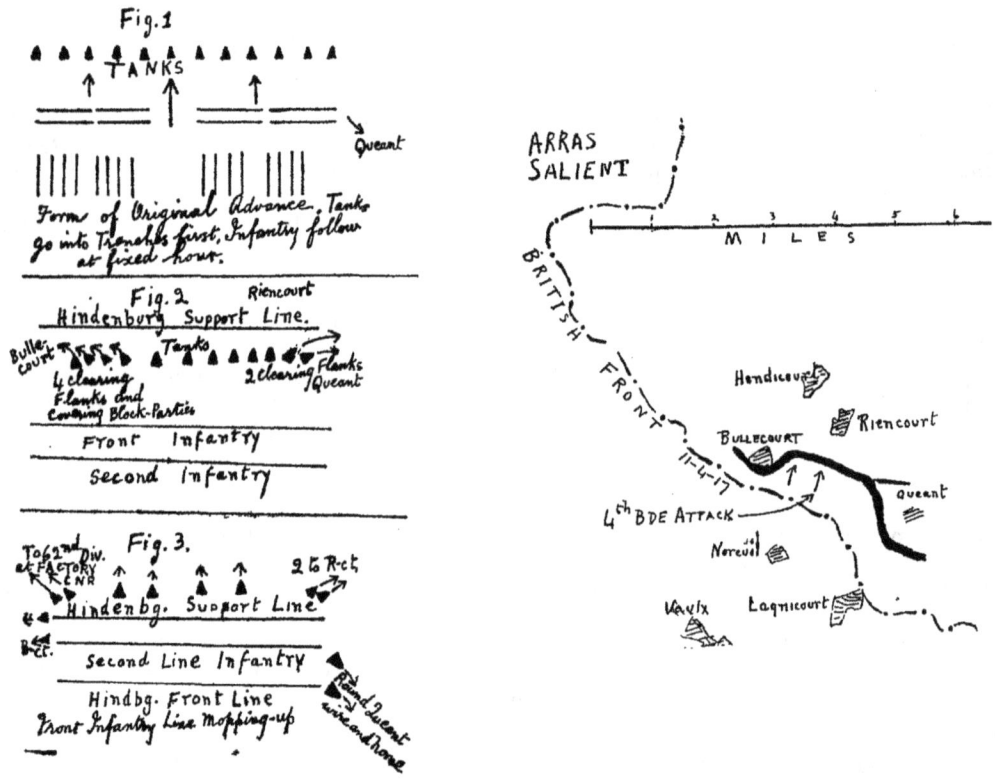

"On reaching the trenches, and, as soon as they have occupied them, the Tanks will display a green disc meaning, "Come on!" Fig. 3 foretold the glorious work that was to follow. The Hun had been crushed out of his boasted stronghold,—teach them to boast—even his Supports and Reserve Line, his machine-gunners had thrown in the towels, their artillery was spellbound. Wonderful Tanks. Two of them in Bullecourt allowing no possible escape for Fritz, and two making posthaste to join the victorious 62nd Division at Factory Corner near Hendicourt. On the right two were in Riencourt; two, finished with Queant were rolling gloriously "Round Queant wire and home", while four eagerly strained on the leash to cross the Rhine. "Home". Nothing more to do now except take tea. These little outings were merely appetisers. "Round Queant Wire and Home". Home, boys, home. Such was the tragically absurd idea of the weakness of the enemy and the Hindenburg Line, and of the miracle-performing Tanks held by some very high authority who had men's lives to play with. And someone higher than our Div. Cmr. Holmes, and Birdwood. At the time we were in Gough's 5th Army. Certainly one cannot name an officer of the 4th Aust. Div. who regarded the scheme as feasible. Regarding the 62nd Div. and its junctioning with us near Hendicourt, the signal for it to attack was to be the appearance of the Tanks in Bullecourt; and, therefore, they did not hop over at all. The Diggers had Fritz's undivided attention.

Let us now see what actually took place with special reference to the 13th. Leaving Favreuil at 10 p.m. they were ready in position in the Railway Cutting, their J.O.L. before 4 a.m. The tanks were still behind Noreuil. Ears were strained for the sounds of their coming by the anxious attackers. The 14th, on the left, and the 16th, on the right, were lying out in the cold, thin snow along their J.O. tape, and the 15th, behind the 14th, and the 13th, behind the 16th, in close support. Guides went back to guide the tanks up. Then a message came on the phone that they could not arrive and that the attack was accordingly cancelled. Streaks of dawn were appearing in the East. To send out messages to retire would take time, maybe short, but Durrant saw how terribly serious was the situation and ran out to his Commanders himself. "Get back for your lives!" he ordered, "Back to Noreuil!" Then men appreciated the situation and started immediately. It was not military precision, but it was the most speedy, and that was what was wanted then. Dawn came on with alarming rapidity, and, whether the Hun saw us or not, his shelling of certain companies increased. Over 3,000 men retiring over snow within ¾ of a mile of his front line should certainly have been seen, but, just when all felt the Bde. doomed to annihilation, snow commenced to fall heavily, the kindest snow we ever experienced, altho' it soon became a small blizzard. Viewed from within this retirement resembled the departure of a crowd from a Test Match, there appearing to be absolutely no order, but officers and nco's were among their own men, and in reality there was as much order and organisation as there could possibly have been in such a hasty countermanding of orders at such a critical time. It would not have suited a drill precisioner, but it saved lives. (Capt. D. P. Wells was told by the Hun that they saw our retreat that morning, and, knowing we would come again, they got more machine guns up.) After rendezvousing at Noreuil, the 13th were ordered to move back to Favreuil. This was hard indeed. So, dog-tired, disappointed and more pessimistic than at any other period in their history concerning the higher authorities, they struggled on over the snow. They had worked all the 9th, marched all night, gone through the tension of preparing for a big battle, and were now marching back over the same ground on the morning of the 10th. No wonder that the last were only limping into Favreuil late that afternoon, falling asleep immediately on arrival without troubling about their meal.

After the gruelling of that night and morning all hoped to be left in peace for this night, but, at 5 p.m. Coy. Cmrs. were sent for and told that the attack was merely postponed 24 hours. Preparations were immediately recommenced, but the men were allowed to rest to the last minute. Still, at 9 they were moving back, and at 3.30 a.m. were again in their position of the morn before. A wonderful performance. Throughout that march the hideous barking of the tanks accompanied them. Gen. Brand had asked for, and had been promised, heavy artillery fire to down these noises, but the firing was totally inadequate, and not at all what it should and could easily, have been.

By 4-20 a.m. three of our Bde., tanks were ready to advance. One had had 'an accident,' one complained of 'engine trouble', and the other had lolloped into a sunken road whither he had gone contrary to proper directions by a 14th officer. These tanks were out of action before the battle commenced, and, not only the three that had arrived, but the others had made squeals, screeches and sparks that must have warned the enemy. Our men cursed them and the 'silent artillery'. On the left of the 4th Bde. there was a gap of 400 yards beyond which the 12th Bde. was to attack, and there were now too few tanks to deal with this big gap. Still the Bde. was determined to do its job, the 14th and 16th to capture the two trench systems and the 13th and 15th to advance beyond them and capture "Riencourt and beyond."

At 4-30 our three tanks went forward. Their progress was disappointingly slow. The day before, after studying them, Durrant had asked that they should leave 15 minutes earlier in order to reach the wire before the men, but, although the other Colonels and the General had supported him, Division had replied "Stick to the programme."

At 4-45 the 16th rose and advanced, and the 13th started behind them. In spite of heavy fire the whole Battalion moved out without a sign of hesitation. It was thrilling to see platoon after platoon in perfect order, and cheerful, climb out of the Cutting, hitch rifles over shoulders and disappear into the dimness. Their intent faces showed that they knew they had a serious task ahead, but that there would be no wavering. The heavy shellfire they ran into on leaving the Cutting, continued on them until they reached the Hindenburg Line. Several fell in the Cutting, and others were soon dotted on the snow from the Cutting as far as watchers could see.

At dawn, owing to a thick smoke haze, those of Hqrs. straining their anxious eyes could see nothing of the advance, but they could see two tanks far behind where they ought to have been. They could be seen as sparkling outlines, for such showers of bullets were constantly striking them that they were outlined as if by electric lights. All passing them had to go through that shower of bullets as well as the storm of shells aimed at them. They had brought this onto themselves and the Infantry by halting and opening fire when only half way across No Man's Land. Then S.B.'s could be seen coming back with their loads, several falling, but others tending the wounded unwaveringly, even near those tanks.

Capt. T. Wells M.C., advancing gallantly with "C" Coy., fell severely wounded by a 5-9. He ordered Lt. C.Kaler, who hurried to his assistance, to inform Capt. A. Lanagan, his Second-in-mand. Kaler was killed shortly after, and Lt.. J. Geary, another "C" officer wounded. Shells and Mortar bombs now smothered the whole area back to the Cutting. About 7 one fell in Bn. Hqrs., killing 6 and wounding 5, Col Durrant being the only one of Hqrs. untouched. Maj. Marks' wounds were so severe that the M.O.'s held out no hope of his recovery, but his determination to get better saved him to return and become C.O. of his Bn. Our M.O., Capt. Shierlaw, M.C. lingered only a short time. Fearless Sgt. P. Kibble (O.P.) was one killed. His record is one to be proud of.

In addition to this shelling, about 600 yards from the Hindenburg Line the 13th came into heavy machine-gun barrages from Bullecourt and Queant, and suffered tremendous losses. Still they advanced, seeing hundreds of the gallant 16th lying in the snow.

So frightfully had the 16th suffered that they had become too weak by the time they reached a belt of heavy wire—one of the heaviest and most super-barbed belts on the Western Front—to attack across it as a body. Much of this belt was overgrown with grass. The 13th saw the 16th in this belt, and some of them well ahead near the Objective. Great gaps were being torn in their gallant lines.

A tornado of lead now swept across the head of the 13th. "Get down till it passes!" called out Murray. Still about 30 of his Coy., including three platoon commanders and his runner, were killed. Gardiner's "B" Coy. on Murray's right also hugged the ground under this hissing hail, but suffered less than "A". This was gallant Gardiner's first battle in France, and the worthy Capt. D. P. Wells was accompanying him to advise if necessary. As the hail swish passed over onto the rear platoons, Murray's voice was again heard: "Come on, men, the 16th are getting hell." As they rose and advanced Murray noticed that the right of the Bn. had closed into the left, the road leading to Riencourt being responsible for this, as it slanted across the line of attack,, and he called out "Get to the right, boys, you're swinging a bit too close." Several of the 16th were now among "A" and "B". Less that 50 of the splendid "A" Coy. of 166 now remained. They struggled through a partial gap where the wire had been somewhat cut. Some of both Coys. gallantly essayed to walk over the belt, jumping from strand to strand in the face of the lead blizzard that had come on them again. Many fell to hang lifeless on its cruel inch-long barbs, others ripped at it with bayonets or smashed into it with rifle-butts; a few crawled under it, anything to get across it. Some of the 16th were now in the first trench and the frontal fire ceased somewhat. The sole remaining tank, solidly outlined by sparks from bullets, was in the second wire, moving slowly and firing its 6-pounder. Ten yards from it, in a hole in the centre of the wire, was a machine gun mowing our men down, 30 falling within a few seconds under its fire. Murray went in where this tank had crushed the wire, to get past it on the left, and got into uncut wire. Moving round to the right he saw this gun, and his men shot the crew of three. Part of "B" also got through here. Others found a few short saps through the wire left by the enemy for patrols. These with a final charge were soon with the 16th in the Trench chasing Germans from bay to bay. The Germans never imagined that it would be possible for attackers to use these saps, so commanded were they by bombers and guns.

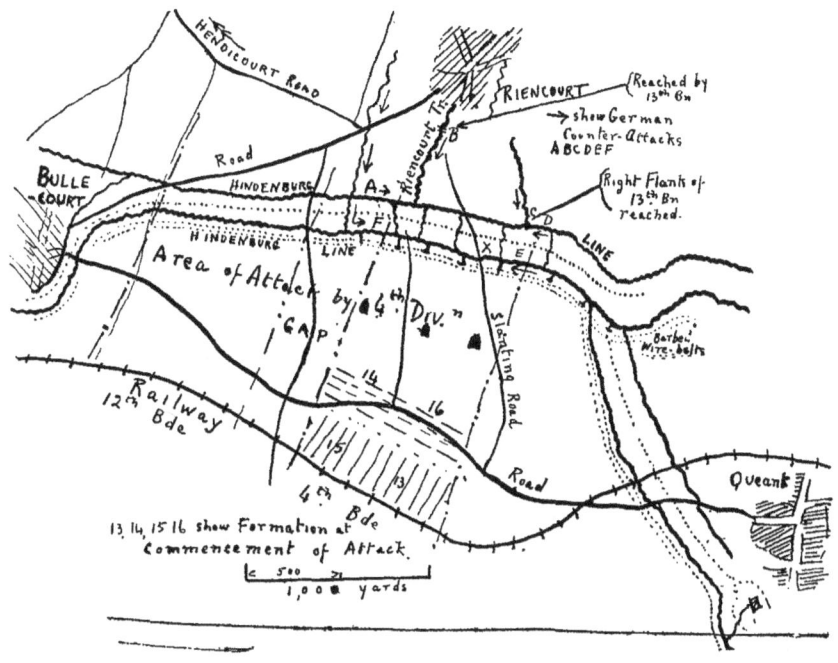

BATTLE OF BULLECOURT, 11/4/1917.

Some of the 16th were preparing to advance to the second objective when their gallant Major Black was shot. Murray saw him dying. It was a hard moment for Murray. They were cherished personal friends and had been Originals on the same machine-gun on Gallipoli, and had since co-operated in many fierce fights.

When looking for a hero with whom to compare Murray the 13th generally coupled his name with Major Black's, and they felt sure that such was the highest honor Murray would wish for.

Not a tank was with them now, although the one they had passed soon moved again and reached the first trench, by which time both battalions had captured the second trench system. Between the two Capt. D. P. Wells fell severely wounded. Capts. Gardiner, Lanagan and Fletcher and Lts. Stones, Parsonage, Gallagher, A. L. Gowing, Cooney, Rose, Gluyas, Brown, Wallach, G. C. Smith and Morgan had all along, been, and were still, setting glorious examples. Lts. Thornley and Shirtley (O.P.) had gallantly died, and Lt. Clasper was fatally wounded. Bullets were still sweeping low over the surface. But the men in the second trench looked over, and some crawled farther to reconnoitre. The tank crew fired into these, their first shot killing 3 of the 13th. They also killed several more of the 16th.

Murray now had 32 prisoners and sent them back, but they were all immediately shot by their own gunners.

The tank now caught fire and the incinerated crew jumped from the top to the ground to die.

With the diminished numbers there was now no chance of capturing Riencourt, the problem being to hold what he had. Every remaining officer and Nco. set to work organising for defence, except a few who continued pushing on. Cpl. W. F. Patten organised a party and, joined by Lt. B. Rose, bombed up Riencourt Trench to within 150 yards of the village. They saw crowds of Germans firing from roofs and upper windows of the village, untroubled by our shells. In full view of these there was no possibility of advancing even with stronger forces. Rose's party reached a maze of strong-posts and was strongly counter-attacked, but not only held fast, but drove the Hun back.

Murray now quickly visited every part of the Brigade position in the second trench advised all and placed posts and guns. He then, at 7.15 a.m., sent a message back stating that they held the First and part of the Second Objective, and that "With Artillery Support we can Keep the Position till the Cows come Home." Truly what a wonderful man was Murray. Here, right in the vaunted Hindenburg Line, with 30 of his 166 left, and most other companies in the Bde. with similar losses—some with heavier—yet confident that, if the guns would only fire, they could keep the position "till the cows come home." And he would have, too. But the guns did not fire.

Those still unwounded of the above-named officers had organised parties and were now either fighting grimly to hold back overwhelming odds, or still advncing up saps. Rose and Patten had, by 8.15 reached to within 100 yards of Riencourt, where they built a block, C. H. Knight helping them gallantly. Four times the enemy attempted to rush this block, but our Lewis-gunners and riflemen, gloriously manning the top of the trench, mowed down all attempting to come over the top, and our bombers kept their bombers in the trench back.

In going round, Murray found some 16th Bombers still pushing ahead and told them to put in a block. "We're not stopping here, Sir, we're going on," replied the Corporal. Murray was showing them where to block when a 16th officer came along. It is not known whether the party pushed on and died or died there. They are "Missing".

The 4th Bde. members now became anxious about the 12th Bde. on the other side of the 400 yards' gap. They had seen one company of the 46th cut to pieces at the first wire. (Only 8 of this company were left). And at 8 o'clock they had seen the 12th Bde. starting to retire. There were masses of Germans in the gap between the two Bdes., the gap unfortunately coinciding with an important enemy C.T. down which they poured their reinforcements, leaving the 4th Bde. holding their 900 yards of the Second Trench with masses of enemy on three sides of them. Some well-protected German cannons were now firing low along the parapets and they shot down several of our bombers attempting to get at the enemy over the top, as at Stormy Trench. We had no artillery to deal with these. Still our men gallantly climbed onto the parapets to shoot into the crowds of enemy hurrying into Riencourt and at others in the windows coolly examining our position. The situation was crying for artillery, but futilely. Six desperate bomb-fights were going on at Points A, B, C, D, E, and F, and the Bde. was beating back every attack, although the Hun had unlimited supplies of bombs to our few, for the battle was intended to be not a bomb-fight—especially one of the first magnitude and lasting for hours—but an open-warfare stunt with tanks cavorting ahead and along the flanks, and bombs were accordingly scarce. Murray and Gardiner had every enemy bomb collected as well as those from our dead and wounded, but the supply was pitifully inadequate.

Between 9 and 10 the Germans made seven overwhelming attacks at the five flank positions. Each time they were repulsed with bomb and bayonet, but each fight lessened our numbers and our supplies. Orders were now given to cease firing on the enemy at a distance, even when good targets offered, the officers recognising that no additional supplies could be got across before night, and that the crisis would come at close quarters before then. The S.O.S. for artillery support had gone up 18 times, but without answer. Durrant, who had received Murray's message: "We hold the first objective and part of the second. Expect heavy bomb fighting in the evening. Quite impossible to attack the village. We will require as many rifles and hand-grenades as you can possibly send, also S.A.A. Look out for S.O.S. Send white flares. With artillery support we can keep the position till the cows come home," had begged for a barrage but had been refused. Why? Not only had the Air men reported: "Australians have taken Riencourt, and two tanks, followed by cheering Australians are going towards Hendicourt," but Rosenthal's forward observing officer reported: "Australians in Riencourt." Hence the guns were kept quiet.

Late in the morning Gardiner sent Lt. Aarons (16th) back to report the situation personally, and called for a volunteer to accompany him. Cpl. R. E. Sullivan, after doing splendid bombing, instantly volunteered, and with Aarons faced the 1,200 yards of raked, level ground. Fortunately they got through safely by rushing yard by yard, but Sullivan's clothes were torn in a dozen places by bullets. Signaller N. H. Bowers (O.P.), after carrying a message from Rose to Murray for bombs and finding none available, went back across the swept area for some. Sgt. C. Trick, M.M., after gallantly commanding the remnants of a platoon, volunteered to carry a message back for Murray.

Bitterly disappointed at the failure of the artillery—the tanks were long before out of consideration—Murray and Gardiner began to think out plans for retreat should such become necessary. Gardiner's message by Aarons was that he wanted a barrage under which he would retire a short distance through the enemy wire, and wait there until night or further orders. Murray also had a similar idea in case he should be compelled to retreat, but his main desire was to hang on till night, when help and supplies could reach him. One of the rear tanks now began moving about aimlessly, but it was soon hit by an anti-tank gun in a pit south of Riencourt, which gun had probably accounted for every tank. Murray got a Lewis gun to silence it, but the last of the tanks had been hit. Lt. A. L. Gowing was now dead, his cheerfulness having been inspiring. Sgts. Bourne, M.M., Cross, M.M., and Ahradsen performed many heroic deeds before falling.

At 11.30 the 12th Bde. retired, suffering frightfully. This allowed the Hun to give all his attention to the 4th. Rose, with proper judgment, retired before enemy showers to the second line. Now the fight became desperate at all points. Not one bomb left, at Points A, C, and D, men charged with bayonets, their rush being irresistible for up to 100 yards. Time and again they climbed on the top to get at the enemy, but each man appearing there for a second was shot down. Although attacking bravely the enemy could never have moved those Diggers had their bombs lasted. Parsonage, on the extreme left near "A," threw the last bomb there and then retired, his party fighting every bay. As officers fell their n.c.o's took command. The strongest enemy attacks were now made up their First Line with the object of pinching the remnants of the 4th Bde. out. The 13th and 16th in the second trench soon heard bomb-fighting behind them, and saw by the overwhelming showers that the Germans were advancing there. There was no time to lose. Helped by the men from the second line those in the Front Line again drove back the enemy over 50 yards on each flank, but some in the second line were already cut off, still fighting in isolated parties until all fell or until the last bomb and bullet were used. Even German rifles were used when their own ammunition was spent, but that also came to an end. Pte. D. Grant, the popular aboriginal, although wounded, was amongst these last fighters. Murray, Sgts. T. Gilday and A. Oswald, and Cpl. G. W. Hickling, who had carried Stokes' shells, and Pte. C. H. Knight were cut off several times and called upon to surrender, but their reply was always fight. In the Front Line Murray organised the parties and placed men on the road at Point X to fire on Germans coming over the top. These grim men fired rapidly until their rifles were too hot to touch. They got others from dead men and fired until their bullets were spent, no German being able to live above ground within sight of them. But the fight was now too uneven, and the flanks were again being pressed back, their numbers diminishing every second under bomb showers. Gardiner could have got back as he had sent a few men back, but while one man was still fighting ahead he himself would not retire. He and his party of four, without a bomb or bullet then suddenly found the enemy around them. Some of them had come through tunnels which ran through dugouts from the first into the second line. Other parties were caught similarly. Murray, still cheerful, went to party after party. "Well, boys," he said, "We'll have to get back, as we've run completely out of ammunition, and Fritz has been heavily reinforced." Most of those able to climbed out and rushed back towards the wire. His flanks still held on in order to give as many as possible the chance to get away. They fought every yard as they retired towards the centre. To the few left Murray said, "There are two things now—capture of go into that." "That" was a hell of bullets from 4,000 rifles and 15 machineguns. Sgts. Buchan (O.P.), Mayo (O.P.), M. White, P. Frost, D. Matheson, and Cpl. Currie (O.P.), M.M., after fighting, leading and organising gloriously, all fell. Sgts. Gove, Paxton

F

(O.P.), Landless, Wynne, E. James and Grierson likewise fought, led, inspired and organised, until wounded and hopelessly surrounded.

Among the last to leave, each from his own area, were Lts. Wallach and Parsonage, Sgts. M. Tague, A. Oswald and T. Gilday, Lewis Gunners E. Butcher, J. White, J. Bertram and P. Ross, Bombers Blaw and Goodwin, Sig. W. Hughes (O.P.), and Cpl. G. Hickling, Murray himself being the last, and only leaving after seeing there was no chance of anyone else being able to leave.

After crossing the wire, those left rested in shellholes awhile before continuing. Murray jumped into one of these holes. The remnant of the glorious 4th Bde. was still being cut down. It was too much for Murray. "This is not war; it is murder," he exclaimed. "Some of those men helped me to get my V.C., and I must help them now." With these words he ran out into the hail to advise in order to try to save his men. And our artillery was still silent, allowing the enemy to pour his lead into us at his sweet will. Thus it was that, after fighting heroically for seven hours, dozens of splendid men were killed returning.

Had the artillery believed Durrant, their barrage could have done any of the following: 1—Harassed enemy during this retreat and so saved losses. 2—Kept enemy back until dark, when we could have reinforced and consolidated, or retired safely. 3—Could have got the 12th Bde. forward.

The gap between the two Bdes. intended to be patrolled by tanks was fatal, coinciding as it did with that C.T. One big German gun fired during the retirement, sending a shell that burst black and killed at least 10 every time, none being merely wounded.

At last the Artillery did fire onto Riencourt, but our poor men who had been captured were then there. However this fire kept the Germans down and so allowed our men still alive to get back.

That evening our bearers went forward right to the wire to rescue the wounded, and it is pleasing to state that the Germans not only allowed them to work, but pointed the wounded out to them, a pleasing contrast to their treatment of our wounded officers and men left in their trenches, for these they mocked, insulted and neglected for days, with the result that scores died who would have lived with even slight attention.

Some of our bearers who were splendid that day were Sgt. P. James, who took charge of the R.A.P. on the death of Capt. Shierlaw, C. Price, J. Campbell, A. Beness (O.P.), A. Brenton (O.P.), C. Kent and J. Holmes. Our bearers were carrying for 14 hours.

Capt. Wallach had gone through the day with a bullet wound in his thigh, having received it before starting. Lt. N. J. Brown, M.C., wounded early, had continued advancing until he fainted from loss of blood.

Murray received a bar to his D.S.O., Parsonage and Rose M.C.s, Oswald, Gilday, Trick, Patten received their D.C.M.s; Rose, Bowers, White, Goodwin, James, Hickling, Beness, Brenton, Kent, Holmes, Bertram, Campbell, Price, Knight, Sullivan, Butcher and Tague their M.M.s. Most of these had had splendid service on Gallipoli and the Somme.

For sheer heroism nothing in the world's history can outshine the feat of the 4th Bde. at Bullecourt. Spartans at Thermopylae fought at the entrance of their own homes, with worse than death to follow if defeated; Balaclava was a mad heroic half-hour; but Bullecourt was at least a two-days' test, every man knowing on the evening of the 9th what a forlorn hope he was up against. Half-a-division to smash the Hindenburg Line, after crossing the widest belts of the cruellest wire. They knew that it was to be purely an infantry assault, for they were not so disillusioned as Gough's advisers regarding what tanks could or would do at that experimenting stage. They knew full well that their Colonels and their Generals were opposed to hurling them on to certain annihilation, although these officers were certain that they had expressed no such opinions that could have reached the men. Somehow, too, they had no faith in or liking for Gough, although they had absolutely nothing tangible to form this intuition on, nothing until the bungling in high quarters became so evident on the morning of the 10th. Still they stuck it without complaint. They would have attacked that first morning without the tanks, but had to walk back eight miles instead, many arriving at Favreuil just in time to get ready to return. A few physically unable to stand up, not to mention march and fight, fell by the wayside, agonised mentally even more than physically at their inability to keep up with their mates. (These unfortunately were harshly dealt with, but almost to a man volunteered to wipe out their red marks in action later on, and made records to be proud of.)

Everything had seemed to work in favor of the Hun as the resolute men left the Cutting behind. Three out of four mates fell, but the one kept on. He walked over, crawled under, or got through the wire somehow, it mattered not so long as he smashed the Hindenburg Line. He got there, smashed it and held it for seven hours, and would have held it "till the cows come home" had his supplies lasted. Then, without a bomb or a bullet, he smashed it again, this time in the reverse direction. Again three out of four fell, but the remainder smashed through, leaving broken, helpless or weaponless men for the Hun to gloat over. And had they been asked to smash through again that same day they would have done it again, too.

The Brigade losses for the battle were:—

	Officers.	Other Ranks.
13th	21	489
14th	19	582
15th	20	380
16th	13	623
4th M.G.C.	5	99
T.M.B.	1	30
Details		57
Totals	79	2260

In the 15th all the officers became casualties, and not one who reached the objective got back.

Records captured later showed the German elation at the defeat of the 4th Brigade. War Office records, according to good authority, show that they specially feared our Bde., and that their front line troops were always warned when the 4th Bde. was opposite them. Also that there was a reward of 1,000 marks for each Colonel of the Bde. and a larger one for the Brig., dead or alive. That they knew all these by name was proved to our prisoners captured at Bullecourt.

Bullecourt is a name for Australians to be proud of. It was not an Australian failure. It was perhaps an unfortunate accumulation of miscalculations on the part of Army authorities, and of non-understandable mistakes on the part of the airmen who saw Australians near Hendicourt in a cheering crowd behind a tank, and of the artillery officer who saw them in Riencourt.

General Brand rightly regards Bullecourt as one of the proudest names in the laurels of the 4th Brigade. The 13th are proud of their share in it, and of their members who took part in it—from Colonel to Digger.

The fact that the vaunted Hindenburg Line could be broken by brave men, unaided by artillery, rudely disturbed the confidence of the Germans, and sowed seeds which later bore a great harvest.

APPENDIX.

Extracts from an Australian Artillery Major's diary concerning Bullecourt:—

9th April.—5.30 a.m.: Snowing; devilishly cold. Morning: Got my guns into action and calibrated in a howling gale, at times having to stop owing to snow. Night: Guns, and ever more guns, making the place hideous, with climatic indications of more snow and rain. Huns began a heavy bombardment.

10th April.—What with Operation Orders and Stop Orders, I was at my wit's end; and the Hun was shelling heavily, too. At 5.15a.m. he got one of my guns. Decided to rest until 9 p.m., only to be awakened by tanks. The Hun must have heard them, for he began searching for them.

11th April.—Had last night further disturbed by another lot of substituted orders. It also snowed. At 4.15 a.m. the Infantry attacked the Hindenburg Line. The tanks looked grotesque. These monstrosities were severely dealt with and only two were left. It appeared to me that they lacked direction and should have been well in advance of the Infantry, who, evidently forced to be close to them, came into unnecessary risk from guns and machine-guns, all of which took heavy toll. . . . For a while, as I saw our boys disappear into the Hun front line, all seemed well. . . . Huns were seen with my naked eye to come out of the ground and counter-attack heavily. . . . . It was evident to me that the attack had failed, and I promptly put down my 4.5 barrage just over the second line until I could get some better idea of the position, advised Headquarters what I had done, and I was advised to carry out the task previously allotted me as they were informed all objectives were taken. I refused on the ground that I had a first-hand view of what was actually taking place. Our artillery was placing a so-called protective barrage behind Riencourt. It made my blood boil to see our poor fellows endeavoring to come back and falling. The Huns came from God only knows where and fairly mopped our boys up. . . . Heavy snow is falling again. . . . So ends a day which promised well, but through Staff blunders ended so disastrously. It ended, too, a period of orders countermanded, orders substituted, orders the like of which I have never before experienced, and hope I never will again. One's work at any time in the front line is bad enough with a straight-out order, but with the heterogeneous litter of literature we have had to put up with one needed the wisdom of Solomon.

APPENDIX II.

Extracts from Official Statement of Capt. D. P. Wells, on his repatriation from Germany as an invalid:—

"After capture no attempt was made to remove the wounded till dark, when German orderlies removed them, handling them very brutally without regard to the nature of their wounds. . . . A German Major put himself out to aggravate me and robbed me of all my belongings and badges of rank. . . . Cpl. Stewart craved for a drink. He died soon after drinking. Then they handed the drink to me, and when I found it to be paraffin, I would not drink. They were determined that I should drink it, and held me down and tried to force me. After that I was prepared for anything. They suddenly hastened out of the dugout pretending that the Australians were again attacking, in order to see what I would do. Knowing it a bluff, I remained still. . . I was roughly assisted out of the dugout. . . . As far as I could see our men were lying everywhere, and scores of Germans visiting and brutally handling them in their endeavour to rob them, but no attempt was made to care for the men or to have them removed. . . . I have no hestitation in saying that hundreds must have died through exposure and sheer wilful neglect. . . . I was surprised at the accuracy of the information they had carefully compiled from time to time. . . . A Staff Officer of high rank said how delighted they all were at having captured the 4th Australian Brigade. He said they had watched our movements very closely for months past, and feared us most of any unit in France. He also added that they feared Australians most of any troops. . . . The good news had been transmitted to all units. He also said that their line was lightly held on the 10th, but machine-guns and reinforcements were hurried to that sector during the night of the 10th. . . . On one station we were left on the platform, being jeered at by passers-by. . . . The medical attention is disgusting. . . . Quite a number of lives could have been saved had the patients received treatment in time, whilst others, instead of being permanently incapacitated, could have been completely cured. I can quote numerous cases of wilful brutality to helpless wounded men.

Chapter XXI.—Messines, Ploegsteert and Gapaard.

THAT road to Favreuil! How well-known to those who survived Bullecourt. Their fourth march over it within 48 hours, a total of over 31 miles with a gruelling battle in between, and the constant nerve-tension increased by the uncertainty. The next morning, the 12th, in rain and snow, they journeyed by train from Favreuil to Albert, whence they marched to Mametz huts, absolutely dead-beat.

That Birdwood was grieved as perhaps never before or since, was evident. His solicitude was sincere. He addressed the Bde. on the 14th and congratulated it on the magnificent work it had done and the glory that would be for ever attached to it for its heroism at Bullecourt. It was surprising how many of all ranks he knew personally, and in individual conversation with the men after parade he touchingly referred by name and history to many of their comrades killed up there.

On the 15th Capt. C. H. Kelleway reported as R.M.O., and soon proved himself a worthy successor to Shierlaw.

April was a cold, snowy, showery and blustery month. Along wet roads the Bde marched back to Ribemont on the 19th to find the inhabitants heartbroken at the absence of so many whom they had come to regard as "old friends." Anzac Day was celebrated here by a Memorial Service and a Bde. Sports Meeting. On the 29th we polled for the Federal Elections.

May was a more comfortable month, glorious weather being the order. We remained at Ribemont at routine training and parades until the 15th, when we entrained for the north again, detraining at Bailleul and marching south to billets in fondly-remembered Doullieu. From here the officers visited Ploegsteert Wood trenches, and Godley and Plumer inspected the Bde. Godley specially remarked: "The smart, brisk step"; that "the men looked him square in the face"; "good transport" and "smart platoon commanders."

The Bde. Boxing Tournament on the 29th was honored by the presence of many distinguished visitors.

We now prepared seriously for another period in the Line, our nucleus going off on the 31st, under Twynam to Morbecque, the remainder marching the same day forward to Vauxhall Camp in Neuve Eglise area, whence officers and specialists visited the Front Line area near Messines daily.

We had now completed a year in France and could look back with pride upon our record. The list of decorations awarded to the Brigade for the year bears a peculiar comparison with that awarded for the nine months on Gallipoli:—

	Gallipoli.	France.
V.C.	1	2
	(Jacka)	(O'Meara and Murray)
C.B.	5	—
C.M.G.	2	1
D.S.O.	5	11
Bar to D.S.O.	—	1
		(Murray)
M.C.	6	41
Bar to M.C.	—	3
D.C.M.	15	39
M.M.	7	241
Bar to M.M.	—	5
M.S.M.	—	3
Foreign	1	12
Totals	42	359

Therefore, a Gallipoli decoration, excepting in the case of Command Rank seems to have been eleven times harder to win than a Western Front one, for 12 of the 42 for Gallipoli went to high officers, while but 8 of the 359 in France did so. No one knowing the facts can deny that the number awarded for the year in France was far below what it ought to have been, many officers and men having been recommended up to five times without receiving an award, and others having been cut out of the lists to make them short enough to stand the probability of being read by busy generals. One feels that the deeds of heroism on Gallipoli in the case of Company Officers and lower ranks were practically unconsidered. The war became more democratic as it proceeded.

A week's active training preceded the departure of an officer and 50 men on the 7th June to Gooseberry Farm to carry to the Front Line for the 12th Bde., and the remainder of the Battalion to Midland Support Trench on the 8th to take their part in the wonderful battles of Messines, of which the 7th was the opening day. Gooseberry Farm and Midland Support were right among the guns and we came in for much of the "backwash," suffering rather severely.

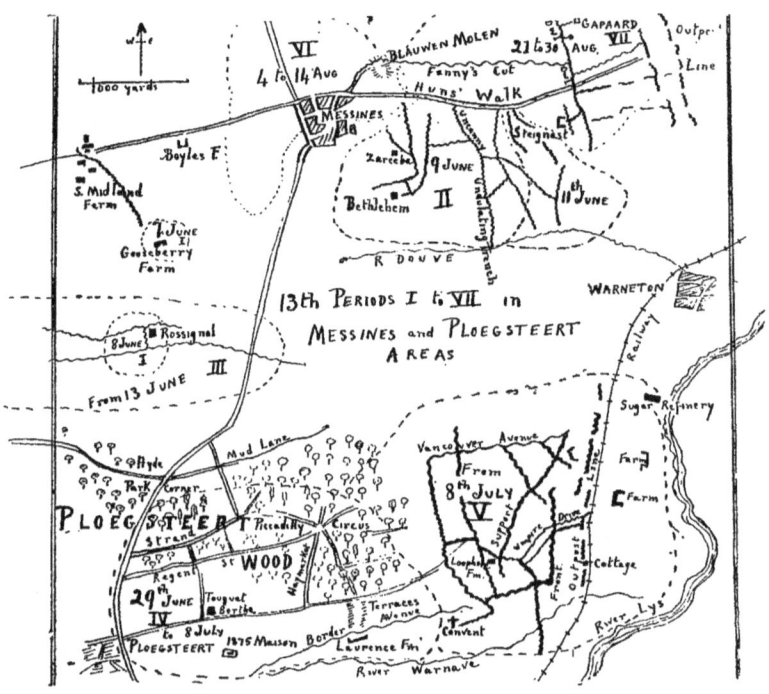

From Support we moved, on the 9th through the ruins of Messines and the litter of the battle still in active progress to the area south of Hun's Walk, near the Zareeba and Bethlehem Farm. Here, from Uncanny and Undulating Trenches, we took an active part in the finalising of the great battle, patrolling to watch for enemy counters and harassing his patrols and outposts, besides continually enlarging the area gained by advancing posts in face of strong opposition from Uncanny almost to Steignast. (Vide sketch.) Lts. R. J. Henderson and G. S. McDowell were the most distinguished officers during this period, their personal patrolling taking them each night right into the German posts in spite of myriads of their flares. They were splendid and daring officers indeed. Henderson received his M.C. for this period, after three previous strong recommendations. Col. Durrant's work in personally reconnoitring the area in front of Uncanny and in organising the advance towards Steignast, although only a minor operation, was admirable, and gained him the highest appreciation from the higher commands. Such minor operations concluded the Battle of Messines, preventing any possibility of a successful counter-attack. The first night had been a night of daring scouting by all hands; the second had advanced the British Line in our area 400 yards. It was a quick and lively period indeed. In 25 hours we marched in, relieved a front line battalion, advanced 400 yards, dug in, handed over, and were again on our way out. Unfortunately, in one of the several heavy enemy barrages, just at relief, Lts. E. Randall (O.P.), "that prince of good fellows," and W. Fitzpatrick, M.M. (O.P.), who had been commissioned for constant distinguished work, were killed, and Lts. Henderson, Player and L. McIntyre wounded in that or earlier shoots. "Lew" McIntyre's brother, Lt. T. A. McIntyre, was killed the same day with the 45th Bn. Both were (O.P.'s), of the 13th with records to be proud of. The barrage during relief naturally caused confusion, but one and all pulled themselves together in a most creditable manner, Sgt. H. B. Brown coolly taking charge of a platoon and extricating it from the shelled area, after which he returned and carried two wounded men out of the zone. He well deserved his D.C.M.

The bearers came in for many hot periods nere, but Cpl. P. Casey set his staff an inspiring example continuously by not only organising squads, but attending cases in the 13th and neighbouring units under the heaviest of shelling. (Received M.M.)

The 13th June found the 13th in the Support Area north of Ploegsteert Wood, where digging and carrying were the order, until the 17th, when we moved back to green fields near Neuve Eglise, where, after a bath and change. we again carried and made roads. On the 23rd we marched a few miles across to Regina Camp, west of Ploegsteert Village where all were again engaged in road-making or cable-burying, the latter generally occupying over 400 men, the cable having to be buried over 6 feet deep.

At the Duke of Connaught's inspection at Bailleul on the 27th 30 of its most distinguished available members represented the 4th Bde., the 13th being represented by Lt.-Col. Durrant, D.S.O., Capt. H. W. Murray, V.C., D.S.O. (and bar), D.C.M., Lt. G. S. McDowell, M.C., C.S.M., A. Oswald (O.P.), Cpl. P. Casey (O.P.), and Ptes P. Ross and A. Brenton.

The 28th found officers and specialists reconnoitring the Support Line in and south of Ploegsteert Wood. It was raining and the Trenches in such a low area promised to be as sloppy as on the Somme, which promise was quite fulfilled. Still the Bn. did a great amount of work in the construction of Communication Trenches, breastworks and roads, especially as, within a week, the sun shone brightly and the ground dried quickly. The woods, though shattered, were beautiful with their long, now historic, avenues named after London's Streets. No one minded the hard work in such a beautiful environment. A Flanders Forest in July! Leafy canopies carpeted bright green dotted thickly with yellow and white—primroses, buttercups and daisies. Each day brought a few casualties, but the forest life and sunshine kept all in good spirits.

From the 8th July, the day after we relieved the 16th, to the night of the 13th, when the 49th relieved us, the Battalion occupied the Front Line, a line of Outposts, and a system of trenches between Ploegsteert Wood and the Lys. near Warneton, Bn. Hqrs. being in a Convent. The ground was so low that in several places breastworks were used instead of trenches. Again our Scouts nightly performed deeds of the greatest valor, crawling through the enemy wire and examining the Refinery and farms on the banks of the Lys, accounting for many enemy parties with showers of bombs. Capt. Murray was again the most daring, working his way through the enemy posts to examine the river itself. The men in the Outposts aver that he even swam the river and examined its farther bank. Sgt. O'Leary (O.P.), gallant and popular, was killed on the 10th. Cpl. S. Wright did splendid work improving this and other areas, often being our Works Officer's right-hand man.

Our losses for the period were 24, including 7 killed. Durrant was wounded on 11th, after which Murray commanded for the period.

On the 14th we marched from the Wood back to Reserve, and on the 19th billeted at Vieux Berquin on our way to Steent-Je again, where we arrived on the 20th. There was a good deal of sickness in the Brigade although the weather remained glorious. The trench life in the Messines area was filthy indeed, the area having been so closely occupied for so long. The foulest of smells were constantly arising, lice and rats swarmed in the old enemy dugouts, and the earth oozed diseased-looking pools. It is a medical miracle that whole divisions were not exterminated by such conditions.

Within a few days, however, after light training and short marches, there was "a very noticeable improvement in the appearance and smartness of the men."

On the 27th Gen. Plumer inspected, and, the next day, Birdwood visited, the Brigade.

July ended and August came in with heavy rains. On August 3rd we moved forward to a tented camp north of Neuve Eglise, and on the 4th to Messines as Supports to the 16th. Here the work was hard and generally under shellfire, the main tasks being roadmaking, digging, wiring, salvaging and cable-burying. The officers in turn all visited the Front Line to the north of Hun's Walk. (See Sketch). From the 4th to 14th we carried on these works, making a tremendous improvement in the Defence Organisation. Casualties were few, but amounted up steadily day by day, Sgt. F. Keep being among the killed, after having proved himself most worthily. On the 10th our transport lines were bombed, 14 horses being killed and 13 wounded. On the night of the 14th we were relieved and marched back to billets in Dranoutre, remaining there for a week, coming back and relieving the 15th Bn. in the Gapaard Area (See Map) on the night of the 20th.

Going in all had hot soup from a soup-stall near Blauwen Molen, Gen. Brand himself supervising and assisting in serving it out. That hillock, Blauwen Molen, had been honeycombed and strengthened by steel and cement by the Hun, who was now regularly shelling it himself; so we advanced past it as quickly as possible, proposing to advance down Fanny's C.T., but, after a few had become solidly bogged in it, the rest kept on the top. During our ten days in there we did our best to drain and improve it, but it remained and would always remain an awful trench. The whole area was waterlogged, all draining arrangements used by the Belgians having been obliterated. On our left was the stagnant swamp of Blauwepoortbeck, overflowing towards Gapaard. From Gapaard to Steignast we deepened the trench to nine feet, drove piles to carry a duckboard floor four feet from the bottom, and still the water rose a foot over the duckboards. Out in the Outpost Line where we linked up a series of isolated posts, the men preferred the dangers of the surface to the waistdeep mud of the trenches. Pumps were used, but still the water rose steadily over the boards put down the night before. Even when the sun was shining the water was oozing up in the trenches. One Company made a long stretch of duckboard track where they felt sure the water would not rise and invited the Colonel to examine it. When he came, ten hours later, it was a foot under water, to the Coy's. intense chagrin. Under such conditions ration-carrying in the dark was as heavy a task as any in our history; and it certainly was dangerous, for enemy machine guns swept the whole surface. Men slipped again and again into holes of filthy water and the bread often became saturated before it reached the outposts.

As the mules crossed the Messines Ridge behind us they could be seen of a moonlight night silhouetted against the sky, and the Huns, unable to reach them there with their bullets, used to sweep, indiscriminately between the ridge and Gapaard. The drivers again proved to be men, while the ration-carriers were absolutely magnificent. Sgt. W. Oswald, (Jerry) a well-known Gallipoli hero, often made four trips a night out to the outposts, carrying bigger loads than his men. Even a dodger would sooner face a hail of bullets than Jerry's sarcasm. Another splendid carrier was "Darkey" Jenkins, well known on "B" cooker. One and all fought trench feet as vigorously as the Hun, the Q.M. sending up dry socks every night as well as two hot meals and a rum issue. "Comforts" also provided "Tommy Cookers" and primus stoves.

Even more annoying than machine guns were "Micky" and "Paddy", two German mortars that sent over right into our trenches tremendous earthquaking shells weighing about 120 lbs. These projectiles could be seen by day rising slowly to the height of perhaps half-a-mile, and men would bet as to where they would lob. At last we located them in farms towards Comines and got our artillery on to them with good results.

In widening Owl Trench near Gapaard a rubber thigh-boot was allowed to project from above the knees, some sentiment preventing men from cutting it off in line with the parapet. It contained a German leg well sealed up. A couple of Diggers polished it and used it regularly as a table, balancing their bread, jam, tea and 'bully' on it to the envy of their mates. How war blunted even fastidious men in certain ways!

Enemy airmen in armored planes came over Gapaard every morning, generally to spy, but sometimes to use their machine guns. They were certainly very brave and coolly surveyed our trenches from a low altitude, bearing a charmed life from the storms of bullets we sent at them.

The 27th August was a bad day for the Outposts as they were heavily strafed. That evening Lt. F. Doust, (O.P.) an officer with a fine record for work at Quinn's Post and since, was sent up with reinforcements. He was severely wounded and still had 800 yards to go. No one of his party was certain of the winding route, so Fred stoically pulled himself up and, staggering in agony, led the way, handed his party over and collapsed. The same night the ration parties were scattered by shells and bullets, but were reorganised by Oswald. One of the carriers, Pte. W. Haley, was severely wounded in the stomach, but, knowing the trials of the men in the Outposts, and the importance of rations to them, he persisted with his load, his example being so splendid that every carrier went through the barrages unhesitatingly after him. After half-a-mile with wound and load he delivered his bags at their destination, turned to hasten back to the R.A.P. and collapsed. Doust received his M.C., Haley his D.C.M.

Every night for ten nights Sgt. N. McGuire, another Gallipoli hero, patrolled No Man's Land, not only up to the enemy posts, but in between them. While this patrol was out our wirers were wiring a belt across our front, Cpl. E. Hanson distinguishing himself at this dangerous work. For dangerous tasks Pte. C. Eason constantly volunteered as he had done on Gallipoli, on one occasion carrying a wounded man and conducting a party of bearers 1,000 yards through heavy fire. McGuire, Hanson and Eason received M.M.'s.

On the night of the 29th we were relieved by the Manchesters who were almost knocked up with their heavy loads even before taking over from us. On the 30th we camped near Neuve Eglise and had a most enjoyable bath and change. We received orders to move back to La Motte Area. Our losses during the last period were 34, including 5 killed. We had now finished with Messines and Ploegsteert after three periods in the Front Line and four in Close Support there; and were not sorry to learn that we were about to get the long rest so often promised us. Each area we had been in near Messines was greatly improved during our periods.

In addition to those mentioned above for special gallantry one must mention the Platoon Commanders, every one of whom was splendid, caring for his men, watching their feet, health, rations and comfort in every possible way. Murray as acting C.O., and Capts. R. H. Browning, and A. W. Davis (Adjutant) were again most inspiring, and Lts. R. S. Swinbourne, S. Harris (Hon. Mjr.), L. Cleland, B. Blythman, A. Brierley, G. Nugent, R. Gowing, E. Hall, A. Lilley, W. Merifield, S. Owen and G. Smallcombe all proved themselves worthy of the men they commanded. Two other most splendid Nco's. were G. M. P. McRae and J. Prescott. They were constantly inspiring. Major Marks returned on 23rd and took command as acting C.O.

For three full months, with about a fortnight's comparative rest, the 13th had been in or near the Line. The whole Brigade was war-weary. Smartness in appearance generally 'slipped' in the line, and the 4th Bde. was no exception. The following is told as originating on one of the Brigade's reliefs from Messines.

We were straggling very wearily back when we passed a billet containing spick and span English officers just fresh from their Officers' School, and soon to go into the line for their first time. A curious Lieut. was astonished at the mud on all from head to foot, and put his head in through the mess window and said: "I say, Skipper, look at these fellows!" "What are they?" meaning "What regiment are they?" queried the inside officer. The "Loot", to answer the question, came out onto the road, asking:—"I say, you fellows, what are you?" also meaning "what regiment?" The weary men hardly noticed him until he repeated the question, "What are you?" when one replied in a voice full of weariness, and sarcasm.:— "Soldiers!"

The Transport also became muddy, and all knew how keen the "Brig." was on that. It was between Messines and Neuve Eglise, and the Transport was looking rather soiled when someone called out that the General was waiting to see it.

"Which side of the road is he on?" asked the officer.

"This side."

"Righto, men; buck in on the near side and give him plenty of spit and polish. Don't worry about the off side."

All hands scraped and shone metal and leather and horse and mule for all they were worth for 10 minutes; then, ten minutes later, they "Eyes-lefted" to the General in great style.

That night the General, who loved to arouse competition among his Battalions, told the Colonels and T.O.'s. of the 14th, 15th and 16th that they ought to see the 13th's Transport. "They came out as smart and as clean as they went in. Plucknett's the one!"

No one enjoyed the joke more than the General when it was told against him six months later.

One of our officers, nicknamed "Nugget," a splendid officer in the line, had always belonged to the Light Horse where he had used leggings, and he could never manage to put his puttees on neatly, nor get a service uniform to fit him. Coming out from near Ploegsteert he was placed in charge of the rearguard and a few prisoners who had just been handed over to the Bn. after being caught back near Calais A.W.L. Again the "Brig." was waiting to see how smart we were. Durrant saw him half-a-mile ahead and rode back quickly to examine his column and to brisken all up generally. "Nugget" looked worse than ever before, for he had lost a puttee and had one leg in a sandbag. The Colonel looked him over and saw that it was impossible to improve him in time.

He had to decide quickly, and he did.

"Nugget", he ordered, "Get in among the prisoners so that the General won't know you are an officer." It was the only thing he could do, both for his own and "Nugget's" sake.

Again we bluffed the "Brig."—or thought we did.

ADDENDA.

July 2nd.—General Holmes was killed as he was taking Mr. W. Holman, Premier of N.S.W., up to Ploegsteert to see the lines occupied by the 13th. He was buried near Steenwerke.

July 6th:— At 7.30 p.m. a shell burst against Brigade Hqrs. Mess. Gen. Brand and three officers were wounded and Lt. G. Mills, M.C. of the 13th, who was now Bde. Intelligence Officer, was killed.

Chapter XXII.—Polygon Wood, Ypres and Passchendaele.

ON the 1st September we rested at Verte Rue in Nieppe Forest and had a general personal clean-up. When Capt. McKillop went along next morning to march "C" off to join the rest of the Bn. to march to the 'buses. he found almost a platoon missing. An excited Flamand with a big key approached, and distant cheers could be heard. In front of Mac, the Flamand was brachially and orally, but futilely, verbose for several minutes until a sergeant came running along to say "The old pot's got my platoon locked up."

Then we heard him repeat "Soixante francs" several times as he led the way back to his farm, where he showed six empty bottles and explained that the platoon locked up in his attic had emptied them, and that he would set them free on receipt of "Soixante francs." He was soon made happy and unlocked the big door. The platoon refunded the amount later and said that they had had a good deal more, but had replaced the empties in their cases.

A bus ride through glolrious country took us to dear old Lisbourg and we felt that the three months promised us here would be heavenly. But something was certainly wrong, for all doors and windows were closed, not even the estaminets showing a welcome. We were the first Australians they had seen and the first troops billeted here for three years. They explained afterwards that they fully believed we would be negroes, for, when they had asked their schoolmaster about us he had told them all about negroes, boomerangs, kangaroos, emus and alligators. No wonder the dear simple souls were terrified.

Soon could be heard from the outside of a hundred doors: "Bonjour, Madame; it's all right; we've got Beaucoup Money and want beaucoup oeufs and pomme-de-terres and tres bon vin blanc," or something similar.

The speeches must have been effective—perhaps it was the "Beaucoup Money"—for Orderly Officers reported within an hour that every Digger was eating freshly-fried eggs or omelettes and chipped potatoes, and that the inhabitants who had been slow in opening were disconsolately beckoning to busy runners and other passers-by. The 13th were certainly a Battalion of courteous gentlemen.

A delightful fortnight passed all too quickly. Swimming in a pretty streamlet daily, Brigade Pierrots—the Blue Dandies—each evening, finalising the cricket competition and a boxing tournament, made a strenuous but splendid musketry and Lewis gun course arranged by Murray seem nothing. The 13th won both Cricket and Boxing Cups, the latter owing mainly to the splendid fighting of Fritz Theiring (middleweight) and Tossey Andrews (light).

So happy were all that the sudden orders to return to Ypres for another period in the line came as a sharp disappointment.

On the 18th September 'buses conveyed us to Wallon Cappel and a march to filthy billets at Staples, whence on the 20th, we marched to filthier farms near Steenvoorde. On the 22nd we again moved by 'bus and marched to Kruisstraat, near Ypres and bivouacked for the night while certain officers and specialists went forward to the Front Line S.W. of Zonnebeke to prepare the way for the Bn. to take over the next night. We were in for another battle—one of those attempts to drive the Hun back from the coast of Belgium.

That night, just as an enemy plane dropped bombs about 300 yards off, some of the 'lads' dropped stones on the helmet and hand of a brand-new arrival who had already told everyone that it was a come-down for him to be an ordinary Digger as he had been a Sergeant on the troopship, and had letters of introduction from two Federal Ministers, his personal friends. "But," he added, "I'm sure to get my commission soon with my credentials. You know that instead of having two different bus-trains to bring us up here, we could have come straight from Lisbourg if the staff had known their business." He was confiding other reasons why all the old staff should be dismissed to a bored section when "Crash!" the two stones arrived. He was assured that they were bits of "Fritz's eggs" and that he was lucky to get such a "beautiful Blighty." At any rate the next morning he had disappeared, having reported shellshock and wounded. A few weeks later he was in London with sergeant's stripes and two wound-bars up, and a month's hospital leave, when an Original Sergeant said to his mates, "I don't know that cove with our colors up."

"And tailor-made duds too!" added another.

"Thought I knew every sergeant in the Battalion."

So over they strolled.

"We don't want to be sticky, Dig, but when did you join the Batt?"

"In September."

"What year?"

"This year; over in Steenvoorde."

"Cripes! And three stripes and two bars for sympathy! No wonder we're winning."

"What Company are you in?"

"C"

"Well, Captain Browning's changed a lot during the last three months to give sergeant's stripes to a man without a lot of line service."

"I got these on the ship."

"Well, they were only temporary. Now, cut them off toute-suite, or I'll call a 'Jack'."

And off they were cut.

"Now, those wound bars?"

"I was wounded near Ypres last month."

"That's one."

"I was shellshocked by a hit on the head, and wounded in the hand."

"Cripes! Now take one off. One's enough for one night. You're worse than the "Eggs-a-cook" crowd."

Our hero left them off until he reached Scotland.

At dusk on the 23rd we moved forward to the south of Lille Gate and had tea under shellfire while waiting for darkness near China Wall.

At Birr Cross-Roads we encountered a terrific barrage, horses, guns, wagons and men from the great streams being hurled in all directions. Never was there a scene of greater havoc. Hundreds of smashed and overturned vehicles were sinking into the mud on each side of the corduroy to form, with horses and mules, foundations of other roads when the present should be blown to pieces.

We rushed across the Menin Road and through the barrage by sections. Darkness had come on and the duckboard track to Westhoek could hardly be seen, but each watched the man in his immediate front. At Westhoek another terrific barrage smashed the long line in several places and many would have been lost but for the voices of their leaders. Over Westhoek Ridge we entered a swamp, the track winding around shell-holes so tortuously that on occasions we were facing Ypres. About 9 another barrage smashed into the file.

At last we reached the Support Line that stretched across a swamp, and "C" and "D" went still farther, into the Front Line, at the north of the west edge of Polygon Wood. Our patrols under Sgts. A. Cormack, M.M., B. Bradney and E. Hall, and Cpls. A. Begg and A. Merrilees were soon out and as familar as circumstances would allow with No Man's Land, a torn and tangled place indeed; dawn showing it to be a miserable-looking area covered with short, shattered stumps,—the remains of Albania Wood. A patrol immediately moved out and occupied Harper House—a pill-box and cemented gun-pit 100 yards out. All night our carriers humped food for rifles, machine guns, and mortars forward, making dumps in many places in readiness for the battle; and "A" and "B" dug over 1400 yards of Communication Trench between Bn. Hqrs. and the Front Line, while the Signallers laid several lines between Hqrs. and the Companies, all under heavy barrages.

About 8 a.m. on the 24th a fog covered No Man's Land, and Lt. J. D. Westwood, Sgt. B. Bradney and 12 men went out into it for over 200 yards, crept onto and cut out from dozens of their friends 9 Germans whom they made prisoners,—a gallant piece of work indeed. "There are more out there," said Joe, as he handed them over to Capt. Browning, and with his party departed to round up some more. This time, however, the fog had thinned, and the enemy were aroused. 24 of them were seen in shellholes waiting. Joe attacked them with bombs and killed 4 before retiring with 2 of his party wounded. One of the most active officers in the Battalion, he deservedly received the M.C. for this morning's work. Bradney, who also remained on duty for 30 hours after being wounded, received his M.M.

These daring actions stirred the enemy up and he shelled our line unmercifully for an hour, one shell lobbing in a hole in which one of "C's" Lewis guns was. Capt. Browning immediately ran out into the barrage to attend to the four men and nobly carried two of them back to the trench before going out a third time to bring back the broken gun to mend. His example was inspiring indeed. On the 25th our artillery ranged in preparation for the great barrage to take place the next morning and one shell fell directly onto Sgt. E. Meadows, (O.P.), one of the finest personalities in the 13th.

That evening strong enemy forces recaptured Harper House, the possession of which would have been fatal to the next morning's advance. Lt. T. A. White was sent to retake it. but the enemy retired without fighting, leaving 3 killed and 1 prisoner. In this stunt in the dark C. S. M. W. Harper (Curly) distinguished himself by following the retiring enemy over 150 yards. He had already been twice wounded that day and could have evacuated, but he had bound himself up and remained on duty. (Received D.C.M.) C.Q.M.S. Franzen and Sgt. Groves were killed that evening.

In the battle the next morning, 26th September, zero was to be at 5.30, the 16th was to capture the Red Line about 800 yards ahead and construct Strongpoints, and the 14th and 15th were to advance through the 16th 400 yards still farther ahead to the Blue Line. The 13th, having then been in the Front Line for 60 hours were to act as Reserves, Carriers and Communication Trench Diggers for the rest of the Brigade. During the battle "A" and "B" were to dig a trench out to the Red Line, "D" to carry supplies forward to both objectives, and "C" to advance to the help of the 14th, 15th or 16th if called upon. In all companies every man that could be spared was to carry with "D". It will be seen that the 13th's task was no light one.

On the night of the 24th Major Marks, Acting C.O., decided to commence the C.T. to the Red Line and had 200 yards of it dug and a party placed at its end to hold it, the idea being to save time digging under the barrages that were certain to crash down on the then Front Line area immediately the battle opened. Marks' mind was one that was constantly alert. He had long before proved himself a splendid leader of men. He was now enhancing his reputation for gallantry and leadership. The main barrage was to be placed at zero 150 yards in front of the tape which was laid on the night of the 25th. It was then to advance 200 yards in 8 minutes and thereafter at the rate of 100 yards in 6 minutes. Smoke was to be added to the barrage at the Red and Blue Lines to mark their positions.

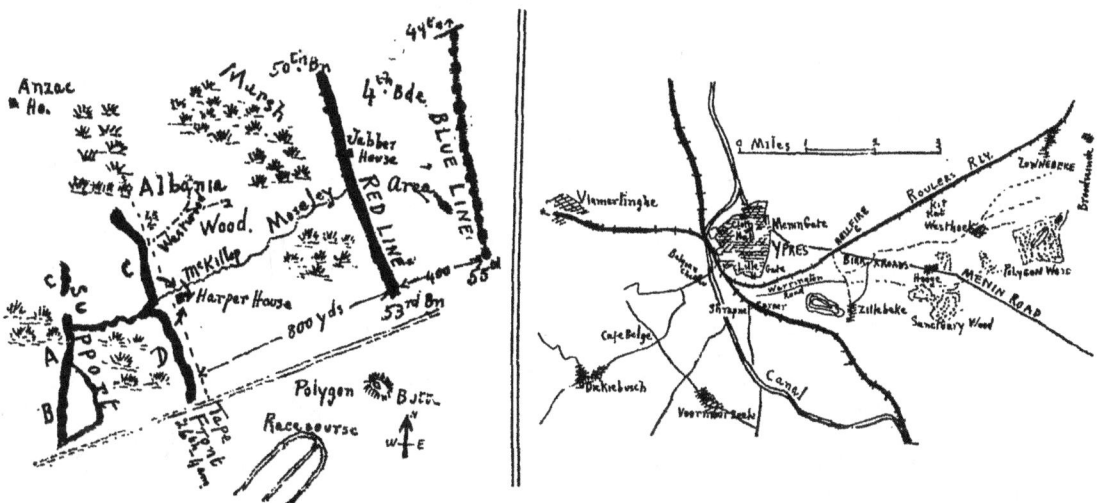

An hour before zero all were lying in readiness with the 13th patrols out in No Man's Land watching, coming back at 5 a.m. At 5.30 the greatest barrage we had ever been under burst over us and swept and ploughed the earth ahead, while hundreds of machine-guns combed the area still farther ahead. Several other barrages commenced at the same time, one creeping back from the Blue Line to meet the advancing one, another sweeping the area in which enemy guns were known to be, and another searching for his long-ranged weapons, while others remained on known strongpoints. It was a perfectly stupendous affair and put great thunderstorms into insignificance, while the number of bullets and balls that ploughed into the earth would have made a great hailstorm had they been ice instead of metal.

While the 14th, 15th and 16th were lying in their lines waiting for zero, our "A" and "B" Coys. were grasping picks and shovels in our C.T. behind the Front Line, ready to follow the waves immediately they moved.

Immediately the barrage lifted McKillop placed his men and set them digging, while Moseley and his men were out at the Red Line almost as soon as the 16th, from where they commenced digging back to meet McKillop. It was a fine sight to see our men digging a line over 1,000 yards long under heavy shell and machine-gun fire, while 200 others humped heavy loads up to the new line and crowds of prisoners hurried back the other way. Every now and again a carrier or a digger would cease work to "souvenir" a few prisoners.

All the Brigade objectives were taken in the times arranged, but a few hidden pill-boxes had been missed. In one of these Sgt. Cormack, M.M., found six Huns, rushed and captured them. With their machine-gun they could have done much damage to the other battalions, but for Cormack's quick decision. (Bar to M.M.)

A dozen times at least shells tore gaps in the line of diggers on the C.T. that they were digging so well, not for themselves, but for their comrades of the other battalions, a fact that made them do it all the more perfectly, so strong was the camaraderie throughout the 4th Brigade. Sgts. H. Curtis and F. Gurney and Cpls. A. Cima, R. Stuart and J. Burrell not only helped Moseley and McKillop to organise the digging, but quickly hastened to the dangerous positions to rearrange parties broken up, setting a similar example to their officers in coolness and determination to get the job done. So solidly did everyone work that within two hours the C.T. was ready for use. Gurney and Stuart received M.Ms.

Every man of the 14th, 15th and 16th who came back or went forward along this 1,200 yards of trench was loud in praise of the New South Welshmen.

And the carriers whose work was as hard, were as splendid, Sgts. J. Osborn, E. Hall (O.P.), and Cpls. A. Walker, F. Brandt, E. Blomquist, who received M.M's., and L.-Cpl. W. McDonald carrying and conducting parties unhesitatingly across to both objectives, coolly establishing dumps where wanted by the advanced battalions. During the day five counter-attacks were hurled against the Blue Line, which was blocked off by barrages, but our carriers manfully pushed through with their valuable loads. In such a position, no matter how splendid and well-trained the attackers were, if supplies had not got forward, the lines won with such gallantry and at such cost could not have been held. The spirit of these carriers was the same as that which had filled the 14th when they had carried to us at Stormy Trench.

The severity of the enemy shelling may be imagined when it is considered that, although we were not the attackers, we had 66 casualties out of about 400 men in a few hours. It can also be seen that our stretcher bearers had no light task, although the Germans were made to help them on their way back. Cpl. G. Thompson (O.P.), who attended the wounded for 24 hours after being painfully wounded himself, L.-Cpl. P Cameron and Ptes., F. Gibson, J. Foster, F. Simpson and A. Swain deservedly received their M.M's. for attending wounded under fire. Cpl. Blomquist was also fine as a volunteer bearer. Ptes. T. Harman and T. Riddock, although badly wounded, attended the wounded for several hours, and Pte. T. Dando was also conspicuous. Dr. C. H. Kelleway attended to 400 cases without a minute's respite. (Received M.C.)

The runners were as splendid as usual, which is saying a great deal, not only running, but guiding parties. J. Leonard, the most distinguished that day and before, and Cpl. S. Cush, Ptes. D. Jones, S. Meade, C. Pepper, L. Wheeler, F. Kingsley and Cpl. A. Begg received M.M's. Runner H. Atkins was also conspicuous. Although a distinguished Lewis-gunner that day, Cpl. H. Dickson made a splendid voluntary guide throughout the period in. (Received M.M.) Our Lewis-gunners and riflemen brought down three enemy planes on the 25th and 26th, the fire of the latter being controlled by platoon officers.

Lt. R. Withers, D.C.M., had charge of getting rations and supplies forward from Div. to Bde. Dumps, which task he performed most gallantly in spite of heavy losses of men and animals each night. Along his route he regularly passed our Cpl. M. Spicer, attached to Div. Traffic Control on Menin Road, one of the most dangerous spots on the Western Front. Here, under hurricanes of shells, Spicer steadfastly remained at his post regulating and guiding the streams of traffic and clearing the roads of the constantly heaped masses of smashed vehicles and animals. (Received M.M.)

But perhaps the 13th's most distinguished heroes for the battle were our Signallers. Lt. Perray, M.M. was O.C. of the Bde. Forward Sig. Party of 38, but when he was severely wounded and his party scattered by shells before the battle started, the 13th Sigs took over the whole of the Bde. signal and message work as well as their own. From midnight on the 25th to midnight on the 26th our signallers and runners handled 111 messages containing, 4,475 words—surely a record—Sgt. G. F. Falkiner, M.M., an Original Sig. and one of the world's best wireless operators, taking charge and working solidly and most gallantly for the period. George received a Bar to his M.M. He had, prior to the war, received the Albert Medal for gallantry. He soon after received his commission as Bn. S.O., remaining so for the rest of our history. Three of his linesmen worked as a team, constantly repairing wires or lying out along them listening to be ready to repair immediately. They were W. Butler, F. McArthur and D. McEvoy, all receiving M.M.'s. Sig.-Sgt. J. Long (O.P.) was killed doing his duty gallantly.

Our cooks also worked regardless of shells.

On the night of the 26th we were relieved, and trudged wearily back along the broken duckboards to Westhoek Ridge, and slept the sleep of the weary until about 10 next morning. Our losses for the period were 147, including 24 killed.

The popular Lt. Fred Doust, M.C., now reckoned among the killed, was "missing" for some time. He was wounded while guiding carrying parties, and although he had only to be carried 300 yards to the R.A.P., neither he nor his bearers were ever afterwards seen or heard of although the most exhaustive enquiries and searchings were made. They disappeared from an area crowded with busy men, big shells and muddy ground.

On crawling out of their "posies" on the 27th all were delighted to receive comforts from Australia, General Brand himself supervising the issue.

We were ready to march out that evening when Marks received orders to send 250 men to bury a cable to Anzac House—1,000 yards, 6ft. deep. The job was done so expeditiously and thoroughly that the Engineer officers specially thanked us.

We reached the Canal Area about midnight, where Murray had arranged hot stew for all, keeping it ready from 11 to 3 a.m., for several, having been lost in the maze of winding tracks, were straggling in until then. Murray made many journeys to guide these men.

The next day we marched back to Montreal Camp, near Ouderdom, but had little rest that night on account of the bombing by enemy planes, the huts constantly shaking violently. About 4 a.m. Lt. T. White and 50 men were aroused and ordered back as a working party for another fortnight, to repair and bury cables west of Ypres, their Hqrs. to be in bivouacs prepared by themselves near Belgian Chateau, Kruisstraat. Reporting there they were given tools with which to dig their "posies," and sheets to form the roofs. It rained continually for the fortnight and they had a very uncomfortable time, their work—anywhere between Zillebeke Lake and Zonnebeke—being also in the mud.

Another party of three officers and 100 men had also to return to Ypres the same day to spend a fortnight laying a pipe line from Lake Zillebeke to Hooge. Their "home" was in the ruins. In their work they suffered severely.

Meanwhile the rest of the Battalion, on the 30th September, went back by 'buses to near Winnezeele, where they remained till the 11th October, on which day they marched back 14 miles to the east of Reninghelst, not one man falling out, and all finishing "in good spirits."

On the 12th they marched into Ypres and camped in cellars under the old Infantry Barracks, where the others who had been on the working parties joined them to go into the Line at Zonnebeke—rather hard on these parties who had been under constant shellfire since the 22nd September but necessary on account of the shortage of reinforcements.

October 13th was a cold and horribly wet day, the reconnoitring officers having an uncomfortable time. On the 14th the Battalion moved up into reserve on Westhoek Ridge near Kit and Kat, where, on the 15th, from 9 a.m. to 3 p.m. we were bombarded with heavy gas-shells, both of mustard and phosgene varieties, necessitating the constant wearing of the uncomfortable respirators. It was the Battalion's first experience of a really tremendous gas bombardment, and our losses would have been much heavier but for the magnificent conduct of Lt. H. S. Baker, who, wearing his respirator, moved about among the men, rendering first aid and carrying bad cases back to the R.A.P. over slippery ground and through shelling. Stretcher-bearer W. Burke was also splendid, entering dugouts in which gas-shells had burst to effect rescues.

On the 16th October we relieved the 15th Battalion in supports, the 15th going into the Front Line to relieve the 14th, who retired to the deep dugouts in Railway Wood.

Here in Support our Hqrs. were in a concrete pill-box near Moulin Farm; "B" and "C" in Zonnebeke and "A" and "D" in the sunken road beyond Zonnebeke. Here we carried, salvaged and dug, finding the wrecked village a "very hot shop."

On the 18th we relieved the 15th in the Front Line, our Hqrs. being near the Sunken Road, the Front Line and Close Supports including the Railway Cutting and extending southwards there from in a curve to Daisy Wood, N.W. of Broodseinde.

In this low, swamy area, with deep bogs on either side of the narrow duckboard tracks, running and carrying were the riskiest jobs, but ever cheerful and reliable men like C.Q.M.S. J. H. Clay (M. in D.), Cpl. A. Parray, Runner V. Morris (Received M.M.) and Lt. W. Merrifield carried rations, munitions or messages, or conducted parties each night with the greatest gallantry.

Patrolling out in front across 800 yards of marsh was also dangerous and uncomfortable, but Cpl. H. Townsend and Pte. A. Watson set splendid examples to their parties, while, as an observer, Pte. G. Hart ("Dad") took every risk to do his work conscientiously. (These three received M.M's.) Concerning the dreary waste so patrolled a 16th officer reported: "In some places an advance of 100 yards in 10 minutes is possible; in others 10 yards in 100 minutes."

On the 20th the 13th took over the whole Divisional frontage and the 16th moved up into close support. Our line was thin indeed, "C," for example, holding 600 yards with 57 rifles, but it was safe in that area with such Scouts and Lewis-gunners. The latter, under such conditions came in for long stretches of duty in isolated and heavily-shelled parts. Still Sgt. A. Wollf and Cpl. W. Phillips by their personal gallantry and magnetism inspired their crews to hang on and even to volunteer for longer periods in order to prevent the bringing of fresh men into the gassed area. Sgt. H. Curtis and Cpl. Cima again did fine work, both receiving M.M's.

The road from Ypres was continually being smashed by the heavies, and the pack train carrying supplies forward had a rough time each night. One night three mules were wounded and the others scattered over the dismal, dark area. Cpl. J. Snowie collected them, transferred the loads from the useless three and brought the whole supplies through. He was used to doing such work. (Received M.M.)

When Lt. J. Stewart, a fine young officer, was killed just on relief on the night of the 21st, Pte. Ibbett acted most gallantly, guiding the relieving platoon in and his own out. He received a Belgian C. de G. For general heroism, in gas, on patrol, carrying, inspiring his men and cheerfully performing all duties even when ready to fall with weariness, Sgt. W. Noble again, as on previous occasions, won the admiration of all with whom he came in contact. Sgt. N. Clinen and A. Jack (O.P.), two most worthy comrades, were severely gassed.

This period from the 15th to the 22nd October was a very weakening one, the weakening not to be judged so much by the actual losses during those days, which, indeed were heavy, being 108 including 12 killed, as by the general debilitation of the whole Battalion, 111 being too weak within a few days of relief for even the slightest effort, many of them being sent to hospital never to return to the Battalion. Never had the 13th looked so truly wretched. Of the 416 who went into Zonnebeke on the 14th 309 remained to come out on the night of the 21st, and of these not one was able to speak above a whisper, that even being agonising in most cases. No officer or N.c.o. was able to call an order, and the general coughing and sneezing were wracking. Throats, lungs, eyes and noses were soon raw, blistered and intensely itchy, and acute vomiting could be heard on all sides, made the more painful by the inflammation. That week left more post-war troubles than perhaps any other week in our history. Throughout the Brigade many of those gassed did not become aware of their dangerous condition until later, when the insidious horror had worked so effectively that cheerfulness and carelessness could no longer deny it a victory. It would have been better had several of these gas casualties paid the full price up there on the foggy, soaked and poisonous Passchendaele Swamps. To the 4th Brigade Passchendaele was almost as disastrous as Bullecourt. Had we known the lasting deadliness of this gas we could have withdrawn all our men from certain areas for days at a time, for the Germans, the pioneers of such murder, would not have sent their men into the areas they had so poisoned. But such knowledge was only to come later.

One can safely say that the big majority of those in the line at Passchendaele were shortly after evacuated to hospital "sick." Some returned to the Battalion, but many were only made aware of the dreadful effects of the Passchendaele poisoned air a few years later, when, too late, as nervous or tubercular wrecks, they sought medical advice.

[These Passchendaele battles were undertaken in order to keep the enemy's attention away from the French. The plans of Nivelle had just ended in disaster. So much had been expected that the failure brought a great reaction, and Haig decided that the British must keep on fighting, hoping at the same time to clear the Belgian coast of submarine bases.]

Chapter XXIII.—A Miscellany.

AS our Signallers were now receiving so many compliments on the name they had won at Polygon Wood, and as our newly-promoted George Falkiner was our last S.O., I propose to review briefly the history of our Signallers. They had another year's hard work to perform, and in this they upheld their reputation, which is as high a compliment as they would wish anyone to pay them; still it seems in order to review their story here.

A few, destined to become the nucleus of the Original 13th Sig. Section, met for the first time in August, 1914, at Kensington Racecourse, whence after a few days, they were transferred to Rosebery Racecourse to receive their first lessons in signalling. When races were on they drilled in Centennial Park, and on their return cleaned the horse-manure out of their "bedrooms." By the time they were transferred to Rosehill the few were already smart signallers, with plenty of interest in their work: still they only became a recognised Signal Section at this camp. Here the indefatigable Lt. Faddy built up that wonderful esprit de corps that the 13th Signallers were more famous for than perhaps any other similar unit in the A.I.F.—an esprit that remains even five years after the war.

At Rosehill the magnet that drew together "the finest body of trained signallers ever collected in one camp" was Petty-Officer W. Jackson, in his naval uniform and badges of Chief Yeoman of Signals—a man with 18 years' Navy service, and one who had climbed from Signal-boy to Chief Yeoman. He had voluntarily transferred to the A.I.F. Demonstrations by "Nutty" Jackson and other ex-Naval Signallers like Tom Morgan, G. Falkiner, F. Warner, Ted Bull and "Wally" Lowen each night would draw around a crowd of hundreds.

With these Naval experts were W. F. (Bluey) Shirtley, W. F. (Billy) Hughes and Jack Allen, trained Signallers of the Australian Citizen Forces, G. Simpson, a trained Signaller of the British Regular Army, with years of experience of Army stations in India, including active service; old "Sammy" Knox, of the old Australia Militia Sigs., and a telegraphist in the Railways; and G. Watkins, with wide experience with cables, and a marvel at sound reading. Watkins would be reading a book when a signaller telegraphing practice messages would rap out a question to him, and without looking up from his book, "Watty" would reply. This trick was tried on him repeatedly by experts like Falkiner and Simpson, who could send or read over 60 words a minute, but he was never known to be caught.

Then into Rosehill one day came W. (Bill) Beasley, an officer of the S.S. Niagara, and one who had sailed the seven seas in all sorts of craft. From then on it was all "deck, poop, bells, leeward and windward," or such talk, and "Bill" soon had all almost up to his standard in cleanliness and neatness of tents and equipment. He became, perhaps, the most popular Original Sig. From Gallipoli he transferred to a North Sea mine-sweeper.

At Liverpool the Sigs. had more freedom in their work than perhaps any other section and they found that the roof of the Auburn Hotel was flat and therefore ideal for signalling to Pennant Hills and Liverpool, as well as desirable in other ways. The big house across the river from the camp was also popular, as morning and afternoon teas always came to the Sigs. there.

On the "Ulysses our Signallers did the whole of the signal work between the flagship and the rest of the fleet for the voyage and were specially complimented officially by the Commander of the Fleet.

At the Landing they carried bigger loads ashore than others, for, in addition to apparatus, they took nine bicycles, useless there as it happened. Big Bill Beasley, from the nose of the boat, was the first Sig. to jump out when their boat beached in the darkness. He called out, "It's all right, only up to your chest." Yank and Wally, short men, took him at his word and jumped out at the stern into about six feet of water. When they were rescued and over the shock they asked Bill why he hadn't said what he meant; that it was up to his chest.

For the first week most of the messages were "Water required" and "Stretcher-bearers"; and they found that flag-signalling was suicide. At the Battle of Bloody Angle, Hughes, M. Crosbie and W. Archer were the most distinguished of the gallant section, Hughes carrying a message across a swept zone and the reply back to Burnage, and Crosbie and Archer waving messages in spite of severe wounds and a hail of lead until their message got through. It was here that Lt. Faddy, with a severe neck wound, disappeared while walking back to the R.A.P. He was never heard of again. Just before this, however, our first Signaller, in the person of popular W. Lowen, had been killed while filling his bottle in Shrapnel Gully.

Without exception every Signaller performed magnificent work on Gallipoli, those mentioned in this chapter being the outstanding ones. The Section landed 34 strong, and, although several reinforcements joined, they numbered eight for the Evacuation.

Then came France. At Bois Grenier they were surprised at the ease and comfort of the work, for telephones were laid on to all Coys. and regular shifts made it easy after Gallipoli; but the Somme smashed the illusion. Here the linesmen got the real war and paid heavily. What wonderful work was done on those lines out of Gibraltar, Pozieres, by T. Morgan, and A. Long, who went out 18 times on repairs one night during the Battle of Mouquet, and F. O'Brien and 2nd.Lt. J. Allen, both of whom were killed in August that year, G. Falkiner, A. Perray, Sol. Wall, W. Shirtley, and W. Hughes. Throughout 1917 two splendid pairs were C. Monday and Sol Wall, and the two boys with men's hearts and minds Ken Bryant and Dave McEvoy.

Others have been or will be mentioned in these pages; the Runners attached to the Sigs. are dealt with throughout our story. Murray once said: "My men will go anywhere and take any position so long as they know there are Signallers like the 13th's to get word through as to what's doing."

Yes, the Signallers were justly admired by all ranks of the Battalion. When the time comes for any old member of the 13th to pass over to the Great Unknown he will probably find our Signallers who have gone before watching for tne Two Blues to snap out a message of welcome and to guide him to his billet as they so often did in France.

. . . .

From the Infantry Barracks' cellars, Ypres, where we spent the 23rd October, we moved by 'bus on the 24th to Reminghelst, where, after a bath and clean-up we remained until the 27th when we entrained near Poperinghe for Wizernes, whence 'buses carried us to comparatively comfortable billets in Fontaine Les Boulans.

The next day, Sunday, as many as could walk the distance, a few miles, visited old friends at Lisbourg, and were right royally received, although tears were plentiful on account of the news of the death of so many up at Polygon and Passchendaele.

November came in cold and wet; still the peaceful village soon improved all, the strained, careworn expressions specially giving way to the usual free and easy and happy-go-lucky countenances of the Diggers. Light training only was carried on.

After so many disappointments we expected to be sent back to fight again any day, but, on the 16th November we learned with joy that we wre now certain to get a long rest, as we were ordered to move back beyond Abbeville into G.H.Q. Reserve.

Billeting parties left immediately on bikes to travel a day ahead of each march, for we were to be seven days on the journey. The march was arranged in easy stages and generally finished each day by 2 p.m., allowing time to rest or visit interesting places along the route, such as Agincourt and battlefield on the 17th, Fressin and its relics of Spanish occupation on the 18th, and Crecy and battlefield on the 21st. Our route lay through Heuchin, Ruisseauville (17th), Canlers, Fressin, Wambercourt (18th), where we rested a day, Cavron, Aubin, Tortefontaine (20th), Dompierre, Fontaine-sur-Maye (21st), Crecy Forest, Hautvillers (22nd), Buigny, Somme Mouth, Cahou, Franleu (23rd), and to Woincourt, our destination, on the 24th. The weather during the march was generally fine, but cold and darkness came in each evening about 4. At Fontaine Capt. Davis was severely hurt in a bike collision with a Frenchman, and Lt. B. Blythman acted as Adjutant for some time, after which he was Asst. Adjt., finishing the war as Acting Staff Captain.

As winter was to be spent in Woincourt all proceeded to make themselves as comfortable as possible, even semi-officially "souveniring" enough hay for all to sleep on from Army haystacks nearby, although they were under a guard. We also prepared for a long course of training in all branches, digging trenches and making ranges, and hiring rooms and crockery and purchasing turkeys for the greatest Christmas dinner ever, especially as, on the 25th November, Orders read: "The Division will now have a long period in which to carry out thorough, systematic training. Owing to never having been out for a long period in which to train, it has always been necessary to carry out more advanced training without having had a thorough grounding." The 4th Division was feeling that at last its luck had changed when, on December 3rd orders were issued to "Be ready to move at short notice." Seven days on the road for eight days' rest, the whole of which were taken up preparing for the future training. That evening all sang "The 4th Brigade are Happy." And indeed they were happy, even when putting the final touches to the cleaning of their billets before marching out from them. The move was definitely fixed for the 5th December, and our destination Peronne, near where we were to be ready to stem the threatened German advance, for they had broken the British line there.

Our departure from Woincourt coincided with our farewell to Col. Durrant on his promotion to A.A. and Q.M.G. of the 2nd Div. His officers entertained him at mess, and although there was no mere flap in the farewell remarks, all were indeed sorry to lose Durrant and so expressed themselves. An Original officer of the 13th, coming to us from the A. and I. Staff, he had risen by merit to be Adjutant, Second-in-Command and Commander. A reader of these pages will already be fully aware of his popularity among all ranks, and the Digger's popularity meant the highest efficiency in the welfare of his command as well as battle efficiency, and the Digger was a keen and able critic. Even those unfortunate enough to appear before him at "Orderly Room" often found enjoyment there, even when receiving the punishment due to them in fines or confinement to camp. No one was ever more careful than Durrant not to "play to the gallery" over unfortunates, or to joke at their expense, his main appeal being always to a man's manly qualities, such as honor and loyalty to his Battalion. After hearing a comparatively serious charge against a delinquent, for even the 13th had its share, the Colonel would search a man through with his keen eye, head tilted. "You a 13th man? A 13th? Surely you forgot you belonged to the 13th when you did that?" Or "An 'A' Company man? Capt. Murray's Company? Do you want to be transferred?"

Having been a soldier so long he knew all the usual excuses, and delinquents got to know this and thought out others. Durrant would appear to take it all in and the man to feel himself successful with his yarn when, "Well, that's a goody," would come in a drawl from the Colonel, "Really, I haven't heard that one before. Now tell me the dinkum about it."

" 'Dolly' rubs it in about the Batt. and you can't bluff him," sadly remarked one who had overstayed his leave, on leaving the Orderly Room one day.

With his officers, Durrant's criticism was always helpful and kindly, not at any time discouraging. No censure was administered in the presence of subordinates, the only known case being the one mentioned a few chapters back, and then there was nothing else to do. He insisted on officers setting good examples, stating that the most effective way of improving efficiency was imitation of such. He wished the discipline of the 13th to be that of a battalion animated by the honor of the battalion, confidence in and respect for its officers and comrades, and by the knowledge that they and their battalion were at least equal to any other unit in the war. In times of stress he was ever a cheery, animating spirit.

An Australian battalion, without a history going back generations, was what its C.O. made it, to a very great extent indeed, and the reputation of the 13th rightly reflects the reputation due to its Commanders. For over three years Durrant had been an active influence on the 13th, and, for several months on Gallipoli and 16 months in France its Commanding Officer. His splendid organisation of Durrant's Post had early made him famous throughout the Div.

In order to give subordinates opportunities Durrant always had a Coy. Commander at Headquarters in order to get them in touch with the working of the unit, and give their Seconds-in-Command the practice in managing the Coy. In accounting for the wonderful efficiency of the 13th as an organisation throughout its history this fact is important. In accounting for its wonderful success in action, among other things it should be remembered that Durrant and Marks insisted on every man being perfectly clear about his own particular task—so clear as to be practically independent of further orders after the commencement of the battle. One can safely say that no one had more to do in making the 13th the Battalion it was than J.M.A.D.

Marks, who had been Acting C.O. on many occasions, now took permanent command.

On the 5th we entrained at Woincourt and reached Peronne about midnight, whence we marched over frozen roads to Moislains, every now and again men slipping heavily on the hard, slippery ground. A lonely billee-goat, the mascot of a Welsh Battalion that had been annihilated in the German attack, was wandering disconsolately over the fields when it heard the tramp of feet. It immediately ran across and placed itself at the head of a platoon, marching along quite at home, refusing to leave its place, even when its smell became offensive. Every now and again it bleated with pleasure; so we let it remain.

Around Moislains and towards Cambrai there were vast areas of Hunnish destruction, vines having been uprooted and fruit-trees slashed vindictively for miles—thousands of them. We did not go into the line in this area, except the officers in turn, but acted as close reserves ready to advance at short notice, repairing roads, salvaging, and digging and wiring a strong reserve line.

The march from Moislains to Templeux-LaFosse on the 19th December, although short, was over undulating, frozen roads, and many slipped and hurt themselves seriously. The horses and mules had to have their shoes spiked to grip in. Each day, before dawn, about 16 officers and 400 men would march out to dig the reserve line or repair roads; the remainder training.

While in this area we felt the winter as keenly as that last dreadful one, as we were in thin tents on a bleak hill until the 10th January. In the tents were an astonishing assortment of braziers or heating arrangements, some made of stones and mud, others of tin and iron, but all had chimneys of a sort with an elbow or two as the smoke had to get out, and the chimney could not go straight up through the tent. Petrol tins made the best elbows.

The days were short, allowing plenty of time for cards for those who liked them, but although gambling was fairly general no complaint was ever made of sharp practices.

Christmas was carolled in by voluntary singers and the band. Christmas dinner could not be taken by Coys., but each section celebrated in its tent, a splendid dinner and tea being provided mainly by our Comforts Committee in Sydney. Ale and wine were issued as well as the usual rum. Officers visited their men to wish them the compliments of the season, which wishes were appreciated and reciprocated. Our Brigade Pierrots put on a fine pantomime—"Cinderella Up-to-Date."

In the New Year Gazette the following names appeared for specially good work during the past six months:—M.C.-Capts. A. W. Davis and N. (Dos) Wallach; M. in D. Col. Durrant, Major Marks, Major Murray, Capt. Wallach and Sgt. Curtis.

The New Year came in cold and snowy, but all remained cheerful, the band playing 1918 in, and then senerading the General who treated them well. Work had still to be carried on, and solid training in open-warfare, often in blizzards.

On the 6th volunteers were called for from among the officers and certain N.c.o's. for Secret Service work. They were to be prepared to sever connection with the A.I.F., to do without correspondence for an indefinite period and to be able to endure extremes of heat or cold, to ride and row and to be of the best health. All expressed their willingness to go if the Colonel thought that they could do better work with the Secret Service than with the Battalion. One officer finally having to go, the hefty, gallant, active, intelligent and cautious Lt. Roy Withers, D.C.M., was selected, and appointd a Captain in the Imperial Forces. As we bade him farewell on the 12th no one had the slightest idea of his destination, some saying the Lebanons to organise the Jews there against the Turks, some Ireland, and some the Soudan. Some months later we heard that he was in Mesopotamia with the Dunsterforce; then we heard that he had been in Baku on the Caspian and that he was "Admiral" of the Caspian Fleet. His experiences in Persia and around the Caspian were many, varied and severe, but he returned safely.

At Moislains Chaplain M. Hinsby joined us, and by his keenness and work on behalf of the well-being of all ranks intellectually, spiritually and bodily, he soon became justly popular. Later, his keenness to give Christian burial to every one killed led him to attempt the dangerous task of conducting the service out near the enemy wire, a task from which he had to be ordered to desist by the Colonel. The fact that he could not have stood upright for one minute out there did not seem to weigh with him.

As the enemy now showed no intention of attacking in this Cambrai area we were again withdrawn, but the period of our "Rest" was ended, and, on our return to our own Corps on the 11th January, after a train journey from Peronne to Bailleul, we were immediately placed on line fatigues preparatory to going in altogether. Arriving at Bailleul at 3 a.m. we marched through knee-deep mud to bivouacs in Meterem, and marched back the same day to Curragh Camp near Locre. We were up north again.

Chapter XXIV.—Hollebeke and the Canal Area,
Jan.—Feb., 1918.

IMMEDIATELY on arrival at Curragh Camp officers and specialists were sent forward to Spoilbank and White Chateau to reconnoitre the position we were soon to take over.

As the frozen ground began to thaw it became sloppy, and constant attention had to be paid to the feet of all. Each day officers had to certify that they had personally examined the feet of all their platoon. This went on even in the outposts near the Canal and Hollebeke later on.

Each day from 200 to 400 men went up to near Spoilbank and White Chateau by decauville train, to dig and wire the Reserve Line, carry material for engineers constructing dugouts and strongpoints or build bombproofs around transport lines. The salvage microbe had now bitten the Battalion more than ever before, and all wholeheartedly collected their bits of salvage wherever such were seen, a great and valuable dump soon being established and sent back to the War Factories near Calais.

On the 20th January we moved forward by light railway and march, and relieved the 49th Battalion in a line of 13 outposts between Hollebeke and the 15th Battalion, whose line commenced beyond our third post east of the Canal, a Support Line stretching from the rear of Hollebeke northwards to the Canal, and the White Chateau, in the ruins of which two Coys. were placed in reserve. The White Chateau had been a beautiful building once, but now its ruins of stone and iron girders formed admirable protection against the heaviest shells to those burrowed under them.

[The defection of Russia released 40 German Divisions for our Front, and so changed the character of the war by losing us the initiative and placing us on the defensive.]

As an overwhelming enemy attack, so boastfully foretold, was likely to eventuate at any time we engaged in a policy of strengthening all posts and trenches, wiring heavily and making dumps of rations, water and ammunition at convenient places. We also tried each night to capture a prisoner for identification, but they were too alert and suspicious, seldom venturing into No Man's Land, but constantly sweeping it and the area to the rear with bullets and shells. Sgt. W. Noble, Lt. H. Davis, Capt. N. Wallach and other daring Scouts took the greatest liberties with the Hun in order to entice him out to be captured, even crawling between their posts and along their wire, but Fritz was stubborn. Night after night our Scouts would lie out in chilly holes in the hope of catching one of their patrols. The ground was low here and the posts consequently wet. "A man got hit outside, and rheumatics inside."

Lt. R. Swinburne had a party of specially-trained rapid-wirers out each night protected by our Scouts.

In our outposts we had five officers and 118 other ranks and five Lewis gun crews, in support one Coy., and in White Chateau two Coys. The Reserve Coys. provided 50 ration carriers, 50 shovel men for strong posts, 12 trench repairers, 10 duckboard repairers, 130 truck-pushers pushing loads for engineers, 12 pill-box cleaners, 52 Reserve Line wirers working in water in gumboots, 44 carriers, 10 bunk-makers working in the chateau, and about 40 others on various other permanent Battalion jobs. Front area life was not merely sitting waiting and watching for Fritz. Joe Westwood, our active Works Officer, soon had our area in as perfect a state of defence, comfort and health as it was possible to have such an area. Details of the work done and stores carried make long lists in official records. Cpl. S. Wright still helped him splendidly.

In the White Chateau, as men came in off fatigues, they were provided with warm water and powder for their feet, and dry socks and hot cocoa from comforts. Along Olaf Avenue, our longest journey with rations, to posts on that side of the Canal, our carriers always found a mug of hot coffee at a Y.M.C.A. shack there.

During both this and our next period up here we witnessed many interesting air fights, our planes generally being the more offensive and successful. Some American planes occasionally worked with the British.

On the night of the 25th our post fired on Germans near Lock 6, a patrol going out later and finding a dead German whose papers provided valuable identification.

On the evening and night of the 29th we were relieved by the 16th, the 13th crossing the Canal by the Sandbag Bridge, "A" and "B" going into Crater Dugouts in the Bluff, "C" to Canal Dugouts, and "D" to Gaspus Dugouts nearby. From here our working parties went forward each night, or by day during fogs. The parties we supplied daily were somewhat as follows:—Two officers and 90 pushing stores for Canadian Tunnellers, two officers and 50 pushing other stores, two officers and 50 revetting the Front Line (using shovels), nine camouflaging posts, 12 camouflaging trenches, seven mending duckboards, 12 cleaning pill-boxes, two officers and 50 wiring and 90 on regular Battalion work. In this area we again suffered severely from gas, but not nearly as severely as the 14th Battalion, which had heavier losses than at Zonnebeke.

On the 5th February the 48th Battalion relieved the 13th, and we were carried back most of the way to Curragh Camp again by decauville train. The only advantage in being back here was that all slept in comparative comfort in huts, for each day 300 to 400 would rise early and be taken to work up near Spoilbank or White Chateau.

As we expected to be called on to raid the enemy during our next turn in, Capt. Wallach and Lt. Marper were given 40 picked men to train as raiders. It happened that they were not used as intended, but that was their disappointment. However they were used as Scouts during the whole of the next period and did splendid service, the enemy being quite unable to send a patrol out.

It was on the afternoon and night of the 20th that we were on the way back to the Front Line again to relieve the 48th, being carried in 'buses to Vermozeele where we had a hot meal. Again we had one Coy. in outposts, one in support, and two in reserve in White Chateau. This period was much the same as the former, except that the enemy was far more active and threatening. Our observers reported him to be massing guns and troops well forward, trains being seen arriving near Wervicq regularly. Special efforts were made to capture a prisoner, for identification was regarded as extremely important at this juncture. Davis, Wallach, Marper, Browning, McKillop and Simpson took many risks for this but the Hun was determined to keep us in the dark. We also took every care to prevent him learning too much in case he broke through, for all papers, letters and maps not actually in use were destroyed or sent back to the Transport. Our Signallers picked up German messages, and information came also from other sources that we were to be attacked that week, and we prepared accordingly, "standing-to" from 2 to 6.30 a.m. on a few mornings, the 14th Battalion coming up to Close Support, but each time we had to stand-down disappointed. In case he should barrage us for days we prepared dumps of rations, water and munitions—enough to do a battalion a week.

During this period of tension our workers carried on steadily, and the regular rations never failed to reach the outposts. Lt. G. Smith made three long journeys with them each night. C.Q.M.S. Clay remained as keen as usual. Out in the posts experienced officers and new but gallant arrivals like Webster, Luscombe and Kelaher kept unceasingly on the alert. Sgt. Strumey continued his camouflaging, working on positions even like the outposts under all conditions, as he had for such a long time. (Received M.S.M.) Cleland (L.G.O.), Westwood (W.O.), Falkiner (S.O.), all from Colonel to youngest sub., remained constant inspirers of their commands.

Great competition was evinced among the Scouts to capture a prisoner, as special leave was the reward for the first identification. Cpl. J. Duncan was the lucky one, and a brave one, too.

Signs pointed to the attack coming on the 28th, so that morning we prepared a special welcome for him, but he did not come. Our relief by the 10th Battalion was arranged for the night of the 1st March, and, on that morning we received word from our Intelligence people that he was to raid us that night. Hence we took special precautions over the change over, making certain that the 10th knew their new position thoroughly before leaving. Wallach took their Scout Officer around every post and the wire in No Man's Land. They heard suspicious movements and listened the more keenly. Yes, sure enough, they were coming this time. It was nearly 10 p.m. Browning, who would never leave anything to chance, and loved definiteness was still in the Outpost Headquarters with Major Henwood, making sure of all details and knowing full well that every second he waited he was adding to the probability of being caught in the attack or the barrage. Most of his Coy. were on their way out, but he was aways the last to leave the line. Wallach put his head down and called out the warning. Immediately a terrific barrage smashed down right on the dugout and all around it. Dos had a charmed life as he rushed back to our Headquarters at Bow to give the news. He used to joke about that run later, saying: "I said to my legs, 'Run, legs; your body's in danger.'" His news was most valuable to our Artillery as the lines were cut to pieces the instant the barrage commenced. So accurate and heavy was the barrage that exit from Headquarters was impossible, and the near posts were quite smothered, too. So perfectly arranged were their plans that every view of their approach was screened, and they assembled in a mass of almost 200, including engineers who blew up our wire with bangalore torpedoes, crept close up to the Headquarters, their main objective, and then, as their barrage lengthened slightly, rushed the dugout with bombs and revolvers. There was no getaway or chance of fighting for the Australians there. Major Henwood rightly surrendered, for his battalion was now in charge of the area, Browning having gallantly remained after his Coy. had gone merely to assist the Major with his valuable advice, which the latter had expressed his anxiety to have. About 100 Germans now surrounded half-a-dozen Australians and were proudly thinking of their success when a burst of Lewis-gun fire cut into them. A 10th officer had hastened forward in time to see the mass commencing to retire, and had immediately fired into them, accounting for over 30. The rest scattered, hastening towards their own line, running however into our barrage, which was now crashing down with frightful severity. Very few escaped unscathed, probably 40 being killed. Unfortunately, however, the Lewis-gun had killed Henwood and severely wounded Browning. The latter was in a critical state in our hospital for some time, but all were delighted to learn later of his recovery. He was promoted to his Majority and transferred to the Staff of the A.F.C.

His Company was caught by the enemy barrage in Oak Avenue, where popular and gallant young Lt. C. L. Luscombe was killed. Many other members of the 13th were caught in his long-distance barrage, but our losses were small considering the weight of the material he sent over, being five killed and five wounded. Members of the Battalion went back next morning and buried our dead near Spoilbank.

Our losses for February and the 1st March were: Killed 5, wounded 15, gassed 18, sick 55.

On the 2nd March we marched to Neuve Eglise.

Chapter XXV.—The Darkest Days—Hebuterne.

NEUVE EGLISE was never a more dreary place than it was in February and March, 1918. Although the approaching Spring was doing its best to hide with its green shoots man's ragged and gaping destruction, and, although the sun came higher each day and shone brighter, there still remained a brooding scowl over those doomed towns around Bailleul and Hazebrouck. Bombs and shells had already begun to shatter homes, shops, farms and factories, and to leave the roads and fields in a disorder of metal and clods surrounding gaping holes from which the litter had been rent.

A few civilians still remained—a surly, boorish Flemish brewer, whom we suspected to be a spy, especially as his home remained untouched by shells, and a few mesdames with their demoiselles, who smiled and cheered us up as they took our francs for cups of coffee, chipped potatoes, postcards and dainty lace. As the screeching shells came nearer, and hurled debris against their walls or smashed their few remaining windows with the concussions, or as a burial party passed carrying a Digger to their churchyard—that ancient, already roofless church with its three gables—they would exclaim from the bottom of their hearts, "Les sales Bosches! Les sales Bosches!" They would remain in deep thought for a few moments. Then: "C'est la guerre! Eggs finish, Monsieur; plus de lait, mais plentee pomme-de-terres." And they would go on cheerfully and smilingly waiting on us.

We advised them to leave as the bombardment was increasing in intensity, but without avail. "Bon pour vous, Bon pour nous, m'sieur!" they would insist. Crash! A neighbour's house is shattered and bricks and dust are hurled into our coffeeroom. "Ah! Les Sales Bosches, les Sales! Neuve Eglise fini tout de suite maintenant." We paid them twenty francs instead of five, again urged them to depart and went back to our duty. We were preparing a field for our Battalion Sports to take place the next day. "Rubber-heels" tore our running track to pieces and we had to make another alongside it. Our 12 strongest men, the pick of 600, were across the road with Lt. (John) Browne, M.C. (O.P.), No. 16, their coach practice-pulling for the Brigade Championship. A "Rubber-heel," its coming unheralded by screech or whine, lobbed forty yards short of them in a ploughed field. It was a "grass-cutter" and hurled its vicious fragments spitefully to comb the surface of the surrounding fields. Our splendid men were taking the strain, "John" watching to pick out the best.

Crash!

We knew that such a crash would mean some casualty, and those nearest hurried to assist, little dreaming they would find the whole team wiped out, five being killed instantly and nine frightfully wounded, two of them, including "John," dying within a few hours. And the shell was one of our own, having been given to the Germans by the Russians, to whom we had given them.

After the sports that afternoon we received sudden orders to leave Neuve Eglise for Waterloo Camp, a few miles further back where we held ourselves in readiness to move anywhere at an hour's notice. Still all remained cheerful, and carried out sports programmes.

The coming German assault was being boasted of by our enemies; our papers were filled with accounts of the tremendousness of the enemy preparations, and surmises as to the probable points to be assaulted in this final war-ending attack. Those on the spot had given over surmising years before. They only awaited orders to move to meet the enemy; meanwhile completing their competitions.

On the 9th March the 13th defeated the 113th How. Batt. at Rugby by 6 to nil. The 12th brought the Lightweight Boxing Championship to the Battalion by the victory of "Tossie" Andrews over Pte. Copeland, of the 4th Field Ambulance, after a 15 round contest; although our popular Sgt. Wollf went under in the Welters to Dvr. Perry, of the 4th Field Ambulance in the 12th round. The 13th was an exciting day, the semi-final Rugby match being one to be remembered, the 15th Battalion defeating us by 5 to nil. Our Soccer team, however, made up for this by beating the 14th Battalion in the semi-final by 1 to 0. On the 16th our Rugby team had revenge for its defeat of the 13th by defeating the 15th Battalion by 16 to 3. On the 21st Lt. Geo. Marper again led his Soccer team to victory by defeating the 15th Battalion in the final by 3 to 1, and carrying off the Brigade Cup.

On the 22nd the Battalion Sports already mentioned were held and followed by the removal from Neuve Eglise to Waterloo, where, the next day, we defeated the 15th in the final and won the Brigade Cup, the scores being 15 to nil.

That evening, although under orders to move to an unknown destination at half-an-hour's notice, we celebrated the victory at a dinner, each cup being filled with champagne or soft "Tack," and emptied by each player in turn.

On the 15th March Major Harry Murray, V.C., D.S.O. (and Bar), D.C.M., had been appointed to command, as Lt.-Col., the 4th Machine Gun Battalion, being sincerely congratulated by the rank and file without exception on this well-merited distinction He had still higher honors to gain, but we were proud to know that it was in the 13th that he had risen from the ranks through sheer merit to the command of a battalion, with a record for gallantry unexcelled by that of any other member, not only of the A.I.F., but of the Allied Armies. In our pride at possessing such a man as Murray, we had not thought of the fact that he was not a New South Welshman. He was an Australian, and that sufficed. His service with the 13th since August, 1915, has been recorded in these pages. As C.O. of his new Battalion he continued his magnificent work and received the C.M.G. and Croix de Guerre.

While Murray had been administering command of the 13th during the "Blighty" leave of Col. Marks we had expected to be ordered to stem the German advance near Messines, and our officers had gone forward regularly from Neuve Eglise to reconnoitre the neighbouring country. But we were not to fight in those parts again.

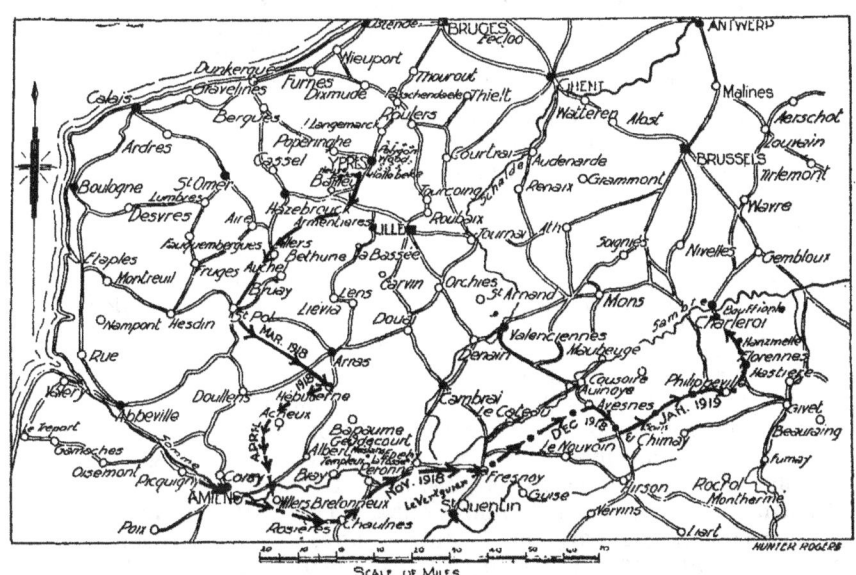

Route from Ypres to Hebuterne and Villers Bretonneux, March and April, 1918. Also the last long trek of 13th Battalion—Picquigny to Charleroi, November, 1918, to January, 1919.

The 24th brought definite news—serious news, too—of the tremendous German attack and rapid advance towards Amiens and Paris. We prepared to embus early next morning, and a Billeting Party under Lt. G. Falkiner, M.M., and our Transport, under Lt. J. Henry, left immediately on a long journey southwards, its destination Busnes, near Lillers, whence we expected to entrain for the Arras area. But these parties were intercepted en route and ordered to a new destination, and we were informed that we would make the whole journey by 'bus to somewhere between Arras and Doullens.

We were up early on the 25th, and after cleaning camp and marching to near Neuve Eglise, we embussed and commenced our journey at 7.45 a.m. Our route was via Steenwerck, Estaires, Merville, St. Venant, Lillers, St. Pol, Roellecourt, Ternas, Maizieres, Avesnes, Barly and Bavincourt to La Herliere, whence we marched a mile before throwing ourselves down in our equipment, ready to move in any direction at an hour's notice. It had been a weary day, and a dusty one except for those in the first few of the hundreds of motor-lorries carrying us down south.

We were well-known around Steenwerck, and the people were lined along the roads to wave and smile to us and to call out "Bon fortune! Bon retour!" Merville and its water-wheels; picturesque, quaint old Lillers; busy, suffering St. Pol, and dozens of sleepy villages had dropped behind us in the dust-cloud. As the first 'buses reached Barly they found the inhabitants with their waggons loaded ready to move back from the oncoming Bosche. They had not seen Diggers before, for they lived between the Somme and Flanders. Each 'bus-load cheered the old people. The loading ceased as they stood and watched the apparently endless lines of lorries, transport and cookers, all with their cheery personnel. Towards Bapaume could be seen the smoke of a burning village which had caused them to hasten their loading. Then, spontaneously, as it seemed, the inhabitants learned that we were Australians. "Les Australiens! Les Australiens!" they were heard calling out to one another by the occupants of some 'buses halted there for a while. Then unloading commenced almost as spontaneously, and later loads saw the furniture being carried back into the homes from which it had just been removed. "Pas necessaire maintenant. Vous les tiendrez," an old man told one of our transport as he drove his empty waggon back to its shed. "Not necessary now. You will hold them." "Vous les tiendrez" may some day be the motto of one of the battalions of the 4th Brigade to whom the remarks were made over and over again that day. "Well, we'd better not let the old chap be disappointed," exclaimed a Digger on understanding what he had said.

All night long-range guns were lobbing shells nearby, and all night could be heard the tramp, tramp of retreating feet and the crunching of metal under the hoofs and wheels of retreating transport; but this did not prevent sleep until the very early Reveille, with which came the message: "Enemy has broken through at Hebuterne. Move to line Souastre-Bienvillers." The position seemed indeed most serious, for these were neighbouring villages.

As we moved out with our Scouts well ahead we saw evidence of rout everywhere in the disordered groups of British troops retiring along every road. In themselves these groups were no more than disheartened and weary, but the various units were mixed together in an apparently-tangleless mass. They all told of the nearness of the Bosche and his tremendous resources of tanks and artillery. "Jerry's got tanks galore!" we were told over and over again. The refugees told us similar news. Nine Staff Officers were crowded on a small car hastening to the rear. They were visibly nettled by the unkind remarks of our men, but they did not slacken speed. "Thank God we've got a Navy," a Digger grumbled.

Sir A. Conan Doyle has written to me that probably these Staff Officers were hastening rearwards under orders to reorganise Gough's Army. I am pleased to accept this view and believe that such, or something similar, was the case; but the thing appeared incongruous to the weary, albeit cheerful Diggers, marching in the opposite direction. The impression that these Officers were setting an unworthy example still prevails among many who marched the other way that day, and it gave rise to a good deal of thoughtless criticism later by our chaps even in conversation with the French and Yanks. The Fifth Army had undoubtedly been broken by an overwhelming enemy concenttation, and, like the French Army adjoining, had been compelled to retreat, and every hasty retreat means disorder. The French were always too patriotic to do aught but glorify their army's retreat, although it was as far as that of the Fifth Army, and the losses were proportionately as great. The fact that Gough, in whose army we had been at Bullecourt, commanded the 5th Army led to many thoughtless remarks.

We were informed by these retreating men that the Germans were in Souastre in armoured cars.

This was serious indeed, and we prepared to go into action on an instant. But our Scouts reported Souastre unoccupied.

Our advanced parties themselves, however, felt dubious, for, almost hidden by clouds of petrol fumes, came a host of iron monsters towards us, and from Souastre. We could hear them crackling and phutting. "There they are! Jerry's armoured cars! They've been after us for miles," we were told. Marks had hurried forward to examine them more closely, while our officers explained to the men the best ways to deal with tanks.

"I think we can fix their drivers if they remain on top like that," remarked Marks.

We were ready to believe that the Hun had many wonderful new ideas and inventions—so persistent had he been in telling the world what he was going to do and what wonders he had up his sleeve—and that these were some of them. Still, in spite of the disturbing ideas that had been forced into our minds, we felt confident of dealing with these tanks quite easily if their crews remained outside as they were doing so far.

They were now within a furlong and we were still uncertain what they were except that they were not likely to be dangerous. They were certainly not tanks nor armoured cars. We did not dream of their being Frenchmen, for we knew that there were no French units in that direction, but French they really were, and their "tanks" were heavy motor plough-tractors. Being farmers, they had been released from line work to plough the fields around Bapaume with tractor-ploughs. They had left their ploughs behind, but had saved the valuable motors.

They were soon rattling along the road between our files, divided to let them have the metal, their crews all smiles and "Bonjours" at knowing that they now had their motors safe.

Then we passed through Humbercamp, and soon left the road to plod across the open fields towards the right edge of Bienvillers. Reaching the Bienvillers-Souastre Road we selected the best fields of fire, and dug in as rapidly as possible. But hardly had we sunk a foot when we received orders to concentrate on the Windmill on the Bienvillers-Fonquevillers Road, as the 4th Bde. was allotted the task of clearing the enemy out of Hebuterne. We were told that a British Brigade would be operating on our right and left, and that Officer's Patrols were to be sent out immediately towards Hebuterne.

By 3.30 p.m. we were in the vicinity of the Windmill, and preparing for the forthcoming attack. Our Scouts and Patrols disappeared into Fonquevillers. Each man examined his ammunition and saw that his rifle was working smoothly. Shovels were distributed as far as possible but there was a grievous shortage, two shovels only being the supply for some platoons.

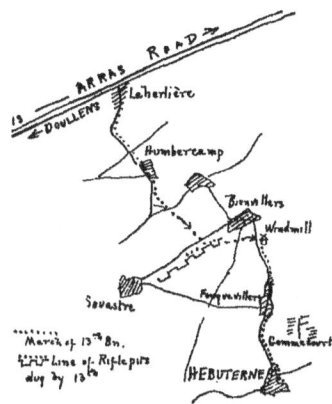

General Brand and his groom had disappeared along with our patrols. At 5 p.m. we saw him hurrying back. He called out "Colonels! Colonels! Get your men assembled here just as they are." All rallied round, and the General opened:— "I've been into the place we are to recapture."

"Silly old Blankard. You'll be getting shot!"

"You're a Dinkum, Steve."

The General evidently did not want to hear these and many other similarly appreciative remarks from the men of his Brigade. To get first-hand information concerning the situation and to ascertain the real strength of the hundreds of disquieting rumors, he had ridden ahead of our foremost scouts right into Hebuterne, officially reported in enemy hands.

As a matter of fact there were a score of Germans in Hebuterne at the time, and a few civilians making final preparations before leaving their doomed homes; but the former had found the villagers' wine, and preferred indoor life to scouting. Great numbers of Germans moreover were hurrying along the roads within two miles of Hebuterne at the time.

It would perhaps have been wise to have ordered an immediate advance towards and through Hebuterne, such an important strategical position as it was; but, had we then moved, there was no knowing when we should have been able to obtain our next meal. So, except for Outposts being pushed out, the Brigade rested until the cookers came up from behind Bienvillers, and all enjoyed a hot meal before advancing.

Then, at 7.30 p.m. the 13th led off. Darkness descended as our Advanced Parties were passing through the long winding main road of Fonquevillers. Emerging from this village they received reports that our patrols had reached Hebuterne.

At 9.15 these Patrols, under Lt. H. B. Brown, D.C.M., M.M., came in contact with the enemy and immediately assumed the offensive, sending back word as to the enemy's position. "B" Coy. under Capt. Moseley was ordered to push on and drive the enemy out of Hebuterne.

The main road was being swept with enemy rifle and machine gun fire, but Moseley and his company pushed on silently and gallantly in the darkness, their progress being naturally slow, for every corner, house and cellar had to be examined. "C" Coy., under Capt. R. A. McKillop, and "A", under Capt. "Doss" Wallach, M.C., were in close support to "B". McKillop gradually worked to the right of the village to become part of the front line and to connect with the 16th Bn., while Wallach cleared the left of the Village.

McKillop's position was soon a risky one, for the 16th had been delayed, and his right was 'in the air'. Guarding this, however, and sending some of his splendid scouts not only to try to locate the 16th, but also to scout ahead, he continued his advance as resolutely and as successfully as Moseley and Wallach. The Brigade flanks were so dangerously weak, the total strength of the 62nd Division on our left being 2,000 and of the 19th Division on our right 500.

Several casualties had already been suffered, and our R.M.O. Major R. F. Craig and his staff kept busy, Lieuts. J. O'M. Jones and M. K. Nolan were among the early wounded, the latter, in spite of his painful and dying condition, remaining cheerful and giving some valuable information before "going west". Both these young officers had been inspiring examples in that weird advance through the dark streets, yards, houses and cellars of the deserted village.

At 11.40 all companies reported "in position." They were right astride the Village—"C" on the right, "B" on the left—with "A" in Close Support and "D" in Reserve, each Company being connected by telephone with Bn. Hqrs. at the Northern end of the village. Whatever happened now we had the Northern two-thirds of the town cut off from the enemy by a line of resolute troops.

Our Scouts had been out behind the enemy posts and had brought back reports, but a definite advance was not safe until the companies had been connected laterally as well as with Hqrs. The enemy were in most places on our front close up against us, their rifles and machines spitting savagely through the darkness. On account of our patrols out in the rear of the enemy there was practically no firing on our side. All who could be spared from "A", "D" and Hqrs. were busy "Mopping-up" in case the front line troops had missed a nest of enemy.

In this mopping-up we found a French Ordnance Store containing big supplies of flour, rice, beans and tapioca, as well as hundreds of French military uniforms and overcoats, which helped to keep all warm and dry. The Germans must have been puzzled at seeing French uniforms in our trenches. Our men in reserve slept comfortably in French overcoats. The greatest excitement these reserve Moppers had was when one of their number fell down a well. He had been searching a backyard when he suddenly fell through some rotten timber into an ancient well. His mates, thinking he was scuffling a German, rushed to his assistance and narrowly escaped falling on top of him for it was pitchy dark. They peered down into the foul-smelling slimy hole, and, by the light of a match, saw their comrade disappear under the scum. He rose up again and clutched at the sides, but the weight of his clothes and equipment pulled him down. His mates were desperate, for they could find no rope and the sides of the well began to fall in. It was then that one of the most heroic deeds in our history was performed. A tall Digger of "A" Coy. stretched himself down into the well, calling out "Catch hold of my legs". Two grabbed each foot and others held onto them, thus making a human rope. The strain became tremendous as the drowning man grasped his rescuer's hands. "Pull! Pull!" the rescuer called out, and all pulled, but it seemed as if they must fail, for the well sides began crumbling. "All Heave!" was shouted out, and over a dozen heaved onto the coats of the four holding the feet. They carried the half-drowned man back to the R.A.P. forgetting all about the hero, especially as enemy machine guns had opened on them with their light. Every effort was made later to find the name of the hero for special honor, but all we could ascertain was that he was "a lanky chap from "A", a new reinforcement." But every lanky chap in "A" who was in that quarter that night denied that he was the one. So this goes down to one of our many unknown heroes.

The next morning a Frenchman was found in his home within a chain of the front line. His home was already like a sieve with bullet holes, but he would not leave it. "Ah, Monsieur, my fowls and my pig, our beautiful things." His wife and daughter had departed the day before with the rest of the poor refugees. While he was talking, a shell blew half of his home to pieces; still he did not want to stir. Two Diggers, however, escorted him back towards Fonquevillers, carrying what they could for him. We had his pig and fowls that night for tea.

In the following strenuous days we forgot about the poor chap who had fallen into the well; but his troubles had not ended. His clothes being wet and foul, the M.O. had used some of the French uniforms to clothe him, and, after resting a few hours, he had been sent back as a "Walking Case" to the Clearing Station. At Bienvillers he had been told to report still farther back, and was making his way when challenged by some French Soldiers who had just arrived from Italy as Reserves for the Arras front. The poor fellow was not only still a bit ill, but he could not speak French at all. They took charge of him as a spy, and, had they been more forward or going into action, they would probably have shot him on the spot.

As it was, it was only after three days' imprisonment and a great deal of explanation, that he was handed over to the British.

By midnight of the 26th the front companies were ready for another advance, which was made still at the point of the bayonet. In this way the whole of the Village became ours by 2 a.m.

The Cemetery with its vaults and old 1914 trenches and dug-outs, however, was held by the enemy in great strength, and McKillop found himself close up against their well-protected strong-posts, from three of which machine-guns enfiladed Moseley's Company as soon as daylight permitted.

Not a shell had fallen all night, nor had we a field gun behind us to fire. The German Gunners evidently did not know where their front line was,, and so did not fire that night.

The Capture of Hebuterne must rank as purely bayonet work. The holding of it for the first few strenuous days was as purely rifle work, for not only had we no artillery, but our ammunition supplies were so short that we could not afford to use machine-guns freely; and our bomb supply was soon exhausted. The Germans, finding Hebuterne held so resolutely, attacked most spitefully again and again, their aeroplanes assisting by firing from the air. In one of these attacks on the morning of the 28th Capt. Moseley received an aeroplane bullet in his stomach, and his splendid C. S. M. "Lofty" Tennant was killed, while casualties came quickly from the showers of shells he was now pouring into Hebuterne. Lieut. T. White, Bomb and Gas Officer, was sent from Headquarters to take charge of "B".

Just before he received the order, however, an amusing event took place at Headquarters. A long-range enemy shell weighing over 50lbs screeched through the air and lobbed on the road near the Hqrs. cellar. All expected it to explode and to hear its fragments hurtling against the wall of the cottage overhead. Instead, they heard it bouncing or skidding along the road before crashing through the wall overhead, and, before one had time to think, amid the sound of falling mortar and bricks, it thudded onto the top step of the cellar. Capt. Davis, the Adjutant, sat calmly looking at it as it rolled down one step after another, hissing in each little pool of water. Col. Marks, who had been taking a little nap, sat up and looked at it steaming, while the rest crouched into corners watching it and waiting. It did not explode, however, for, although it was not a 'Dud' its nosecap had not struck anything direct. A few minutes later two runners carried it outside, and all relieved the tension by joking about it.

The 28th was indeed a most trying day. We occupied a scrappy line of muddy sunken road and old crumbling trenches stretching across the southern end of the village, with the enemy strongly holding a commanding network of the 1914 system, including the cemetery with its vault, in most places within a few yards of us. Every approach to his front trenches was swept by him from the other trenches. We could not aford to let them look towards our weak position in daylight; so we kept up a policy of vigorous sniping, rifles and Lewis guns constantly snapping out at German heads that chanced to show even for an instant. Cpl. W. Dixon (O.P.) especially excelled in Lewis Gun sniping, his wonderful bravery and offensive spirit leading him to take his gun out fifty yards in front of his trench in order to fire into the rear of the enemy in the cemetery. He knew he was facing certain death, but faced it unflinchingly and on his own initiative. He knew the position was critical, and that was sufficient, and so he willingly sacrificed himself to help the men of another Company..

How many enemy were massed in the Cemetery we knew not, but they continued rushing small parties towards it and the Quarries on its right all the 27th and morning of the 28th. "B" and the 15th Bn. made splendid execution among these parties. "C" was the company directly threatened, but they were unable to see more than a few yards in their front. Hence they were being saved from an overwhelming flank and frontal attack without knowing it. Marks, however, had the situation well in mind, having at daybreak followed his usual practice of visiting all his newly-established posts; and on his return he had sent every available Lewis and Machine Gun to the positions whence they could sweep across the approach to the Cemetery.

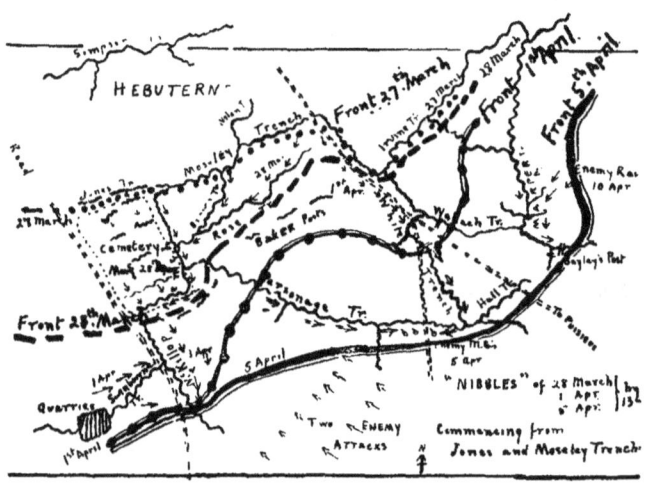

Hebuterne "Nibbles" by the 13th.

Evidently these small parties did not meet with the success the enemy expected and they determined to launch an overwhelming mass. At 11 a.m. our aeroplanes, just arrived, reported them massing, and at 1.45 the left of our front line caught him advancing in 12 waves towards the Quarries, the right edge of the Cemetery, and the New Zealanders on our Bde. right. They simply could not miss. The first wave melted away. The second hesitated, and the third and fourth came up to them, forming a massed target, and they fell like ninepins. A few officers ran to the front to lead them. They fell. All their waves were now close together in the open to "B" Company and the 15th Bn. Our guns and rifles were burning hot but they worked as smoothly and continuously as they had in competitions for which they had so often specially prepared in the past. A jam in a Lewis-gun then would have meant the lives of dozens of the enemy. There were no fire orders; each man judged his own distance and fired rapidly as long as a German was in sight. It is safe to say that fewer bullets were wasted at Hebuterne than at any other time in our history. Murray, though a machine-gunner himself, had, as Company Commander and Second-in-Command, trained the Battalion to as perfect a state of efficiency with the rifle as any battalion ever was trained. In this he followed Durrant's plans and in his footsteps. No prize markmanship about their training, no special sights or gauges, but every contest under active service conditions. Cpl. Mutton was typical of a hundred "rapid-loaders" the Battalion could boast. Any platoon could charge across a hundred yards of rough country, take cover, fix sights and open out on any target that might suddenly appear for a few seconds on any part of their front.

THE DARKEST DAYS—HEBUTERNE

(Durrant gave Murray charge of the Bn. musketry in April, 1917, in order to take his mind off Bullecourt.)

At 4 p.m. on the 28th about 150 of the enemy were seen approaching in the distance, evidently feeling safe for they were in column. It was too good a target to miss, so three Vickers were quickly rushed to a suitable spot, whence they opened at 1600 yards, smashing and scattering the column immediately, several remaining lying were they fell. The survivors, however, kept to the dead ground and rushed towards the Cemetery in twos and threes wherever the ground was open.

Although these attackers had been so severely cut up McKillop's flank was still 'in the air' as the 16th had not been able to join up with him, and the Cemetery was threatening to become an impregnable fort judging by the masses of the enemy our scouts reported there and the sounds of a hundred picks and shovels that could be heard consolidating. If we allowed the enemy to hold the Cemetery we should have to withdraw our line to the centre of the village at least, which would have been a serious matter to other parts of the line. Marks with characteristic decision, ordered McKillop and White to prepare for immediate attack, the former to make a frontal, the latter a flank, attack.

Within a few minutes all were ready, and "B" and "C" commenced trickling forward while Lt. Waterford's Stokes-mortars poured a tornado of shells onto the spots where the enemy was believed to be strongest. After showers of bombs the attackers entered several deep trenches and, at the point of the bayonet, advanced from bay to bay. The bombs used in this attack were rather risky, for they had been 'souvenired' from a 1916 dump in Humbercamp, Lt. T. White and Sgt. H. Townsend having, on account of their dangerous condition, taken to pieces and rearranged 500 of them, for which they were specially complimented. While the Bombers of "B" and "C" worked along the trenches the remainder of "C" and a Platoon of "B" followed across the top. The greatest heroism was shown in the bombing and rushing of machine-guns; and "C" bombers, by 1.30 a.m., 10 minutes after zero, found themselves in undisputed occupation of a very deep trench on the far side of the Cemetery, with "B" bombers guarding their left flank and a deep trench leading into their left front. Most of the enemy had bolted in the darkness but some still remained behind "C's" new position. These soon ran or surrendered when Lt. "Dick" Swinburne led his platoon of "D" in and mopped up every vault and strong-point.

Their rear and left safe, the ambitious "C" bombed out into the new No Man's Land and along a trench system in their right front until they linked up with the 16th Bn., the whole operation being done with such rapidity that a party of eight from enemy advanced Hqrs. were astounded when they found that they had walked right into "C" instead of their own strong point.

The result of this 'Minor night operation' was that Hebuterne was now entirely ours for keeps, and we gained complete observation of the forward slopes and a command of the Quarries and all approaches to them to such an extent that the enemy there was in such a state of siege that they were glad when the New Zealanders walked over and took them prisoners.

This final loss of Hebuterne so annoyed the enemy that he vented his spleen by terrifically bombarding every portion of the village. Every minute some cosy home would crash to pieces, every minute some part of our trench or nearby tree would be hurled skywards. His supply of heavy shells was unlimited, for he had captured from the Fifth Army thousands of guns and millions of shells, and these he turned on us. The heavens hissed and screeched and the earth spat clods and jagged iron in all directions. Shells of every calibre from whizbangs to 12 inch mortars tore into and over our lines. The German gunners must have been joyful at being allowed such extravagance.

And we could not retaliate, for our artillery, except for a few guns, had not yet come up. There was no counter-battery work at all; and, except in the Cemetery, there were no dugouts for protection in the front or support lines, all having to remain scattered in the shallow smashed trenches or shell holes in the drizzling rain. In addition to the shelling of our lines the enemy put down a heavy smoke screen all along our front, so heavy that we could not see more than a few yards into it. We believed him to be massing behind it for an assault on us, and prepared to receive him. Our men were scattered in ones and twos for safety from the shelling, but were ready to rush back to their firing positions the instant the enemy barrage should lengthen, for then we believed he would come. Each instant we expected to see his hordes emerging from the screen. All knew that if they were broken there were no reserves behind to prevent the enemy reaching the Arras-Doullens Road, which would have been a tremendous disaster. The front-line companies were completely isolated for all telephones were cut to pieces in spite of the splendid gallantry of the linesmen who patrolled and mended the lines unceasingly. Stretcher-bearers, too, had one of their most trying times, but never for a moment flinched. Every now and again a watchful rifle or Lewis gun would crackle out at an enemy machine-gun flash or at one of their patrols. The fact that no gas-shells fell on our front-line told us to expect his assault early. Out in their smoke could be heard the voices of thousands but not one could be seen except occasionally. At least a dozen times during those first six dreadful hours of shelling did the Diggers rush to their firing places, but each time were they disappointed. It seemed, from the shouting of orders and the exhortations going on in the smoke that the German Officers were urging their men on to the assault.

Never were Diggers more serious than at that time. Since Reveille on the 25th they had had practically no rest or sleep, and the fight against weariness on the afternoon of the 29th was as gallant a struggle as that against the Bosche. Their cigarette supply had given out two days before, but, knowing how valuable they were, several officers had saved their own and now distributed them singly. The Diggers had the name of being a hard-swearing lot, but, like many 'Home' impressions concerning them, this was an exaggerated one. The Diggers were expressive, but far from filthy in their swearing. But even this swearing disappeared those early days at Hebuterne. It was good, when things got less serious, to hear them express themselves as—so it seemed then when an hour was an age,—as of old. Each man felt the world-seriousness of holding the over-weening and vaunting Bosche at that stage, and each felt a tremendous personal responsibility in the matter. The shelling was so terrific that even veterans of Gallipoli and Pozieres were dazed. Several were absolutely worn-out and trembling with weariness and concussion, but they steadfastly refused to evacuate. Their only disobedience was that they would get together in twos and threes instead of keeping apart. In a few cases at least it was in order that they might share the same cigarette, but there was an intense feeling of loneliness in the front of Hebuterne never felt at any other time in the front line even on Gallipoli. Some were afraid that their feet would become "trenched" in that mud, especially as no foot-soap or powder was available, and changes of socks were scarce and these got their mates to restore circulation by hard rubbing. The general opinion of all is that there was not one man then at Hebuterne who would have left the front line without being carried.

It may have been that all the exhortations of their officers could not bring the Germans to the assault, or it may have been the determined and accurate rifle and Lewis fire at every possible target and into the smoke every time the sound of movement came close, that kept them back. The fact remains that after a final lot of talking they were heard retiring, and, when the screen thinned, they were out of sight. But he continued his terrific shelling for nine hours that day, and then all that night, now adding gas in great quantities. Mjr. Craig was wounded attending to his cases, Capt. S. M. O'Riordan joining us in his place the next day. This lanky Doc., "Mick", soon became as popular as any of our "Docs." had been. In Sgt. E. Robertson and Cpl. McIver we had now lost two valuable men.

In addition to the disturbing rumors we had heard regarding tanks and enemy successes we had been filled with stories of spies, who had certainly, in the garb of British Officers, mixed up with the retreating 5th Army and given orders to hasten the retreat. Anyone giving such an order to us was to be instantly shot. So when four English officers were found in our front line, whither they had arrived without our Colonel's authority, they were sent back for inquiry under escort of Lt. H. "Bill" Simpson (O.P.). A shell caught the party near Hebuterne church. "Bill," knowing his wounds to be fatal, ordered the Bearers to leave him and hasten to a Digger lying wounded nearby. "You can't save me; you might save him." So passed away, amid the crash and tearing of bursting shells, another of the 13th heroes. "Bill" had risen from the ranks through sheer battle work. One of the "Tommy" officers killed was a V.C. Major, for the party was a geniune one of English Artillery officers who had just come to the Hebuterne area, but who had neglected to report at our Headquarters before going forward.

On the evening of the 31st "D" Coy., which had not only been helping "C," but had been

THE DARKEST DAYS—HEBUTERNE

in the front line against the 16th for a night, moved across onto the left of "B," relieving a company of the 15th Battalion. That same evening "C" wounded and captured two runners, the bearers of an important despatch which they attempted to destroy, but which was pieced together, however, and translated, giving details of a German relief at 3 a.m. next day. Our artillery, now in strength, was warned, and sent over an encouraging strafe, resulting, we learnt, in heavy enemy casualties. The sound of our own guns was pleasing indeed.

At 1.15 a.m. on 1st April "C" was ordered to co-operate with the 16th Battalion in an attack on a strong post some distance ahead of the junction of "C" and the 16th. This attack was another with bombs and bayonet and was wonderfully successful, 71 prisoners and 4 machine-guns being captured and over 100 dead Germans counted. We had again definitely taken the offensive and all were in great heart. "B" advanced a post 200 yards into enemy territory, rushing it in broad daylight on two minutes' notice; "C" sent out another post on its own left, and "D" sent another well towards Puisieux. So well planned and swift were these stunts that we had only two wounded. Another very successful stunt was the rushing of a nest of troublesome enemy machine-guns after a short "hurry-up" by Waterford's Stokes' Mortars. As the only German left alive near these guns was being sent to the rear he caused amusement by pointing to the Stokes and exclaiming disgustedly, "No bon cannon!"

With these posts established the rear of the Battalion could rest a little more comfortably, well assured of plenty of warning in case of attack. During the next few days we fortified the village so strongly that it became practically impregnable. The old Catacombs, 100 feet deep and capable of holding a battalion, were opened out and provided with steps so that our reserves could sleep safe and dry. A "Rubbing Post" was also established here and all threatening to have trench feet were sent to be tended.

The next three days passed without any rumour of relief for the three front-line companies. All knew they could expect no relief while the Allied Line was so thin. Still fighting Nature was hard—harder than fighting Fritz. We kept up active patrolling, our patrols working even between and behind the advanced German posts, Cpls. F. Massey, M.M., and E. Rawdon and Pte. W. Coady specially distinguishing themselves in this work. Smiling little Frank Massey's record for 19 nights was 40 important patrols and the guidance of two raids.

We also built weather-shelters in our trenches, shovelled hundreds of tons of mud out, and carried out as complete a trench draining policy as possible. The Companies were now much weaker and wearier, for their short scraps of day-sleep were constantly broken, and all night every man not on patrol or outposts carried heavy loads through trenches knee-deep in mud, or across slippery fields. It is not surprising then that men had begun to wonder how long they could remain vigilant against the fresh hordes of Germans reported several times each day of that first week to be pressing on. It was noticed how easily such men were cheered when, after the first black four days, a new team of Vickers Gunners arrived. The news was passed even to the outposts and cheered all wonderfully.

On April 5th the Tommies on our left attacked and we arranged a diversion in the form of a raid on a nest of machine-guns that had been irritating us a lot. Two Bomb Sections from "B" under Lts. H. B. Brown, D.C.M., M.M., and E. A. Hall, covered on their left by patrols from Wallach Trench, and on their front by a smoke screen arranged by Lt. L. Cleland, worked down White Trench to meet a similar party under Lt. W. Parsonage working down Parsonage Trench. The raid was a great success, the nest being destroyed and the sole remaining gunner captured with his gun.

That these minor operations were of value is seen from the following message sent from down near Amiens: "The Div. Commander has just rung up to thank the G.O.C., officers and men of the 4th Brigade for all their good work to-day. He fully realises that, though the enemy has made very determined efforts to get a footing in our lines he has failed to do so, suffering severe casualties in the attempts."

On the 8th "B" Coy., after having been in the front line for 13 days and nights, was relieved by "A," also a very tired company on account of having been providing most of the working and ration-carrying parties. While taking over the outposts, two enemy machine-guns which had been brought close up in the fog, brought sparks from the wire belt through which "A" men were passing. All flopped down except the lanky Lt. Harry Baker, who stood coolly taking the bearings of the flashes with a view to later action.

The same day the 4th Brigade received a splendid tribute from the Corps Commander, who stated that he was afraid to let the defence of Hebuterne to anyone else. General Brand wrote to the 13th as follows: "**Dear Marks,**—The Corps Commander is afraid to let the defence of

H

Hebuterne out of our hands. Consequently Headquarters stay where they are at present with the 13th and 14th in the line." Col. Marks, in reply, pointed out to the General the severe strain his men had been under for so long.

The 4th Brigade has reason to be proud of the following letter from Corps, received on the 8th April:—

Fourth Australian Brigade. (Through 37th Division).—

"The Corps Commander desires to thank all ranks of the 4th Australian Brigade for their gallant behaviour in the defence of Hebuterne against all attacks during the past 14 days. Without relief and without complaint they have held their positions, and, in many cases, have advanced and improved their lines.

"Heavy attacks on the Brigade on the 1st and 5th April were repulsed with severe losses to the enemy.

"Skilful enterprises carried out on the initiative of local commanders have resulted in the capture of several enemy posts with a gain to us of 80 prisoners and eight machine-guns, besides inflicting heavy losses on the enemy.

"The Corps Commander considers this a very fine performance, which reflects great credit on all ranks of the Brigade."

HEADQUARTERS FOURTH CORPS,

7th April, 1918."

General MacLagan also congratulated all ranks on "one of the best things done by them in France."

On the 9th, after a detailed inspection of the front lines, General Brand sent the following to the 13th Battalion:—

"I regret that the relief of your Battalion has been postponed from the 10/11th April to the 13/14th. After 15 days' strenuous work all higher Commanders would have liked to see your men get a few days' rest, but the holding of Hebuterne is all important to the Fourth Corps. It has been decided therefore that the 4th Brigade carry on the good work instead of being relieved. . . . The importance of the British holding the Germans and allowing him to expend his fresh divisions while the French and American counter-offensive is maturing will be appreciated by all thinking officers, N.c.o.'s and men. From what one can gather the British have very few fresh Divisions, so that all our efforts have to be re-doubled.

"It is gratifying to note that the cases of trench feet are practically nil, whereas, in flanking units there are several cases. Credit is due to all concerned. Keep up this good record.

"Please let all ranks know that the best service they can do is to stick it.

"(Signed) C. H. BRAND."

With daylight on the 11th came a repetition of the previous hellish tornadoes; only this time "D" received more than their share of the "hate." Their trenches were smashed to pieces and many had to move out into shell-holes; but, on account of the fog and a smoke screen they could not see their advanced post just beyond the junction of Wallach and Marper Trenches. So smothering was this barrage on the whole of "D" area that all wires were cut faster than Falkiner and his gallant linesmen could repair them. A hissing sleet of shells and bullets swept into and along the surface of the earth. Capt. Wallach expected an overwhelming attack on his sector. His runners got through to Headquarters with a message that he was ready. Lt. T. White was ordered to stand-to with "B" Coy., just relieved, to move to his help. The Germans were again using our own shells most extravagantly. But their three-hours' "strafe" only led to a raid into the most advanced post. Here Cpl. Bayley and his four men, all with splendid records, were helpless, when, the instant the barrage lifted off them, they found 50 Germans around them. It was the only post the 13th ever lost, and it would not have been lost but for a peculiar misunderstanding on the part of the English unit on "D's" left. They were supposed to guard Marper Trench, but withdrew their posts at daylight without informing Wallach or Cpl. Bayley. Hence the Germans were able to move along this trench into the rear of Bayley's Post. A Welsh machine-gunner just out of the barrage said that he could have wiped out the raiders had he "been ordered to fire." He saw them in the open wearing British steel helmets, but did not fire because no one ordered him to do so. "My gun was an S.O.S. gun," he explained.

The remainder of the 20 officers and 506 other ranks who had gone in Hebuterne 19 days before, won it at the point of the bayonet, cleared it and the fields beyond, fortified it and assaulted the enemy in his own trenches twelve times, were so weary that, on the relief on the night of the 13th April by the 13th Battalion English Rifle Brigade, many were quite unable to walk. Officers and men helped each other along to the bivouacs at Coigneux, but many dropped along the roadside and slept until transport could be spared to pick them up. It was less than four miles to Coigneux, but dozens took eight hours to cover it. The General himself was at Sailly helping to issue coffee to the weary troops. In the line men who had been cheerful and active to the very last lost their reserve of strength all at once upon relief, and the strongest found themselves forced to sit on the road bank and then unable to rise.

Our casualties at Hebuterne were more than a quarter of our strength—16 killed, 79 wounded, 39 evacuated sick, and five lost as prisoners. Had not our weakness made us hold our lines so precariously thin they would have been much higher. The defence of Hebuterne was, notwithstanding the splendid work and heroism and incredible endurance, very greatly a matter of sheer bluff. A single line, a very patchy line, of determined Diggers, without artillery, and an inadequate supply of ammunition and bombs, had signally defeated an overwhelming army of cocksure Germans, backed up with more artillery and munitions than any other army ever had. From the moment he met the Australians his advance ceased; from the moment they attacked he fell back. Some day the epic capture and holding of Hebuterne will move a poet. Although 70 per cent. of the English battalion on our left were evacuated with trench feet within a week—and they were used to the climate—the Diggers were so determined to remain that the 13th, for example, had not a single case of trench feet in twice that time. During our period in Hebuterne the 4th Brigade was attached to four British Divisions in succession, on the relief of each being handed over "as trench stores" to the next.

The officers found it difficult to decide on the N.c.o.'s and men to be recommended for special work, so wonderful had been the conduct, spirit and valor of all. The names of more than half of the Battalion were sent to the Colonel for special devotion to duty. Of course, these were too many to send on, and the names were gone through over and over again by the officers and senior N.c.o.'s until 70 were selected as outstanding even their mates. This list was again revised and ultimately Capt. R. A. McKillop, Lts. R. S. Swinburne and H. B. Brown, D.C.M., M.M., received well-merited M.C.'s, and Sgt. W. F. Hughes, Cpls F. E. Massey, M.M., and E. Rawdon received D.C.M.'s, and 23 M.M.'s, including a Bar to Sgt. F. Forbes, went to other N.c.o's and men, many of those receiving them being keenly disappointed at their mates' missing.

Writer's last wish is that this history should be taken as an "Officer history," but he cannot help mentioning the high sense of duty of the 13th officers. At Hebuterne 39 men were evacuated sick—a very small number indeed—during those 19 strenuous, muddy, hissing and crashing days, but not a single officer. The men of the 13th have always been the first to recognise this devotion of their officers, with remarkably few exceptions. The first concern of the 13th officers from Colonel to sub. was always the comfort and wellbeing of their men. They were often more dog-tired than the men, or than the men guessed, but they gave cheery service on every occasion and were animating spirits in times of stress like those at Hebuterne. They were never heard complaining by the men, although the latter saw that their officers were no better off in the trenches than themselves. Some units were rendered much less efficient than others by the fact that their officers lost spirit and energy and infected their men. And, in the 13th, what can be said of the officers in this respect can most generally be said of the N.c.o.'s. And the men imitated these good examples, thus improving in the most effective manner, the efficiency of the Battalion. Onerous, disagreeable and irksome duties were cheerfully performed because they were known to be in the interest of the comfort, health and safety of the men.

The 13th did not leave the Hebuterne area for the next 10 days. After a few days' rest and clean-up we moved back into Close Reserve, where we dug and wired the Purple Reserve Line, built splinter-proof shelters, cleaned out old dugouts and gun pits and the cellars in Sailly-au-Bois, made sand-bag strong-posts, camouflaged all work with clods and brushwood, and salvaged a great dump of all sorts of material from a wide area.

On the afternoon of the 23rd we were relieved by the 2nd Auckland Battalion and moved back to Coigneux. We had finished with the Hebuterne Area.

It has not been in my power to investigate the authority of the statement so widely circulated at this time that the 4th Brigade had been selected by the French Government for a special honor—a Brigade Croix de Guerre—or of the statements that our high authorities had refused to allow it.

Chapter XXVI.—Villers Bretonneux.

FROM Coigneux, on the 24th April, the 13th moved farther south by motor-bus to the Amiens Area again. Passing through the pretty villages of Thievres and Marieux we were soon waving to old friends of Rubempre and Rainneville before debussing and marching to the Bois de Mai of Allonville. At Rainneville the Chasseurs Alpins, just arrived from Italy, welcomed us with fanfares. In the beautiful Bois de Mai we pitched tents and for a few days spent a delightful time among the budding trees and flower-starred grass. We were back with our own Division again after having been in four British Divisions—the 19th, 62nd, 37th and 42nd—since leaving Belgium, each G.O.C. lavishing unstinted praise on us. General Williams, of the 37th had personally addressed the men on their relief from Hebuterne to express his admiration and appreciation, facetiously remarking that although he knew we had lost many of our horses and mules near Hebuterne, he also knew that our Transport was still at its full strength and that our animals were better than ever before, although the Imperial Transport people, who had suspiciously visited us had been unable to recognise any of their missing quadrupeds. "At any rate even my transport people believe that it's been worth while having you with us," he added.

There was good reason why the Imperial Transport had not been able to recognise their lost steeds among ours. The animals we had "souvenired" to replace our worn-out and dead ones had been sent down south, per medium of the 7th A.S.C., to the other battalions of the 4th Division while their "souvenirs" had been sent up to us. Perhaps the G.O.C. 4th Div. was pleased at the scattering of his command. At any rate, Major Walsh, M.C., of the 7th A.S.C., was always a popular visitor to any battalion in the 4th. Division.

Anzac Day we kept as a day of rest, Padre M. Hinsby conducting a most impressive service in the Bois. Enemy planes bombed our area each night, but we luckily escaped.

The 27th found us, after marching past General Birdwood, moving into desolate Daours. The inhabitants had left hurriedly as German shells and bombs rained over them, and the evacues of Villers Bretonneux reported the enemy occupation of that commanding town. We were in high spirits, however, for we knew that Villers Bretonneux was now in Australian keeping, having been gallantly recaptured by our comrades from whom we were going to take over. Half the officers went forward to examine the line area, remaining there all night. The rest of the Battalion slept on deep soft beds.

On the evening of the 28th, in small parties, we crossed the fields to Advanced Brigade Headquarters on the Fouilloy-Villers Road before following this road into the eastern outskirts of Villers Bretonneux, whence the four companies in the darkness branched off to their outpost and support positions, relieving the 59th Battalion, the relief being complete by 11.15 p.m.

The front line was a series of short, hastily-dug trenches and pits with level bullet-swept areas all round them, making communications extremely dangerous. There were no landmarks to guide runners and officers from post to post; so Col. Marks, who visited every post after midnight, immediately gave orders for these isolated posts to be connected up and wired in front.

In many places we were within 40 yards of the strongly-entrenched enemy, rendering active patrolling on our part a necessity. Our first patrol, out protecting a party advancing a post, captured a prisoner.

We had moved in astride the Peronne Road, but soon moved all our posts across to the left of it, allowing the 14th Battalion on our left to shorten their long frontage.

The policy of nibbling forward was one at which the 13th excelled, no night passing without our advancing a Lewis gun or a few snipers to form a post which later became a J.O.T. for another nibble, which irritated Fritz so much that he became extremely jumpy and nervy sending up all night continuous streams of flares and bursting out spasmodically into fits of hurricane strafe.

So reliable were our patrols and so continuously bright was No Man's Land with their flares that we ourselves used no flares at all. Indeed, it was always the policy of the 13th to trust to active patrolling instead of using flares. It was often claimed for us that we used fewer flares than any other battalion of the A.I.F., and the 4th Brigade fewer than any platoon of the enemy.

Thirteenth Headquarters were established in the basement of what had been, until a few days before, the magnificent chateau of a French woollen manufacturer, whose factory was next door. From this factory we obtained a cardigan jacket for each member of the Battalion, the French Mission giving us authority to use for our own ends anything in Villers Bretonneux. We also sent back to the Mission many cwts. of wool and tons of machinery.

Each cellar and standing building was full of the most deadly gases which had to be cleared out by fires and fans, many of the cellars containing heaps of dead Germans or Tommies.

. . . .

Although the most tremendous assault ever made had been stopped, and although the Australians had immediately assumed the offensive and regained Villers Bretonneux and the commanding hill on which it stood—a hill overlooking Amiens and its rail junctions, and the Somme Valley almost to Abbeville—all felt that the enemy was just taking a breath before repeating his assault.

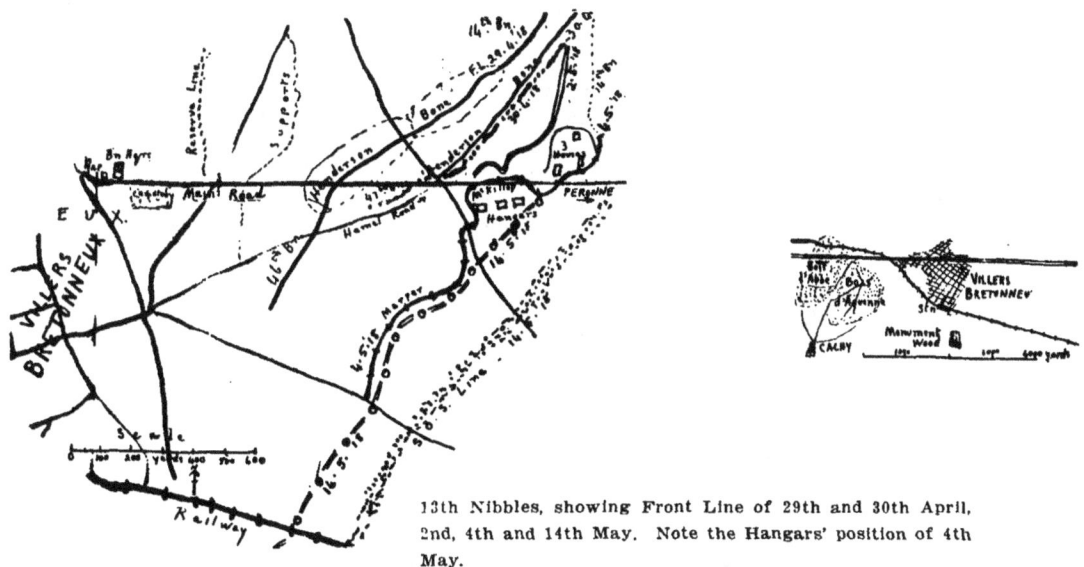

13th Nibbles, showing Front Line of 29th and 30th April, 2nd, 4th and 14th May. Note the Hangars' position of 4th May.

Feeling this, we may have been regarded as doing the correct thing had we gone in merely for building up defences. True our Support Company and Reserves worked hard at digging and wiring night after night, and the town was filled with wiring, strong-point and tank-trap parties from other units at work every night, still we allowed the enemy not an hour's rest, for, in addition to our constant nibbles, our airmen and gunners strafed him night and day. Each night his airmen came over and dropped tons of bombs all over Villers Bretonneux and the area behind, but daylight kept him to his own side, except on one occasion when he came over flying British colors and bombed us, and a few others when he hurried across and back after a quick observation.

Several times he poured showers of gas-shells into our trenches and the town. After one specially severe strafe we asked our artillery to retaliate, and never will those present forget that terrific bombardment of the enemy in Monument Wood. Five thousand gas-shells were poured into the small wood in ten minutes. All that afternoon our observers on the roofs of Villers Bretonneux could see their stretcher-bearers at work, and no wonder, for our artillery was using the new British gas, stronger by far than anything the Germans with all their start, possessed, one cubic foot of it being powerful enough to dilute fatally 100 million cubic feet of air. This was not the only way in which our nation, although caught unprepared, surpassed the Hun with his own weapons.

Another day our observers from the roof of our chateau saw a Transport column of 20 vehicles near Warfusee. Our signallers immediately got busy, and within a few seconds our artillery had annihilated the column.

Three aeroplane hangars just in our front were a great advantage to the enemy, hiding his machine-guns and movements from us, so permitting him to mass unseen within 50 yards of us. They were constructed of steel ribs covered with a non-inflammable material through which our shells went with little effect. The 4th Field Engineers were given the task of destroying them. In the darkness the 13th crept out beyond the first and lay down in No Man's Land to protect the Engineers who carried petrol, sprays and tinder. Unfortunately they could not get the flames going and the enemy gunners were especially lively, sending bullets through and from both ends of the hangars. From an enemy strong-point in the second hangar especially, our scouts saw many machine-guns spitting. Our Lewis-gunners fired into the enemy flashes, but their guns were too numerous and well protected; and the hangars would not catch fire in spite of attempt after attempt on the part of the Engineers and the 13th to light them. Then a change of wind came up and rendered any attempt futile.*

On several occasions the 13th had done more dramatic stunts than these nibbles at Hebuterne and Villers Bretonneux, but none were more risky, required greater gallantry, or worried the enemy more. An overweening enemy flushed with a great victory, was bearded again and again in his own trenches. He could not keep an outpost or patrol in No Man's Land.

The mere holding of Villers Bretonneux was something to be wondered at; that the Diggers should advance nightly was sheer wonder. It was again a matter of consummate cheek accompanied by reckless gallantry. If our commanders had been willing to risk it and had asked our Scouts to work through the enemy's lines to Peronne, miles into their territory, the majority would assuredly have got there and back, especially if accompanied by men like Cpl. M. Roach, who did such splendid patrolling at Villers Bretonneux, often purposely drawing the enemy's fire in order that he might get their true position and strength. They did not ignore the prowess of the enemy, but they repeatedly attempted what he believed the impossible, and were therefore successful.

Some idea of the riskiness of these nibbles may be derived from the maps. It will be seen that each advance on the left of the Peronne Road caused our right flank to be more and more in the air, but Marks, Bone, Henderson and McKillop knew that with the men they had they could take the risk.

On the night of the 29th April Henderson and Bone, after personal reconnaissance, gallantly led their companies forward to beyond the Hamel Road, where they dug in rapidly in isolated pits, their scouts lying out in the open to protect them. Capt. W. S. Bone was unable to take part in our further advances, for, on the morning of the 1st May a shell lobbed in his shallow trench, killed his runner, J. Leonard, M.M., one of the best, and shattered Bone's feet, both of which he lost. He had just finished his sketches and notes for the Colonel. His loss was indeed a heavy one for the Battalion, for he was second only to Murray as a Company Commander. Were one who knew them all asked to name the finest Company Commanders in the A.I.F., it is safe to say that Capt. Bone's name would be among the highest, bracketed with that of Major R. H. Browning, although they were two quite distinct, and, in many ways opposite, personalities. Bone, like Browning, insisted on correct details in everything, "Get down to facts" being an expression frequently heard from him. No vague definition, position or excuse was accepted by him without "Come on, now; get right down to tintacks." His smile and his "Goodo," when pleased, were regarded as sufficient rewards by those earning them.

The 1st May was a rough day for 13th officers. Lt. R. N. Jones (promoted from the ranks for good work) was wounded, and the two "subs." of "D," while conferring with Capt. N. Wallach, M.C., were also wounded by the same shell that killed "Doss." They were Lt. "Joe" Watson (O.P.), and Lt. G. J. Smith, the latter being wounded in 37 places, and recovering.

That same night Henderson took charge of his own and Bone's company and again pushed ahead in spite of the fact that the 47th Battalion on the right of the road were unable to advance, necessitating the forming by Henderson of a strong right flank facing south. (See map.) His Platoon Commanders quickly marked out a new trench line on which all again dug shallow pits. Henderson, knowing his position to be a critical one, for the enemy in the

*[After reading the above in MSS., Cpl. Blaw, who took a prominent part in the stunt, writes: "We had four tins of petrol sent up by our ration carriers; also the usual water supply in petrol tins. When we tried to light the "petrol" we found we had taken the wrong tins. 'A' was short of water that day."]

strong posts in the Hangars could fire into the rear of many of his posts, hurried from post to post supervising, advising, assisting and setting a splendid example of coolness and carelessness of self in that midnight darkness during which streams of bullets constantly swept the areas over which he was passing and repassing. Before dawn, however, the inevitable happened. A bullet smashed deeply into his thigh. One of the gallant runners accompanying him quickly brought bearers who carried him back to the R.A.P., whence, in spite of terrible agony, he sent for the Colonel and gave him the dispositions of his posts, and recommended his bearers for their gallantry in attending to him and carrying him slowly back under extremely heavy fire. We never saw him again, for he died of the wound at Etaples just before the award of the Bar to his M.C. for his work at Villers Bretonneux. Generous to a fault, his hand was always in his pocket to give a man due for leave, but without the means to enjoy it, the wherewithal. His main weakness in the eyes of some was that he overlooked the faults of some of his men; but these faults were probably fewer on that account. "Bob" was unanimously beloved. His bearers, L. Greenleaf and S. Smith, received well-earned M.M.'s.

Just prior to his wound Henderson had learnt that his right was really more "in the air" than he had believed, on account of the withdrawal of the flank battalion. Lt. G. Marper, who succeeded him, set himself assiduously to the task of making this right safe by rearranging bombing and Lewis-gun sections. Marper's enthusiasm inspired his tired men to still further efforts.

Our Scouts, out far ahead of our outposts, and in between the enemy posts, were surprised on the evening of the 1st May to find a wounded English soldier, who had been lying in a shell-hole for nine days. He had been wounded before the Germans had captured Villers Bretonneux and had heard them each evening passing him, but had refused to attract their attention. For nine days he had eaten nothing but grass, having endured not only the pangs of hunger and wounded thirst and the heat of a shadeless sun and the cold of wet nights, but the agony of a fractured thigh rather than surrender. Although behind the German posts their patrols had missed him. Ours found and carried him back, while he, learning they were Australians, hysterically drew them down and kissed them.

Capt. McKillop, M.C., now took charge of our front line and again advanced our posts on the left of the road a considerable distance and occupied the area of the Three Houses from which the enemy had previously annoyed us considerably. That night was a particularly lively one, the Hun being especially jumpy. Our most advanced patrol, out covering McKillop's advance, pushed right up against a strong post containing overwhelming odds and was showered with bombs and squirted with machine-guns. Cpl. J. Stewart brought his Lewis-gun into action, firing at the enemy flashes until he found himself being rushed by 30 Huns, when he fired into them. They came at him from three directions, however, and were firing at him. His third pannier jamming, he coolly shot the two nearest with his revolver, which made the others take cover. Sgt. Purssell, M.M., utterly fearless as usual, repeated the splendid work he had already done on many occasions before being wounded.

At 1 a.m on the 4th May McKillop took over about 800 yards of new front line from the 47th Battalion. His notice to do this was extremely short and he had entrusted the operation to Lt. Marper, who, after rapid but keen reconnaissance, had successfully led his Company across to the south of the road occupying the area that had previously been held by three companies. His men were soon at work digging, wiring and patrolling, Lt. J. D. Westwood, M.C., lining out the wire. McKillop's line of 4th May is shown by a barred line. (See map.)

Although it was only to be expected, considering his reckless gallantry, the death of our popular Sgt. A. Wolff, one of our best boxers, was felt considerably. He had developed the habit of taking his Lewis-gun right out into the enemy wire and even in between their posts, having in this way, over and over again, inflicted heavy losses on the Huns, and, by silencing their machine guns, had saved us many casualties. As all correctly guessed, he died right out there on the other side of No Man's Land surrounded by enemies.

The repeated consolidation of new front line after new front line at Villers Bretonneux was greatly helped by bombers like Cpl. J. Prowse, who on several occasions sent bombs or rifle grenades on top of enemy machine-guns; and to splendid signallers like P. Turnbull and H. Sweet, who night after night repaired lines, on several occasions working in heavy gas and under terriffic shelling. One night one of Prowse's grenades lobbed on a dump of enemy bombs, exploding dozen to the delight of our front line. M. Weatherell (O.P.) was most helpful and inspiring (M.M.), Cpl. O'Brien also (M.M.).

On the afternoon of the 3rd our men attracted a German message dog into their advanced post and sent it back as a prisoner, naming it "Digger," although its German name was "Roff." The message he carried was from a German platoon commander complaining that his men were tired and had not had food for 48 hours. His O.C. had written on it: "Weber has been in longer than you, and he does not complain. We will send you food to-night. Give Roff any further messages. He does not complain."'Roff evidently thought that desertion was preferable to complaining. (Roff reached Australia as a stuffed dog, having died after being a long time in quarantine in England.)

Right out ahead of the new line "C" patrols discovered a considerable force of Bosches digging and wiring. They sent word back to our artillery which quickly smashed the parties up.

Early on the 4th May 42 British planes crossed over and bombed the enemy heavily, being followed during the day by a dozen similar squadrons.

That the enemy did not take our repeated successes and strafing calmly may be seen from the following brief official records in addition to the furies already mentioned.

1st May.—Villers Bretonneux shelled with Blue-Cross gas-shells. Heavy concentration of high-explosive and gas-shells repeatedly during the day and night.

2nd May.—Heavy barrages at dawn on supports and reserves. At 11.15 our Stokes fired 14 rounds into an enemy post. Their S.O.S. went up and was followed by heavy enemy barrage.

3rd May. 2 a.m. Enemy S.O.S. went up and was followed by heavy shelling. Enemy artillery active during the afternoon.

4th May.—Bosche propaganda balloons came over. Enemy sent pineapple bombs and rifle grenades into our posts all night. Three attacks in force during the night. Each attack driven back.

On the night of the 4th we were relieved by the 16th Battalion, and went into support on the western and northern outskirts of the town. We were almost as silent a lot as on our relief from Zonnebeke for practically every throat was red and raw with gas. Most eyes were also bloodshot and watery; still, whenever opportunity offered, everyone did his best to forget the war and to make up for past and future hardships by present fun. When we awoke on the 5th we found that we were among a score of dead horses which we soon buried.

It was still expected that the Hun would hurl another tremendous assault and so, although in support, all dug, wired or carried several hours daily. The Pioneers who had fortified Villers Bretonneux as strongly as any town in France was fortified with wire entanglements, strong points, mines and tank-traps, and Col. H. Murray's Machine Gunners, who had been placed in special positions right across the Brigade Front where they were daily visited by Murray himself, generally in shirt sleeves and on a push-bike, almost prayed for such an assault, well satisfied that, by no possible conglomeration of men and weapons could the Hun get through all their obstacles.

After their work the 13th would stroll back into the town to admire these contrivances, to souvenir anything from a bunch of onions to a piano or motor-car, or simply to wander about to satisfy some curiosity. A piano was brought out from under a heap of ruins on a hand-cart and installed under a shrubby tree, whence hymns, ragtime, dance, sentimental or grand opera music issued every afternoon. To make these dances and 'afternoon teas' more realistic several Diggers dressed themselves in the finery from the wardrobes of the ladies of the town, to the delight of the French sentries on the Railway Bridge. Some indeed looked very dainty. Several discarded rough flannels for silk nightdresses near their skin. The din of our own guns just behind us and the screaming and bursting of occasional enemy shells were unnoticed at these 'afternoons'. Back at the Clearing Stations in Amiens and at the hospitals at Crouy and Abbeville, however, heaps of ladies' finery stained with Diggers blood told mute tales of the lighter side of the life at Villers Bretonneux and the simplicity of the Digger's fun. A few were buried in their finery with their uniforms alongside them.

From the 4th to the 9th the 13th remained as Support Bn. working mainly on Villers and Banana Switch Trenches. On the 10th they went back to Blangy for a bath and change of clothes before going into Reserve in the Bois l'Abbe and Aubigney Line, Hqrs. being for a time in the Chateau, and later in the railway cutting nearby. Our extreme right post was an International one, containing Diggers and French who agreed admirably.

On the night of 13th May we relieved the 51st and part of the 48th, sending "B" and "A" Coys. into the front line and "C" and "D" into close support. Our line was from the railway to the Peronne Road, and although now continuous, was practically where it was ten days before. Cpl. Chapman, D.C.M. (O.P.), was killed on the 14th. Our work this period was mainly digging deeper, wiring, carrying and patrolling, although a great amount of salvaging was done as well. The German shelling on several occasions during this period was terrific. Cpl. J. Watt received his M.M. for attention to wounded and stretcher-bearing during these barrages.

About midnight on 18th-19th we were relieved by the 16th Bn., going into Supports in and near Cachy Line, our right post again being an international one, containing French and Australians, the extreme right of the British Army. The Diggers loved the French bread which was a change from, although not as good as, our ordinary issue; and the French loved our cigarettes and tobacco.

There had always been a wonderful comaraderie between Australians and French civilians, but that between the soldiers of the two nations was far stronger. Each had much to learn, even in war matters, from the other. The French did not appear to do nearly as much trench digging as we, crowds of them lying out in small groups in shell-holes day after day. Their Support Line was a continuous trench like ours, but could not compare with ours or the British trench for tidiness or sanitation, a laissez-faire policy evidently being followed. Quite unlike the Australians their officers did not live the life of their men in the trenches and posts, far more responsibility being placed on the Sergeants.

On the 20th May, just before relief by the 42nd Bn., a Hun plane flew low over Villers Bretonneux flying British colors, and bombed and machine-gunned us before scurrying back to his own side, wounding Capt. T. A. White, O.C., of "B," and several men of the Brigade. That evening the Bn. moved back to Blangy-Tronville area as Reserves and bivouacked in the fields. The 21st was spent cleaning up (and swimming in the Somme). On the 22nd we were relieved by the 38th, and after a hot march reached Allonville where we spent a week of light training for Open Warfare combined with sport including four Cricket Matches. On Sunday, 26th, after a Brigade Church Parade, Birdwood presented medals and ribbons to 133 recipients in the Bde. Birdwood's address on this occasion was regarded as one of the finest ever made to the A.I.F. He bade us farewell after 3½ years in charge of us. Still, he added proudly, "The Commander in Chief has promised to let me have the Australians again." His address comes more within the province of an A.I.F. history than a Battalion's. Still every member of the 13th sincerely felt he was losing a personal friend. We agreed with him when he emphatically remarked, "The Australian soldiers have done more for Australia than all the politicians since Adam."

The 30th found a few officers and n.c.o.'s from each company back beyond Daours inspecting the area between there and Aubigny and Corbie where on the 31st, after a swim in the Somme, we relieved the 59th as Reserve Battalion. Here we remained supplying working parties of every description and enjoying daily swims and occasional fish meals from fish bombed although orders forbade such, until the 16th June, when, during the night, "A" and "C" took over the Front Line, "D" the Support, and "B" the close Reserve Line from the 14th Bn. Two shells had lobbed on the 14th back at Allonville, killing 18 and wounding 68, many of the latter dying.

We were now north of Villers Bretonneux in what was later part of Albury Line, and facing Vaire Wood with Hamel Wood behind it. Our Support was called Digger's Support. From the 17th to the night of the 26th we held this position, the companies changing over, our main worry being short shooting by our own artillery, which, however, luckily did little damage. Active patrolling was carried out, often in heavy fogs which lasted till after 8 a.m. In these fogs several interesting patrol encounters took place in one of which our bombers, after a long duel, silenced a machine gun. A great deal of enemy movement was constantly seen in and behind Vaire Wood our scouts observing while our artillery practised on these bodies. Capt. C. D'Arcy Irvine (O.P.), was killed and Lt. A. B. Lilley severely wounded, by our own men unfortunately, on the 20th. Both most splendid officers and most popular, they had gone forward in bright daylight to examine the Quarry without informing "A" Company. The latter, seeing movement in the tall grass out near where they knew the enemy to be, naturally fired, with such distressing results. D'Arcy had been promoted from the ranks for brilliant service in Gallipoli and France. Sgt. W. Noble, remarking "I can't see my officers lying out there," climbed out of the trench and most gallantly advanced. Noble by nature as by name. However, our bearers reached there first.

Morn of the 27th found us back near Aubigny after a night march across fields to Fouilloy and along the Canal to our cookers. On this march we had heavy casualties, one shell almost annihilating a platoon.

Here, as Reserve Bn., we had the unique experience of having 244 Americans, including 7 officers, attached to us. Several Americans had been with us for short periods previously for experience, and we had met many attached to the French near us at Villers Bretonneux, on all occasions forming very high opinions of them for their keenness and manliness; but now we had them living with us with the result that our appreciation of them increased. Before the attachment of this large body small preliminary parties were sent, each for a few days' line work, the notice arriving with each party being somewhat as follows:—

Fourth Brigade Hqrs., 20th June, 1918.

C.O., 13th Bn.

Herewith personnel of 33rd American Division who will be attached to you for a tour of duty in the line for a period of 4 days. Please afford them every facility for obtaining as much experience as the brief time of their attachment will allow. A short report on each officer and Nco. should be forwarded to Bde. Hqrs.

Signed:— Bde. Mjr.

All knew that our period in the line near Vaire Wood was only preliminary to a big stunt in that area, for not only had we improved communications more than usually, but every possible officer and Nco. had been in our Observation Posts and on patrol. Moreover we had not done as much wiring as usual. The attachment of the Americans made all guess that the stunt was near at hand. Still we went on with our Cricket Competition, the nucleus of the Bn. supplying the team while we were in the line. New South Wales will not be ashamed of the record of its Fighting Battalion at cricket, the competition being won by the 13th with 8 victories in 9 matches to its credit.

CRICKET MATCHES PLAYED BY THE 13TH BN., JUNE 1918.

Date	Versus	Won by
9	14th Bn.	13th
11	4th Div. Hqrs.	4D. Hq.
13	4th Bde.	13th
15	4th M. G. Bn.	13th
17	16th Bn.	13th
19	3rd D.A.C.	13th
22	16th Bn.	13th
26	3rd D.A.C.	13th
28	4th Bde.	13th

Before dealing with the Battle of Hamel the reader may be interested in some other aspects of the 13th's efficiency.

Chapter XXVII.—Efficiency.

THE 13th was not merely a Battalion of splendid fighters, but a unit of the highest efficiency in all things pertaining to the welfare of the A.I.F. and the British and Allied Nations. Such should be apparent from the following pages although details covering long periods are not given on account of the monotony of long lists, typical short periods merely being dealt with.

The wastage of war was indeed stupendous, and all were urged to do their utmost not only to prevent it but to collect material that could be re-used in the manufacture of munitions or equipment. Special Salvage Units cleared up Back Areas but, especially during the period of trench warfare, much material would have sunk into the mud or rusted hopelessly but for the salvage work or Line Battalions. In the fortnight from the 19th February to 5th March, 1918, during its stay in the Hollebeke Area, the 13th salvaged list was as follows:

Bayonets, 46; Brass parts, ¼ ton; Bombs, 24 boxes; Box Respirators, 18; Mule Shell-carriers, 18; Howitzer brass shell-cases 1368, weighing nearly 2 tons; Eighteen-pounder brass shell-cases, 1910; Camp-kettles, 2; Oakum, 42lbs; Rifles, 78; German rifles, 8; Gun Lanyards, 8; Rubber, 56lbs; Steel Helmets, 13; Rifle Ammunition, 32,500 rounds; Ammunition Chargers, 3210; Bandoliers, 150; German Bandoliers, 200; Ammunition Boxes, 12; Broken Sets of Webb-equipment, 250; Rum-jars, 24; Picks, 2; Pick-handles, 130; Lewis-gun Panniers, 63; Pannier Carriers, 8; Large Casks, 5; Lead, 4 cwts; Cable-drums, 2; Telephone wire, 2 reels; Underpants, 2 pairs; Ramrods, 2; Recoil Springs, 2; Fire-extinguisher, Gun-sight, Ladder, Pump and Hose; Swingle-bars, 2; Wire-cutters, 2; Gun-mat, Horse-rug, Saw, Machine-gun Stand, box and belt; Large Thermos; Small parts, 15 cwt.

The above was salvaged while the Battalion not only held the line, but strengthened it by digging, carrying and wiring. Every man returning from the front line or supports seemed naturally to look for something valuable to carry back to the Salvage Dump.

In addition to a list corresponding to the above the 13th sent back, during April and May, from Villers Bretonneux, the following which went to the French:—Cardigans, 384 complete; 23 dozen woollen bodies and 144 sleeves; Reels of Sewing Cotton, 16 gross; Lining, 20 large rolls; Hessian, 78 rolls; String, 170 balls; Wool, 5 tons; Wire-netting, 26 rolls; Wire, 12 coils; and several tons of machinery.

The following Works Report for the week from the 19th to 26th February, 1918, one of the weeks included in the above Salvage List, gives some idea of the activity of the Battalion in addition to the work and salvaging already mentioned. Be it remembered also that of the 460 men in the Line, after allowing for men on Outpost Duty or on the Special Raiding and Patrolling Party, and for Runners and Stretcher-bearers, less than 300 were available for manning' the Support Line, ration carrying, anti-gas work and other permanent fatigues, leaving the following list for about 100 men.

Front Line:—Wiring:—130 yards Double-Apron Barbed-wire interlaced with French Concertina wire; 50 yards wire thickened with barbed; 40 yards interlaced with French wire; 100 yards Double-apron interlaced with French wire; all posts drained; all gaps in wire repaired.

Support:—Wiring:—600 yards D.A. wire; Draining:—8 men, permanently; Revetting, 120 yards parapets with sandbags and 30 yards with sandbags and frames; Duckboarding, 2 men continuously; Digging, 30 yards new trench, 4ft. 6in. deep and same width at bottom; 12 "A" frames placed in positon, 2 new shelters made, and all work camouflaged.

Reserve Line:—10 new bunks constructed and 10 repaired; 2 men daily repairing duckboards.

Communication:—100 yards Duckboards laid; 200 yards of Hand-railing erected; 2 men daily repairing duckboards.

General:—1 officer and 15 men made Signal Dugout, 15 ft. by 30; with roof of iron girders, wood, paving stones and earth all material being found and carried by the party; 1 officer and 10 men working with Canadian Tunnellers; 1 officer and 30 constantly carrying supplies.

So, being "In the Line" did not mean simply sitting and watching for the Germans.

Now, men fighting and working like these require food, munitions, material, tools and many other supplies. The 13th could never blame their Quartermaster's Section or their Transport if supplies failed, and all generally and generously recognised this. Not only did they get the stores forward but they got all the salvage mentioned back to Brigade or Divisional dumps. An idea of the work of the QM. people may be got from the following typical report. "During June the following rations were drawn from A.S.C., split up, bagged and carried by First Line Transport to the Forward Area:—

Fresh meat, 10,500 lbs; Meat and Vegetable Ration, 3150 lbs; Tea, 656 lbs; Sugar, 3937 lbs; Milk, 1313 lbs; Cheese, 1800 lbs; Jam, 2102 lbs; Bread, 15.600 lbs; Butter, 1137 lbs; Biscuits, 1500 lbs; Cigarettes, 9600 pkts; Tobacco, 120 lbs; Matches, 2800 boxes; Dried Vegetables, 150 lbs; Potatoes, 2400 lbs; Onions, 700 lbs; Sauce and Pickles, 125 lbs; Salt, 112 lbs; Mustard, 12 lbs; Pepper, 4 lbs; Dried Fruits, 525 lbs; Pea-soup Powder, 60 lbs; Oxo, 80 lbs; Bacon, 2625 lbs; Candles, 450 lbs; Rice, 600 lbs Flour, 200 lbs; Oatmeal, 600 lbs; Kerosene, 50 gals; Lime Juice, 50 gals; Water, 6,000 gals; Creosote, 10 gals; Chloride of Lime, 224 lbs.

Also comforts as follows:—Oatmeal, 7 bags; Sugar, 1 bag; Milk, 3 cases; Coffee and milk, 17 cases; Tommy Cookers, 4 cases; Cards, 40 pkts; Chocolates, 2 cases; Tobacco, 1 case; Cigarettes, 1 case.

The above refers only to rations and takes no account of the far greater supplies of war material. In addition, the QM. section sent back to Railhead during this period the following by-products and scraps collected in the camps:—Dripping, 1040 lbs; Paper, 113 lbs; Cardboard, (cigarette boxes, etc.), 3065 lbs; Pulp, 20 lbs. It will be seen that Capt. Plucknett, our very efficient QM., and his efficient staff, were kept busy.

Plucknett, an O.P. of the 13th, had been promoted for consistently good work. He often went with the supplies right to the Outposts to ensure their safe arrival. For his splendid services and gallantry he had already received a Serbian decoration and mention, and, after the 8th August he received his M.C. His R.Q.M.S., B. Hobson (O.P.), was a great help to him and deservedly received his M.S.M. later.

Our Transport also shared in the Battalion's efficiency, its work being almost as arduous and risky as that of the ordinary Digger. Before his promotion to command of a Platoon, Lt. J. Geary, "Old John," as he was popularly called, had managed our Transport very efficiently throughout those most trying days of 1916 and 1917 on the Western Front. "John" was our original Transport Sgt. and had been promoted for conscientious work throughout long and trying periods. As a Platoon Commander his conscientiousness won him the admiration of his men and superiors. At Hebuterne, after a long period of inclement weather and severe shelling, he was relieved from the most advanced outpost, where, with five men, he had remained in the open sap day after day. After reporting to Capt. McKillop at Coy. Hqrs. and drinking some hot tea, John commenced putting on his equipment again. "Aren't you going to have a sleep, John?" asked Mac. "No, I think I'll go out and stay with Merifield; it's awfully lonely out there," replied John in his slow heavy manner, as he pulled himself up the steps on his way back to his old post. Just after gaining his Captaincy, the height of his military ambition, John went west at the Battle of the 8th August.

Our next Transport Officer was Lt. H. J. Henry, from the 12th A.S.C. whence he came with an excellent record, which he upheld with the 13th. His successor towards the end of the war, was Lt. Keeler, M.M., (O.P.), promoted for consistently conscientious work.

Practically during every period the Bn. was in the Line in France and Belgium, the Transport men had to bring laden mules up to dumps well within bullet range of the enemy and to accompany their stolid animals through shell-swept areas while all others took to shell-holes or trenches. Night after night, below Messines, they unloaded rations and munitions, and loaded salvage under a spiteful machine gun barrage, and similar work was as gallantly performed over and over again on all parts of the Western Front on which the 13th served, their casualties proving the danger of their work. In Corbie Area, in June 1918, while the 13th was Support Bn., and engaged in digging and wiring night and day, they were repeatedly bombarded, especially by gas-shells. During several severe outbursts the Diggers and wirers took to their trenches, but the Transport drivers had to stand by their mules and horses, to the great admiration of all.

Every member of the 13th remembers the Transport's mascot, the bantam rooster already mentioned.

The efficiency of Bn. Hqrs. was helped vastly by Sgts. Plasto, Strumey and Pickup, and our famous footballer, "Roger" Bradley, each in his own sphere. The three Sergeants received commission for long commendable service. Our very able, courteous and gallant Adjutant, Capt. A. W. Davis, was the best of examples for these Nco's. to follow.

In considering the efficiency of the Bn. one must take off his hat to the ladies of our Comforts Fund. Their work has already been mentioned, but chapters would not do it justice. The ladies must not judge our appreciation by the space—too limited—this book allows them.

At a meeting of the Queen Victoria Club in July, 1915, it was decided to establish a Comforts Fund for the 13th. Mrs J. Kell was appointed Hon. Sec., Mrs. A. J. Brierley, Hon. Treas., and Mrs. T. Henley, Pres. Mr. A. J. Brierley gave the first donation, Mr. Lysaght the free use of a room in Atlas Building for a depot and work-room. Lady Henley held the position of Pres. throughout the war, her office being filled during her absence in Egypt and England with her husband by Mesdames Fox and L. Pattrick, Acting Presidents. In September, Mrs. Kell's health failed—all the committee had anxieties because of their nearest and dearest being on active service—and Mrs. F. Laseron became Hon. Sec. retaining that strenuous position "for the duration".

January, 1916, found the Committee installed in Manning Chambers the room being lent rent free by the City Council. Mrs. H. L. McDonald now became Hon Treas., remaining so also "for the duration." Real hard and constant work was now the order of each day for these energetic women. Materials and money had to be obtained. Entertainments, gift-afternoons, competitions; sales of cakes, fruit, jams, anything at all donated; raffles, bazaars, etc., were held constantly. Buying, sewing, knitting, packing, collecting and writing were always going on too, still these ladies shared in a refreshment tent at the Sydney Show, and organised an "Old Clothes" Business in Paddy's Markets, the latter especially bringing in a big sum. It was indeed hard and trying work, but our women folk were as brave and splendid as the best of our men. It was Mrs. Stephens, the mother of two gallant 13th sons, who suggested this "Old Clo." Business.

When the 45th was formed the work was doubled, the cases and money sent away being halved between the two Bns. Misses E. Hobbes and N. Pearce assisted Mrs. Laseron in her arduous, yet happy, duties. The names of the many other devoted women are to be found in the Committee's records.

During 1916 the Committee raised £1009 and sent to the 13th the following:—

814 Shirts
846 Pairs Socks.
86 Balaclavas.
73 Scarves.
124 Pairs Mittens.
51 Handkerchiefs.
1203 Tins Fruit.
483 Tins Cocoa and Milk.
298 Tins Sardines.
37 lbs. Tobacco.
2090 Tins Cigarettes
10 Gross Chewing Gum.
86 Bags Nuts.
1102 Plum Puddings.
984 Xmas Boxes.
12 Tins Honey.
129 Tins Curry Powder
517 Private Parcels.
98 Pairs Underpants.
1 Case Sheepskin Vests.
60 Boxes Soap.
150 Fly Veils
54 Washers.
12 Pairs Kneecaps.

Mr. Foote was specially thanked for packing these goods and other valuable assistance. The 45th received a proportionate list.

In 1917 £1550 was raised and the following list sent between the two battalions:—

From Sydney:—1270 flannel shirts, 1728 tins of sweets, 1920 pairs of socks, 1728 tins meat paste, 660 balaclavas, 864 tins cheese, 1800 Xmas parcels, etc., etc.

From London, with money cabled to Sir. T. Henley, who worked untiringly for our Bns. among others:— 65 cases of cocoa and milk, and £300 worth of Tommy Cookers, primus stoves, sport material, etc., etc.

In 1918 £2300 was raised, including £1300 from the "Old Clo." Stall, and £363 from Show refreshments. In addition to a list of comforts similar to the above £900 was cabled to London.

After the Armistice the Committee donated £600 to the Voluntary Workers for the erection of two cottages at Matraville, one for a 13th man and family, the other for a widow of a 45th man.

The above is a mere—far too mere—sketch The husbands, sons and lovers of such women could not help making splendid battalions.

Chapter XXVIII.—Battle of Hamel, 4th July, 1918.

JULY 1st found the 13th bivouacked in the Somme Bank near Corbie, overhauling equipment and replacing shortages. Supplies were more plentiful than at any other time in our history, and the equipment was soon perfect to the last button. About 200 of the Bn. had been taken during the past three days back to the snug little village of Vaux, a few miles N.W. of Amiens to take part in tank demonstrations which were some of the most interesting and enjoyable demonstrations ever attended. Diggers and Tankmen were soon great pals and also treated their tanks as such, the monsters being given petnames, addressed kindly, admired loudly and, when occasionally scolded, scolded as one would scold a faithful dog. The Diggers climbed all over them, inside and out, rode across trenches and over walls and banks, and even drove them.

"They'll do us," was the general opinion. What a change to the feelings about the tanks of Bullecourt when the very name was anathema! But these Mark 5 Tanks were really marvels and a great advance on the clumsy, imperfect and more weighty monsters of 1917, which took four men to drive instead of the one in the Mark 5. They were now going to be used for the first time in battle and we were to have the honor of trying them out. Dummy machine-gun posts were quickly seen and dealt with by the crews as they lolloped over the fields of Vaux. "This is how we squash Jerry and his gun", proudly remarked a driver as his tank pirouetted on top on one of these positions.

All remarked the tremendous improvement in the morale of the tankmen since Bullecourt, the crews themselves feeling that they had in the minds of the 4th Div., something to wipe out; and they were proud of the prestige they could see they had gained already. We knew that they would be on their mettle to uphold this inthe real thing.

On the 30th June the Tank officers detailed to work with the 13th visited us to get to know those with whom they were to co-operate. Our Battalion was now a most interesting one, containing Americans, Tankmen, a few liaison officers and Nco's from Artillery and Engineer units as well as the Diggers.

On the 2nd July the Americans were astounded to hear rumors of their withdrawal before the battle. Indeed three companies were withdrawn from the Brigade that day, loud in their disgust and indignation, but our Commanders opposed the withdrawal of the remainder, as such would have seriously affected plans already formed. Had all been withdrawn at this last moment there would certainly have been chaffing on the part of the Diggers, which may have caused a little ill-feeling. Fortunately, both for the goodwill already established between the two nations and for the friendship soon to be cemented by blood, the remaining companies were allowed to remain.

[General Monash, we believe, told G.H.Q. that if any more Americans who were committed to the battle were taken away, he would cancel the whole plan. Perhaps it was carefully arranged by a smart Staff Officer, but it is said that no further orders on the subject reached the General until after the battle started.]

[Mr. Hughes, Sir. J. Cook and General Birdwood visited the Brigade on the 2nd.]

Final details were settled at a conference at Battalion Headquarters on the 2nd. This was attended by all 13th officers and officers of American, Tank, Machine-gun, Trench-mortar, and Engineer units co-operating with us. Even many of the officers learnt for the first time at this conference what the stunt was going to be. Some had a fair idea, but there had been the greatest secrecy in all matters pertaining to it. Any operation to be successful with the smallest possible loss to ourselves must be a complete surprise to the enemy, and so, during the past few days, no movement of troops, transport or guns had been allowed during the day, and every new gun was carefully camouflaged and ordered to remain silent until the hour of battle. Men moving towards the threatened front were told that a big German attack was expected and that they were moving to resist it.

On the night of the 2nd three platoons of "D" and all "A" relieved part of the 50th Battalion, "D" going into the front line between Pioneer Switch and our Right Divisional Boundary, and "A" dividing its platoons between the support and reserve lines behind "D" and between the same flanks. Sgt. Merriel was killed. Both companies formed strong liaison parties on the right with the 21st Battalion. The other platoon of "D," under Lt. L. Player, was specially detailed as an Engineer Platoon for the construction of strong points for which they had had a special course.

BATTLE OF HAMEL

At 6 p.m. on 3rd Col. Marks learnt that zero was to be at 3.10 a.m. the next day. He had already moved his Headquarters well forward and had arranged all details so perfectly that everyone felt confident. All had felt for some time that the Colonel, though youthful, was a veteran as a Commander, not only in action, but also in matters of detail preparatory to action, and this battle was to enhance his reputation, especially among his own men. During the past month he had, as a Birthday Honor, received his D.S.O., and well-merited had it been, not only for his work at Hebuterne and Villers Bretonneux, but also for splendid work for at least a year prior to Hebuterne as Commander and Second-in-Command. His officers especially admired him for, among many other sterling qualities, his quick decision and his constant determination to have accuracy in all details affecting the safety of his Battalion, even when such meant personal visits to dangerous outposts and wire belts night after night. This feeling had its effect on the high morale of the Battalion which, despite the recent loss of so many of its experienced Company Commanders, was now as high as ever before.

At midnight "A" (Capt. Marper) moved into the Front Line alongside "D" (Capt. Geary) and both Coys. were soon ready to move out onto the tapes already stretching along their fronts on which they were to be lined up before Zero. At 1.45 a.m. (4th) "C" (Capt. McKillop) and "B" (Lt. Merifield) arrived in that order at the junction of Pioneer Switch and Reserve Line and were led by guides to their Jump-off positions; and at the same time "D" commenced filing out onto their tape in No Man's Land. The Battalion was quite familiar with the area between the Front Line and the tapes, for not only had they patrolled it during their previous stay in this area, but that very night they had pulled down and rolled up 250 yards of double apron wire and 400 yards of double-trip wire in order to clear their front and also to allow the tape to be laid straight. Other tapes for the alignment of rear platoons had already been laid.

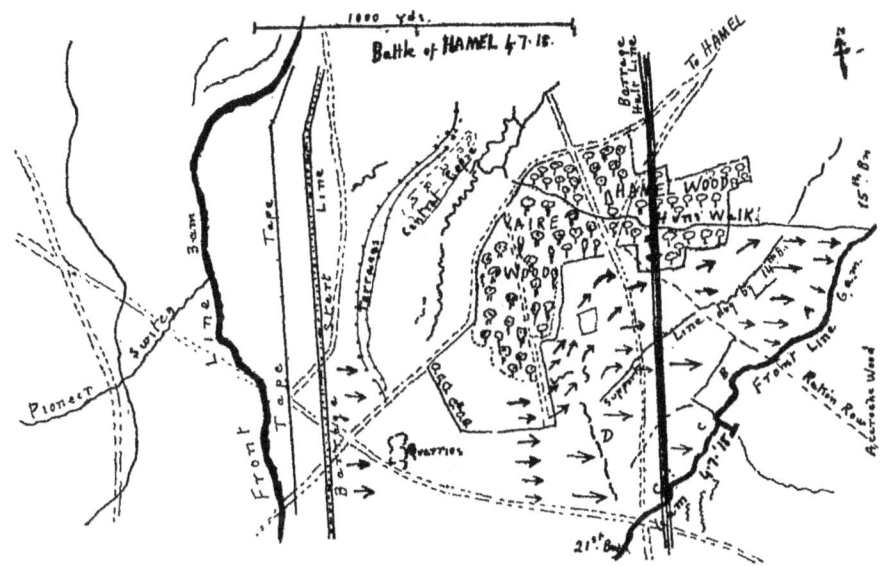

At 2.15 a.m. all Companies and attached details were in position, and the tanks were drawn up at their start point in rear of Support Line just north of Pioneer Switch. The din they had made moving up from Hamelet, where they had been hidden in ruined houses, was drowned by the harassing artillery fire and the whirring and droning of our aeroplanes flying low up and down the front, which firing and flying had gone on nightly for the past week.

At 3.2 a.m. the usual morning heavy fire was opened on the enemy and smoke-shells were again used with the heavy stuff in order to lead Fritz to put on his gas-helmets. We had been sending gas over mixed with smoke many times lately in order to lead him to believe that "where there was smoke there was gas." But no gas went over this morning for our own men were going into the area. Still Fritz got the "wind up," put his masks on and thus inconvenienced himself considerably.

During the 8 minutes between 3.2 and 3.10 the tanks were hastening forward the thousand yards to get in line with the Infantry.

At 3.10 the real battle opened with a crash that made the previous firing seen nothing. Our 326 field guns and our 302 heavies, as well as 111 Vickers machineguns, swept and dug into the enemy across the 6,000 yards of the attack front, while our aeroplanes dropped 1,100 25-lb. bombs and 58 1-cwt. bombs in the same area. The field-guns barrage, consisting of 60 per cent. of 18-pounder shrapnel, 30 per cent. of high explosive with delay action fuse, and 10 per cent. smoke was placed for four minutes 200 yards ahead of our tape; while the heavies commenced work 200 yards farther ahead and also dealt with every known enemy gun and strong point.

Immediately the barrage opened the men of "D" crept forward to within 60 yards of it and lay down, the rear companies also moving forward a little, our four waves being close together in order to get quickly through the area likely to be swept by the enemy S.O.S. barrage. A few German S.O.S. signals did go up, but their response was rather weak for a while. At 3.14 the tanks reached the waiting infantry, the barrage lifted and crept forward, and all advanced into the smoke and dust and ground mist. The nearest enemy posts were quickly captured and within a few minutes prisoners were streaming back. The barrage advanced at the rate of 100 yards in 3 minutes, rather slow for the eager infantry. At 3.37 Marks received a telephone mesage from our advanced Battalion Headquarters that they were established in the Quarry and that everything seemed to be going well. Our Signallers were as usual well up with the infantry.

After advancing nearly a thousand yards the barrage halted for 10 minutes in order to give Capt. Marper and his "A" Coy. time to make a double wheel round the south of Vaire Wood and to line up behind the stationary barrage in line with the rest of the advance. A wheel in the heat of action is a risky movement, and can only safely be entrusted to first-class troops, but George and his "A" Coy. splendidly carried out a double wheel.

The Battalion had started the action on a limited front, only 400 yards across, having been ordered to skirt Vaire Wood on the south before increasing frontage to the 1,250 yards, the length of its objective, the 16th and 14th Battalions having the tasks of capturing and mopping-up Vaire and Hamel Woods, carrying supplies and digging and wiring supports for the new front line. The sketch shows the formation of the 13th at Zero, and the arrows show Marper's double wheel and shaking-out into line with "C" on his right, during the 10 minutes' barrage halt. It will also be seen that "C" had to pivot on its right near the Crossroads and swing its left forward considerably. "D" had an intermediate objective—a line on which they had to dig in at the south-east end of Vaire Wood—a position intended to become a support position to the Front Line. The tank on their right unfortunately received a direct hit from one of our 18-pounders, which killed our Scout, T. Parrish, who was guiding it from the conning tower, and put it out of action for the rest of the stunt. Parrish's brother had died of wounds the previous week. Without this tank, however, McKillop and Merifield gallantly led their companies forward, their Platoon Commanders, Lts. C. Kelaher, C. James, A. Turnbull, M.M., A. Hall, M.M., Markusson (U.S.A.), J. Buckle, Strumey, Squires (U.S.A.) and Hodge, supporting them magnificently. Lt. Hall was killed and Merifield and James wounded, but their N.c.o.'s carried on their good work. Not only did "C" soon dig in on their objective, but they raided several strong points still farther out, capturing many additional prisoners. They also set to work and wired their front with wire brought up on a tank. Altogether "C" had captured 80 prisoners, 2 minenwerfers and 10 machine-guns, and had counted 150 dead Germans on their front.

"D," having gallantly led the assault to its intermediate position, were digging in rapidly when Marper made his first wheel northwards towards Hamel Wood. So that the members of "D" could be recognised as the troops to be "leapfrogged," they had had their helmets streaked with red. The Yanks also had blue patches on their hats to distinguish them from the Company attached to the 15th Battalion.

In this northward move "A" soon came under a hail of bullets from an enemy strong point defended by determined men. Casualties came quickly, one whole section being wiped out in one sweep. Marper instantly rushed the position and shot three Huns with his revolver, his action being so rapid that he was there with the gun in his possession before several other eager men could have a say in the matter. Rapid action was necessary, for the barrage was halting for only 10 minutes. "A" was completing its second wheel, towards the east, when they suddenly found right in their near front, another enemy trench, so well camouflaged that it had not been seen by airmen or on photos. Two machine-guns in this trench, firing point-blank into "A" threatened to hold them back. Marper again immediately, quite regardless of himself, rushed across the swept area to attract the attention of a tank, and in doing so was severely wounded in the chest and arm. He remained to see the tank lumber over the top of the stubborn enemy and, spinning like a top, crush the guns and crews into nothing. Then, seeing the trench captured and his Company following the now moving barrage correctly, he handed over his command to Lt. "Tommy" Dwyer, who soon had the misfortune to lose two very gallant officers in Lts. G. Nugent, who was so severely wounded that he died shortly after, and R. Smith, M.M. "Tommy" himself was wounded (his fourth time), but, saying nothing about it, carried on as long as possible. (Received M.C.). Lt. McRae was the only "whole" officer left in "A" and came in for a great deal of responsibility, and shouldered it all magnificently. Marper most deservedly received his D.S.O. His career had been an extremely gallant one.

At 4.18 a.m. "A" reported on the final objective and in touch with the 15th Battalion on its left.

"B" had followed "A" and were not called on to fight until on the final objective, when two platoons were drawn in on "A's" right and joining with "C" The remaining platoons of "B" were drawn in later. The whole objective had been won and was being consolidated within 90 minutes. The 13th had captured 200 unwounded prisoners and many wounded, as well as 14 machine-guns and much other booty.

At 4.40 a.m., in answer to Klaxon horns from planes, ground-flares were lit along the new line. Shortly after, boxes of ammunition were dropped from aeroplanes onto or near white V's (Vickers) spread out on the ground. These heavy boxes descended slowly under their parachutes.

At 5.20 Marks reported to Brigade that he was connected safely with the 21st and 15th, and at 5.25 he was in telephone communication with all companies. Lt. G. Falkiner's Signallers had had another particularly heavy time, for, not only had shells cut their wires, but every time a tank had crossed them it had cut them in four places. Especially fine was the work of Signallers J. Harris, M.M., P. Turnbull and R. Kirkwood. Harris's mate being wounded, he himself ran over 500 yards of wire across an area constantly swept by snipers and shells, and kept this line in repair all day, setting an example of cheery duty that won the admiration of all who saw him. He worthily received a Bar to his M.M. Turnbull anl Kirkwood kept four lines in repair throughout the day, working cheerfully quite regardless of self, for which and previous distinguished work they now received M.M.'s.

In addition to the Signallers the Runners played their usual part in the work of communication. It is safe to say that anyman even chosen as a Runner in the 13th was a gallant and conscientious man, for otherwise he was not chosen. At Hamel the Runners all had a trying time and all did splendidly, but the work of Runners W. Tong and E. McLaughlin was selected as specially worthy and both received the M.M.

So splendid, without exception, were the N.c.o.'s this great day that one feels he must be unfair to some to mention any. Still heroes like Cpl. J. Lihou, M.M., and Sgt. W. G. Phillips, M.M., and C.S.M. J. Meek, who gained D.C.M.'s for battle, and Cpl. R. E. Sullivan, who gained a Bar to his M.M., Sgts. F. Drake, E. Stanford, F. Higham, L. Canning and A. Settle, Cpls. M. Roach, S. Jarrett, A. McLaren, E. Curley, H. Conway, R. Carroll and J. Walsh and Ptes. G. Smith, W. Jones, W. J. Jones, G. Rowe, C. Partridge and T. Henderson were seen to do such conspicuous work that their names must be recorded, although there must have been a hundred similar acts of gallantry unseen. Lihou was especially clever in firing his Lewis-gun from his hip as he advanced, being one of the pioneers in this, his example being followed in later stunts with great success. His cheerful, careless gallantry was such that he was regarded as a certainty for a V.C. had he been spared. The one disappointing thing in the history of the 13th is the fact that gallantry resulting in immediate death was generally omitted from the Recommendation Lists after actions. Whether this was from the desire to have living decorated men in the Battalion, or whether there were so many splendid living men in the Battalion for the few decorations allowed by higher authorities that those gone west had to be omitted, writer is not prepared to say. But every dinkum 13th man can name scores of dead heroes whose evergreen memories are connected with V.C. deeds.

I

[There is a regulation that the one recommended must be alive at the date the recommendation is signed. The V.C. and Albert Medal are exceptions.]

Sgt. Phillip's special deed during the battle was the charging, at the head of three men, a stubborn machine-gun crew, and shooting five of them with his revolver and capturing their trench and several prisoners. In addition to his D.C.M., he worthily received his commission shortly afterwards. Cpl. Sullivan had also done a similar thing. Cpl. Roach gave his life to save an American platoon that, having lost its officers, was advancing through our own barrage. Roach, seeing their danger, due to inexperience, gallantly ran through the hail of shells and turned them back, but died next day as a result of the wounds received in the barrage. Roach, with other V.C. deeds to his credit, remains one of the undecorated heroes of the 13th. Sgt. Drake, who had assumed command of a platoon of Americans on the fall of its officer, also found them far too eager to get forward and had the greatest difficulty in keeping them out of the barrage, frequently risking his life in heading them back. He later on used their eagerness in leading them out to raid two enemy posts 200 yards beyond the Objective. Although but a L.-Cpl., McLaren, seeing that a platoon of Americans had lost its leaders, and was confused as to its movements, gave his Lewis-gun to his No. 2, and took charge of the Americans, led them to their proper objective, superintended their digging-in and then calmly returned to his gun. The other N.c.o.'s mentioned all performed sterling acts of leadership, both of Diggers and Yanks, several other brave but inexperienced parties of the latter having been wiped out but for the impromptu Digger leaders. James, Rowe, Partridge, Henderson and Jones are mentioned because of their splendid work as Stretcher-bearers, crossing swept areas repeatedly and attending the wounded even in No Man's Land. Sgt. Lewis (O.P.), ever reliable, and R. Lecder (O.P.) were among the killed.

Just after we settled down a German counter-attack developed along the sap between "B" and "C" and resulted in several more prisoners falling into our hands.

The most up-to-date battle ever fought was over, and the Diggers and Yanks had been successful along on the whole battle front, having captured Hamel village and Hamel and Vaire Woods, which three places had threatened to become second Pozieres.

The news created a wonderful revival of morale throughout the Allied Armies and soon the Huns were being pushed all along their front.

The Hamel Ridge was a valuable observational and manoeuvring advantage to us, for it allowed us to see enemy movements in the valley beyond, and prevented our troops being cramped on the east of the Daours Bend of the Somme as they had been.

The battle created a bond of friendship and sincere respect between Diggers and Yanks that should last for ever.

Of 227 Americans attached to the 13th for the battle, 57 were killed or wounded, including four of their five officers, which losses would have been much heavier but for the general guardianship of them by the Diggers. Our losses were 126 out of 510 engaged. When they said good-bye to us on the night of the 5th we really felt like losing old comrades. The 90 minutes had made them soldiers more than all their previous training. "You fellows have shown us how to deliver the goods all right," and similar expressions were frequently heard from them, and they spoke sincerely. And they were indeed fortunate to have such concerned advisers during such a time. Battalions of their countrymen near Reims attempted far less and were annihilated. In our friends those 90 minutes had changed parvenu seriousness into veteran sang-froid.

We had expected them to be anti-English, but to our agreeable surprise they were generally lavish in their praise of England, her people, scenery and interesting places. They knew a good deal of British politics and spoke familiarly of Lloyd George. Their broad nasalisms were not as general as we had expected, rather to our disappointment. Still a few came up to our expectations. "If we could only get some of those old *carstles* over to the States I guess they'd soon pay for their transportation," one remarked to the writer. And the following yarn is vouched for as true:

"I guess we're shark troops now," one of a party of Yanks visiting us after Hamel remarked.

Thinking he was referring to collecting souvenirs from Fritzs, and not being willing to take second or even equal place with anyone at that, our "Souvenir King" took out a heap of

German watches, marks, photos, soldbuchs, feldpostbriefs, revolvers and daggers, and proudly retorted, "You'll have to be Some Shark troops to beat that little heap, I guess, Guy."

"I wasn't referring to souvenirs, Aussie. I said I guess after that battle we'll be regarded as shark troops like you Australians. Shark Troops—SHARK troops, like you. S-H-O-C-K—shark; t-r- double-o-p-s—troops." The Digger's perplexed look vanished.

On the 6th "C's" patrols captured three more prisoners. Our area was also heavily shelled with gas, "D" Coy. suffering severely. That night we were relieved by the 16th Battalion and moved back into reserve bivouacs.

Some statistics of the Battle of Hamel may be interesting. The 147 machine-guns used 427,000 rounds of S.A.A. Extra shells from 13-pounder to 6-inch, 200,000 approximately. Each fighting tank carried Lewis gun ammunition and water; each supply tank, 12,500 lbs. (equal to 300 men) of barked wire, pickets, corrugated iron, bombs, S.A.A. and 100 gals. water.

Total prisoners were 41 officers and 1,431 other ranks.

That grand old man of France, Monsieur Clemenceau, hastened to visit the Division to thank the Australians for their work. On the 7th July he addressed a large assemblage of those who had fought at Hamel. He concluded with: "I shall go back to-morrow and say to my countrymen: 'I have seen the Australians; I have looked into their eyes, I know that they, men who have fought great battles in the cause of freedom, will fight on alongside us, till the freedom for which we are fighting is guaranteed for us and our children.' "

Sheafs of congratulatory telegrams from distinguished men far and wide reached General Monash immediately after Hamel, but none affected the Diggers more than that old man's visit.

The Americans were loud in their praise of our help and courtesy to them, and also conveyed this feeling to us through the official channels. They also sent us gifts of cigarettes and tobacco later.

Chapter XXIX—A Happy Interlude.

THE 13th remained in close support in terraced bivouacs behind Hamel, suffering a few casualties and doing plenty of carrying, digging and salvaging, until the 11th July, when we moved back to the Querrieu area, where we spent one of the most enjoyable fortnights in our history. After bathing, changing and cleaning up generally, all engaged in sport of every kind—swimming, cricket, racing and athletic events—and every evening there was a concert. Company sports, inter-company cricket, battalion sports, brigade sports and a divisional race meeting, kept all sport organisers busy. All seemed to "let themselves go" this fortnight, from General to Digger, for the interlude was to be followed by big things.

On the 13th our Band returned from a tour which had taken them to Rouen and Dieppe. They were at their best both in looks and in form. The main fault we had to find in the Band was its excellence which resulted in its being taken away to represent the A.I.F. musically in other places. Although he had lost most of his band personnel on several occasions when shortage of men had resulted in their being taken in on line fatigues, Bandmaster Percy Copp, by training others, managed to keep up the reputation of the 13th Band as one of the best in the A.I.F.

In addition to the sports, lorries conveyed parties to spend a day in Abbeville or Doullens.

The 4th Brigade Sports on the 20th were the best ever held in the Brigade, the morning being occupied by aquatic events, the afternoon by athletic. Among the many sideshows was a splendid circus from the 7th A.A.S.C. A score of well-got-up fancy costumes added to the amusement, while a tote run by Capt. MacIntosh, of the 15th, and bookmakers created greater interest in the races. In the evening an American concert party gave a most enjoyable show in front of Querrieu Chateau.

The Divisional Race Meeting on the 22nd was one of the greatest sporting events held anywhere on Western Front during the war. Motor lorries of troops — Australian, American, French and Imperial—came from far and wide to Allonville. In addition to races there were sideshows and fancy costumes galore, and a tote. An enemy plane came over from behind the clouds during the afternoon and destroyed an observation balloon near the course.

Unfortunately a tragic event marred the total enjoyment of the day—two Divisional officers being killed in a race.

But sport could not last longer, and within the next few days advanced parties proceeded to the line South of Villers Bretonneux to arrange for taking over, and all went through the gas-chamber at Allonville to test their respirators.

On the night of the 27th the 16th Battalion had three killed and 12 wounded by an aeroplane bomb. Luckily we had escaped the showers of bombs that nightly had fallen around us.

On the 29th Colonel Marks went forward to inspect the position the Battalion was to occupy, and on 31st we relieved French Zouaves in support in Aquenne Wood, south-east of Villers Bretonneux, finding the Zouaves most punctilious in even the smallest details in the handing-over.

On the night of August 2nd we relieved the 24th Battalion in the Front Line in Monument Wood Sector, just south of Villers Bretonneux, rain falling heavily all night and making trenches most uncomfortable, in addition to which the enemy was very active with bullets and shells.

In this position our line faced south and cut through the Wood. Our stay here was short; still a policy of vigorous patrolling was carried out, as well as constant worrying of the enemy by machine- and Lewis- guns.

At 2.15 a.m. on the 5th August our relief by the 50th Battalion was complete, and the 13th moved north to billets and bivouacks in and around Vaire-Sous-Corbie. Something big was again being prepared for us.

Chapter XXX—Battle of August 8th, 1918.

THE fortnight's rest back near Querrieu had been so enjoyable that it seemed really more than a month since Hamel.

The big thing before us was already generally regarded as a success, although the enemy was much more active than just prior to Hamel. His shelling was at times terrific, and his long-range stuff searched all areas back as far as Amiens. His planes came over and "laid their eggs," too, every night, and even by day. In one of his "shell-strafes" on 6th we had 12 casualties, including Cpl. Hewett, among the 45 in the Brigade. Col. McSharry, the most popular Commander of the 15th, admired unanimously throughout the Brigade, was killed in this same strafe, which was part of a German offensive across the Somme in which they drove the Tommies back 2,000 yards.

Still arrangements went on for our attack. A company of 4th Pioneers, a section of 18-pounders from the A.F.A., two Vickers and crews, two Stokes mortars and crews, and two troopers from the 13th Regiment A.L.H. were attached to us. Three Mark 5 tanks each for the 13th, 14th and 15th Battalions, and three extra as Liaison tanks between the 13th and 14th joined the Brigade, and nine Mark 5 Star tanks were also to assist by carrying 10 Vickers of the 4th Division M.G.'s, and 16 Lewis-guns of the 16th Battalion, under Capt. Lynas. Our Tank Guides were Blaw, Penman and Sullivan, all splendid Scouts.

All preliminary arrangements were made with even greater secrecy than before Hamel, no advance bodies going up to the line to have a look over, the tanks and guns that came in gradually being carefully camouflaged, and no registering being allowed. Our own planes flew over each day to see that we were not moving about too much.

The battle was one of the big ones of the War, but, in a story such as this, one can deal with only a small part of it. Moving out from Vaire-Sous-Corbie at 2.45 a.m. on the 8th we were by 3.30 formed up with the 14th and 15th Battalions on the first forming up position (F.U.P.) just west and north-west of Hamel. The morning was very quiet and the weather promised to be fine. Harassing fire was going on, and giant planes were flying up and down the line as had been done every morning of late, in order to drown the roaring of approaching tanks. We felt confident that the enemy was going to be surprised, and events showed we were correct.

Zero was at 4.20 a.m., at which time the barrage opened. This time, however, we were back near the guns firing and not up against the bursting shells, for the 3rd Division formed the first wave in our area. At the first crash all held their hands to their ears, so deafening was the burst. We expected to be shelled heavily by counter-battery guns, but, luckily only a few stray shells lobbed near us, our losses being only four in this position. At 5.50 a.m., with all tanks in position in our rear, the Brigade moved forward in lines of small columns to its second F.U.P. This move was likely to have been much confused owing to a very dense fog thickened by smoke and dust to such an extent that vision beyond five yards was impossible, but all details had been so carefully arranged that very little readjustment was necessary. At 7.30 we again halted for 10 minutes in rear of the Green Line, the first objective, which had been captured by the 3rd Division. The 45th Battalion was on our right. During this advance, our Field Artillery, having quickly hooked up, passed through us as they hurried forward to occupy new positions just behind the Green Line, and crowds of intensely delighted prisoners came streaming back, openly marvelling at all they saw.

On the second F.U.P. we waited until 8.30 a.m., at which time the barrage which had been protecting the 3rd Division digging in, was lifted to allow us to leapfrog them and to proceed to the Second Objective, the Red Line, which stretched roughly south from between Morcourt and Mericourt.

There is nothing of individual importance to narrate before the crossing of the Green Line, for until then, the Battalion was simply a unit in a wide advance. After the crossing of the Green Line companies, platoons and sections became important units.

The 13th had the task of capturing the right of the 4th Brigade's Red Line, the 14th the centre, including Morcourt, and the 15th the left, including Cerisy. The slight opposition we met at first allowed us to hear the tremendous machine-gunning from Cerisy and Chipilly, and we felt sorry for the 15th, for the fog had now cleared. They would have had no more opposition than we, had the commanding Chipilly Spur been in the hands of the Third Corps of Imperial troops, as we had been assured it would be by 8.20 a.m. That Corps had, on the 6th. been driven back 1,000 yards on a frontage of 1,000 yards, losing an area just won by the 3rd A.I.F. Division. After repelling the Tommies to-day (8th August), the German gunners and machine-gunners slewed their guns round and dealt with the 4th Brigade and our tanks, knocking the latter out one after another by direct hits, easily obtained over open sights. However, the 15th captured Cerisy and 350 prisoners as well as other booty; and the 14th entered Morcourt from the south-west and north and captured 400 prisoners with much valuable booty.

On the 13th front there were three obvious enemy centres of resistance—the spur running north towards Cerisy, Morcourt Spur and Red Line Spur. When the fog lifted this undulat- country offered delightful scenery. The Somme Valley on the left with its canal, swamps and foliage, backed up by the Chipilly Ridge, and the waving crops on the ridges in our front formed a veritable picture.

We were soon sending crowds of prisoners back to the 3rd Division, as they had done to us during the first stage, our two Light Horsemen rounding them up and escorting the bigger batches, one of which numbered 387. Our runners also enjoyed the novelty of having messages back to Brigade Headquarters carried by these horsemen.

About 9 a.m. we commenced ascending the Morcourt Spur and came under direct fire from 16 field-guns on Chipilly Ridge and many machine-guns. Still all gallantly pushed forward, and by 9.50 we were ascending the Red Line Spur, Capt. Ken. Pattrick's dash, quick decision and gallantry at the head of his Company being specially encouraging to his command. Unfortunately he met his death soon after, being the second of two fine brothers to give his life on the Western Front, a third brother also serving with much distinction. Their mother was one of the most active of the splendid women who worked so untiringly for us during the whole of the war, and she and her gallant sons had, and will always have, a warm spot in the hearts of the 13th and 45th Battalions. Capt. Geary also fell about the same time.

The 14th had sent two companies to help the 15th and so required help from us. We sent "C" to take over part of their front on the near right of Morcourt. It was here that C.S.M. W. Oswald, M.M. (Jerry) did some splendid work for which, and previous distinguished service, he received his D.C.M. "Jerry" was in charge of a mopping-up party when he noticed the gap between the 13th and 14th, and, without waiting for orders, led his party into the space, silenced several enemy machine-guns, and linked the two battalions up again. Later, as his party was ascending Red Line Spur, they were subjected to a most galling shelling from Chipilly and naturally wavered, until Oswald led the way. His example was so inspiring that not only his party, but others on his flanks, rushed ahead. There was never a braver or harder-working N.c.o. in the 13th than "Jerry." A worthy namesake—Sgt. A. Oswald—was mortally wounded.

By 10 a.m. the 13th was consolidating its objective, "B" on the right and "D" on the left. The Pioneers, who had fought magnificently, although fighting was not their real work, were moved up to help "B" and "C." Capts. McKillop and Swinburne had treated the battle with such joyful coolness that they had infected their men, one and all, with their spirit. Never have men joked so and laughed so heartily throughout a long battle as did the 13th that great day.

Soon, however, our casualties came quickly, 57 falling within a few minutes on the objective. The "assured" field-guns on Chipilly ridge were still firing point-blank on us two hours after they were to have been captured. Our two mobile 18-pounders came into action against them at 10.15, but they were outnumbered. Still they drew a certain amount of fire from the men consolidating.

The 45th Bn., on the right, were still co-operating with us, their I.O., Lt. Love, being most gallant and active.

The 13th now had 700 prisoners to its credit, 400 having been taken from Dudgeon Wood Valley, in addition to four field-guns, 20 machine-guns, two mortars, 40 horses, a complete M.G. Coy. transport, and a wireless installation. Two machine-guns, hidden in Morgan Wood, fired onto our men digging on Red Line Spur. Lt. McGuire rushed into the wood, followed by two unknown men, and captured both guns and crews.

The Red Line being held, it was the task of the 16th, who had come up to beyond Morcourt in large tanks and scrambled out of them under heavy fire, to go through us and exploit the country ahead, which difficult and hazardous task they performed splendidly, but, at 2 p.m. they sent back an urgent request for relief. The 13th instantly responded, three companies, "C," "A," and "D," taking over, in that order from right to left, the right half of the 4th Brigade's final objective—the Blue Line.

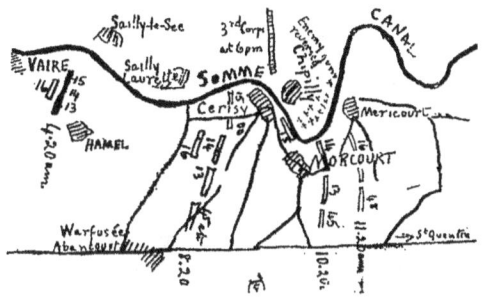

On the night of August 9th we again advanced, this time about 800 yards, without much opposition, right into the outskirts of Mericourt-Sur-Somme, which greatly improved the general position.

In all this great advance into the unknown, from the time we crossed the Green Line, our Scouts and Lewis-gunners were naturally the first to come onto the enemy or under their fire, and without exception, they were wonderful, over and over again rushing posts, or drawing enemy fire while their mates did so. The Lewisgunners generally fired from their hips as they rushed ahead without thinking of their safety in order to get better shots at runaway bodies of enemy, or at machine-guns holding up any part of the advance. Cpl. Gerald Sexton* saved many lives by the almost incredible, even uncanny, promptness and skill with which he used his Lewis-gun, quickly silencing enemy opposition on four occasions. While advancing through crops south of Morcourt a hidden gun fired into the Battalion and caused several casualties. Sexton stood up in full view of the enemy, calmly noted the position of the gun from the flashes, and still standing, fired a magazine at the flashes and put the gun out of action. He received his D.C.M. for the day's work. Pte. C. Finch vied with Sexton in this Lewis-gun work. Although the only one of his section left, he carried the gun and magazines—three men's load— to the final objective, on several occasions silencing enemy guns. During consolidation he saw an enemy machine-gun on our flank and engaged it. The enemy moved to a safer posi-

*Correct name was Maurice Buckley.

tion and fired at Finch, who, unable to get a good shot at them, rushed forward, killed two of the crew with a bomb and brought the remaining five back as prisoners carrying their own gun. He received his D.C.M. Pte. R. Sloan, without a Lewis-gun, charged a machine gun, terrified the crew into surrendering, and made them carry their own gun back. Cpl. Bourke, seeing a machine-gun enfilading us from the south of Morcourt rushed it, firing his Lewis-gun as he ran. He also, single-handed, killed or captured the whole crew. Cpl. A. Williams fought a duel with his Lewis-gun against an enemy machine-gun at short range. He rushed forward through their bullets, occupied a suitable position, and fired into the enemy. When we arrived there a few moments later we found that he had killed the crew of seven. Cpl. J. Banks and Pte. A. Peacock did equally gallant and effective work with Lewis-gun. These last named five received M.M.'s. Lt. L. Cleland, who had long been our very capable Lewis-gun Officer, although in charge of a platoon in this battle, personally used a Lewis-gun as courageously as the men he had trained. Les received his M.C. and his Captaincy shortly afterwards.

From the above list one can see how important was the Lewis-gun as a weapon for open warfare. Still there were many other deeds of heroism by others without these weapons. Lts. A. D. Turnbull, M.M., N. McGuire, M.M., and L. Player received well-won M.C.'s, and Sgts. E. Stanford and J. Prescott, M.M.'s for specially distinguished leadership qualities and gallantry during this and the following days in and near Morcourt.

A particularly splendid deed was that of Pte. W. Waite, whose three comrades had been killed by a Hun machine-gun. Waite crawled out to get a shot at the gun and had his left arm shattered. Still he advanced, crawling fifty yards farther until he gained a position whence he with his one arm engaged the enemy with such success that the gun was no more worry to us. Cpl. F. Burton was another to rush a machine-gun post singlehanded, killing two and capturing five and their gun. Cpl. J. Bashall showed great initiative and daring in connection with the trench mortars attached to us. Those in charge having been hit, Bashall, seeing the importance of the weapons, and instinctively knowing where the shells were required, took charge of the two and shelled several strong points. The lastnamed three received M.M.'s.

Stretcher-bearers J. Edmunds and G. Kelly and Signallers H. Sweet and A. Woods received well-earned M.M.'s also.

In such a battle the keeping up of hot meals was almost an impossibility, most units finding it so. Still, although the 13th had advanced eight miles that evening, owing to Sgt.-Cook A. Lowe's energy and determination, a hot meal was received in the front line soon after nightfall. Sgt. Lowe had done similarly splendid work on many previous occasions and had been wounded three times doing his duty well forward. He had still some splendid work to do before the war ended for which and previous work he received a Belgian C. de G. Of course our Transport and Q.M. section helped him considerably.

Our R.M.O. Major O'Riordan, received his M.C. for gallant and constantly efficient work in attending to our casualties well forward under heavy fire. Sgts. Lundie (O.P.), Curley, Webb, Jamieson and Langham, and Cpl. A. Wilson (O.P.) were mentioned for several distinguished actions as leaders. Lundie, Curley and Webb gave their lives, the remaining three were wounded.

On the night of the 10th we were relieved by the 11th Brigade, and, after a long and tiresome march during which, however, all sang heartily for hours, we crossed the Somme and bivouacked near Sailly Laurette. The men were in tremendous spirit, speaking volumes for the efficient working of all things connected with the battle and following period.

Our losses had been 2 Captains and 11 other ranks killed, and 61 other ranks wounded; sick or missing nil. Small losses indeed considering the gains, but our Army could ill afford to lose even a few such men.

Chapter XXXI.—The 23rd of August, 1918.

WE were not to remain long amid green trees and wrecked homes of Sailly Laurette, for, after two days' resting, swimming and cleaning-up in glorious sunshine that made all long still more for their own sunny land, we marched to the south-west of Harbonnieres, via Hamel, Lamotte-en-Santerre and Bayonvillers, a few long-range shells whining over us or ploughing into the road and fields nearby, one lobbing in a platoon of the 15th at Bayonvillers and killing 9 and wounding many. We bivouacked in and near the railway embankment in "possies" recently occupied by the Hun.

The next morning all Company Commanders, with their Scouts, went forward about six miles to make a reconnaissance of the trenches to be taken over from the 9th Battalion near Auger and Crepey Woods, being followed that evening by our advanced parties of an officer, three sergeants, Nos. 1 of Lewis-guns, and H.Q. Scouts. The next night, August 15th, the Battalion moved into the line, the relief of the 9th being complete by 11.25. "B" and "D" were in the Front Line, "C" in support and "A" in reserve, the 15th Battalion on our right, and the 14th on the left.

The 16th was a rough day for the rear areas, hurricanes of heavy stuff bursting repeatedly from reserves right back to Villers Bretonneux, the Front Line troops having a quiet time in spite of an advance of 500 yards along old trenches into a new system. We were following up our policy of keeping in touch with Fritz, and, after this advance our patrols, under Cpl. Blaw, pushed out another furlong, while our supports and reserves also moved forward. Our patrols found many signs of very recent enemy occupation. (Blaw received M.M.)

The 17th brought a tremendous concentration of enemy artillery of all sizes onto our front lines, special attention being paid to the Woods. It was a trying day, indeed, for it seemed that the enemy knew the exact positions of all our posts. Still, that evening, at dusk, we advanced another 600 yards by "peaceful penetration," "B" and "D" occupying Lihu Farm and Verger Trench without a casualty, the 15th and 14th also moving forward on our flanks. Our night patrols immediately pushed forward again, and, finding the trenches in our immediate front unoccupied, the Battalion once more went forward, occupying part of the old front line of 1916. The Brigade strengthened this part in order to give sufficient ground to hold the tactical features of Lihons in case of enemy attack on our thin line. That night our "C" cooker was smashed by a "5.9" and three wounded. C.S.M. Meek, D.C.M., one of our bravest—was killed.

Daybreak of the 19th brought another terrific barraging, so heavy that we prepared for an enemy attack; but he missed us to attack the 2nd Manchesters on our Brigade left, and got into their trenches, staying there until dislodged by the 14th Battalion. His terrific bombardment remained on us all the morning, and his planes came over by scores to bomb and machine gun us. (Capt. Rose, M.C., D.C.M., and Lt. E. Hall were among the wounded, the latter fatally. He had always been reliable and gallant). It really seemed that he was recommencing his big offensive. But he evidently had something else in view, for, on our officer's patrol pushing ahead, they found that he had just evacuated Satrape Alley. We again prepared to push on, but received orders to make no further offensive, but to begin strong defensive works. Our period of "peaceful nibbling" was at an end, and we had to sit, for this and the next two days quietly under his unmerciful shelling. These days he spared neither front nor rear, but poured H.E. and gas shells into us day and night. The weather had been very hot and dusty, the traffic having cut up the roads and fields. Gas-masks on top of this added to the discomfort.

We felt a little bit revenged, however, on the 21st, when news of great victories by the English on our left, and the French on our right, reached us. We also received orders to attack again on the 23rd, and, from the reports of our Scouts, expected a tough proposition. Then we learned that only "C" Coy. of the 13th was to be in it, the 4th Brigade being represented mainly by the 16th Battalion.

At 4.45 a.m. the barrage came down, and "C" went out under it on the right of the 16th. Great was the astonishment of all to find the Bosche fighting as gamely as at any period of the war, several severe hand-to-hand encounters taking place, and every foot of trench being stubbornly contested, but those Diggers who revelled in tough propositions were delighted, and the contempt they had recently begun to feel for Fritz changed to admiration.

For its 50 prisoners the Brigade had seldom had a harder fight, the Hun evidently being determined to prevent us reaching the Somme, which now ran behind him. It was in this fight that Lt. McCarthy, of the 16th, won his V.C., the winning of which forms one of the most wonderful stories of the war. We were a very tired battalion when, on the morning of the 24th, after a 10-mile walk, we embussed west of Harbonnieres for a rest back at familiar old Poulanville. The 15th Lancashire Fusiliers had relieved us.

It was during this period that Capt. McKillop's runner came in without him. "Where's Capt. Mac.?" the runner was asked.

"I asked him to let me come on ahead."

"Why?"

"He's been taking photos of shellbursts all the afternoon, and trying to get close ones. It was 'Come over here, Runner, where the big ones are lobbing,' or 'Wait a minute, they're coming closer,' for over an hour, so I thought I'd ask him to let me go."

Although all this period had been particularly heavy for runners and ration-carriers, the posts being so scattered and their positions being so often changed, not to mention the shelling and gas through which these men had to be continually passing, Cpl. S. Hensby did splendid work in charge of Front Line carrying parties. He had, on account of his gallant zeal, reliability and cheerfulness, long before deserved the M.M. he now received. Runners V. Graves, F. Good and B. Gough received M.M.'s not only for distinguished message work, but also for carrying supplies forward when returning to their companies. Several others were recommended for special gallantry, particularly in "C," but, as the one most distinguished in the Battle of the 23rd August Cpl. P. Bourke was awarded the M.M. After "C's" advance Bourke saw a large body of Germans coming down a sap to counter-attack. The position was critical. Without hesitation or waiting for orders, Bourke climbed out of his trench, called on his section to follow, which they did in face of machine-guns, and attacked the advancing enemy with bombs, driving them back with heavy losses, although they outnumbered his party by ten to one.

Since 19th August the 4th Brigade had been under the command of Lt.-Col. Drake-Brockman, of the 16th Battalion, General Brand having gone on a month's leave.

Chapter XXXII.—Battle of 18th September, 1918.

In order that a successful attack might be made on the farfamed Hindenburg Line it was necessary first to capture the tremendously strong lines of outposts in front of it—systems of trenches and belts of wires as well-placed and as strong as the Line itself, stretching out ahead for miles. The last great battle for the 13th was to be an attack on this system—a finale matching in tremendousness the Battalion's first feat of arms.

From the 24th August to the 7th September we remained at sleepy Poulanville, cleaning-up, resting, training and sporting, the 13th again holding its own, winning the Brigade Boxing Championship, the scores being:—13th 11 points; 15th 6 points; 14th, 16th, 4th F. Amb. and 4th F. Eng. 1 point each; our Boxers being Barham (Bantam), Haley and Austin (Featherweights), Haydon and Anderson (Lightweights), Hawkesworth (Welter) and Doody (Middle). Our phenomenal success in the boxing was mainly due to "Dad" Hart (who, although 60, was one of our best soldiers. For splendid line service "Dad" had received his M.M. He became very indignant when told he could stay out of the line because of his age, and insisted on doing his share. His was a powerful influence for good on the young men. "Dad" was appointed our trainer, and saw to it that his boxers trained properly and solidly.

After regular night bombing by the Hun planes our chief excitement was a fire, for which the owner of the place burnt claimed damages, but it was conclusively proved that the Diggers were in no way responsible.

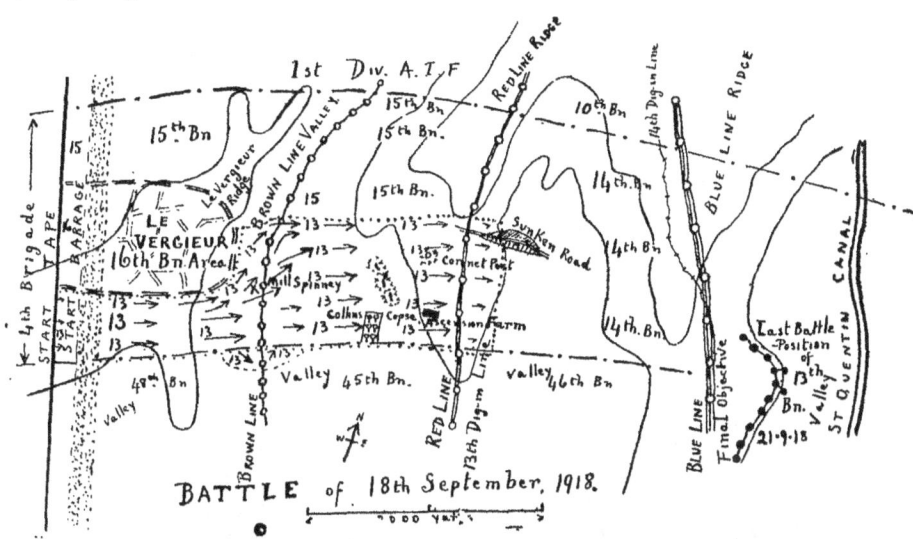

On the 7th our Transport moved to Morcourt, and the rest had baths and changes preparatory to moving the next day. An early reveille, a thorough cleaning-up of Poulanville and a march to the 'buses on the Coissy-Allonville Road, occupied till 9.30, when we were carried through Allonville and up the beautiful Somme Valley again to Biaches, where we arrived at 3 p.m. bivouacking in terraces near the Canal within a short distance of Peronne, the "bivies" of sheets of iron and small canvases soon becoming uncomfortable in the rain. Baths and changes again on the 9th. On the 10th, in heavy rain we crossed the Somme at the south of Peronne and marched into Reserve Area near Mons-en-Chausee, whence we gradually moved forward until on the 14th, Marks received word at a Brigade conference that there was to be a big attack on the Hindenburg Line outposts. The 4th Division was to be represented by the 12th Brigade, on its right, and the 4th Brigade on its left; and the 1st Division was to be on the left of the 4th Brigade. Other British and French troops were also to co-operate. Part of the 4th Brigade Orders for the battle reads:—

"The 16th Battalion will capture and mop up Le Verguier, and the 13th (right) and 15th (left) passing on the flanks of the village, will capture the Brown Line and form up there for Phase 'B.' The 16th, after mopping-up village, will occupy Brown Line.

"(B) The 13th on the right, and the 15th on the left, jumping off from the Brown Line, will capture and consolidate the Red Line.

(C) The 14th Battalion, passing through the Red Line, will exploit the success with a view of establishing themselves on the Blue Line."

Three tanks only were allotted to the Brigade, but dummy-tanks were carried out and placed across the attack frontage to draw the enemy's fire. Four additional machine-guns and two light trench mortars were allotted to the Battalion to the Red Line, after which they were to go on with the 14th.

On the night of the 16th the 13th relieved the 49th in trenches east and west of Vendelles, and outposts were pushed out almost to Le Verguier. Colonel Marks held a conference with his Company Commanders, each of whom afterwards held one with his Platoon Commanders.

By midnight of the 17th/18th Lt. East and his Scouts had laid the tapes in the face of constant machine-gun fire. The wide white linen J.O. Tape stretched in a straight line across the front of the attack, about 150 yards behind our advanced posts which, accordingly, half-an-hour before Zero, were withdrawn to take their place on the tape.

The laying of this tape and others in rear for other platoons and for guidance of troops coming up, on such broken country, with all landmarks smashed beyond recognition, in darkness, was a fine performance. East and his Scouts had still more good work to do in the battle, helping to guide the First Wave to its position on the Brown Line. For this John was awarded his M.C.

At 4.30 a.m. all were in position on the tapes ready to attack They had for hours been thoroughly saturated, but now as they took their places another downpour occurred. All were carrying heavy loads, too, made heavier by the soaking, and every now and again someone would slip and fall heavily into the clay or old trench. He would curse, but would be asked if he didn't know there was a war on.

Some of these men had been stumbling under heavy loads going into battle at these uncanny hours, year after year, and carrying heavier loads of rations in between times to outposts, across seas of mud and liquid gas, through hellish tornadoes of shells and bullets, so that their cobbers, huddled up in muddy outposts, or standing shivering waistdeep in freezing slush, could get their hot drink of tea. They knew there was a war on, and said so most emphatically, especially if the questioner happened to be a new arrival. A few of the most splendid of these men of longest service had been getting Australian Leave each month lately and arrived in Australia to hear "stayat-home-patriots" discussing whether their comrades should have help or not. Whether hurt more by the insulting remarks of bigots who preferred alien flags to the one protecting them and the one the Diggers had been fighting under so long, or by the flap of windbag "loyalists," who were prepared to use the name of the Diggers for their own ends, is hard to say. They generally felt for both the contempt both deserved. Had these cancers left their warm bodies to stand even one night in a saturated uniform, waist-deep in slush, with sleet cutting into their gas-raw faces and making music on their steel helmets, they would probably have been less malignant on their return to their hosts, if, indeed unfortunately return had been their lot. Some Diggers returned mere ghosts of their pre-war healthy selves, their strong minds and bodies wrecked. "Weaverism" fortunately doesn't worry them; they have lost the power of appreciating such. They are not likely to hit back. But it does hurt those who went through the mill to have their weakened mates weavered by a healthy young "Too-Blanky Later." Some lay down in the rain; others stood up. It was a long lonely hour; not a word spoken above a whisper, no comforting fag or pipe; and the pelting rain.

'I can't get any wetter; so here goes!" mumbled one as he threw himself on the ground, cuddling his rifle, however, under his armpit to keep its mechanism dry; and many followed his example. A light strafe was going over from our guns to drown the noise of the very few tanks, but the one allotted to the 13th didn't arrive owing to the slippery ground—according to its commander—but, according to others, owing to funk on his part—a contrast to the tankmen of Hamel and 8th August. It seemed as if Zero would never arrive.

At 5.15 all stood up and faced enemywards, felt the pins of their bombs, and saw that their bayonets were firmly fixed. "One minute!" was soon whispered, and all put cigarettes into their mouths to light the next minute when lights would not matter. Those not clever enough to get a light from a match got one from their mates' cigarettes.

As the swishing and crashing of the barrage broke forth a line of dense smoke arose about 150 yards ahead from smoke shells. The machine-gun barrage fell about 150 yards ahead of the artillery and travelled accordingly. It seemed heavier than at any time previously, and was indeed so, for Monash on account of the scarcity of tanks, had sent many extra machine-guns to assist in the barrage. We always knew that he would do everything to save the lives of men. For three minutes the barrage remained stationary, and then lifted by stages every minute. Although generally regarded as splendidly accurate and intense, it was not so on the 13th front, for we were continually worried by "shorts" and, at every lift, when we ran to catch up with it again, some would not lift with the others. Lt. N. J. McGuire, M.C., M.M., proud in his first command of a Company, was killed by one of these "shorts" at Zero. He had joined the Battalion as a private early on Gallipoli.

The smoke-shelling was overdone and led to confusion, as it hid the bursting line of shells after each lift, and prevented men seeing more than a few yards. On several occasions parties were lost, and some advanced too far and had to bomb their way back.

The 13th again had a double change of direction to perform during battle, starting out on a frontage of less than 600 yards and extending to the left after passing Le Verguier to meet the 15th Battalion, before advancing again in line on a front of 1,000 yards.

In the map the arrows show the area captured by the 13th, and their extension northwards after passing Le Verguier, which was then being mopped-up by the 16th.

Heavy wire was encountered over and over again by the 13th, and several enemy strongpost and trench systems; many of the former being surrounded by heavy barbed belts. The heavy smoke had this advantage—it enabled our first line to get close enough to bomb and rush enemy machine-guns before they could do much damage.

Le Vergieur stands on a ridge which extends southwards across the 13th area. In the valley before this ridge a machine-gun was gallantly rushed by Sgt. G. Sexton, of "D," who killed the stubborn crew who had continued firing to the last. Sexton then advanced with his Lewis-gun at his hip, slung from his shoulder, far ahead of the rest of the company that had been delayed by wire and other posts. Just as our barrage passed over their dugouts a platoon of Germans came up, manned their trenches, fired into us and hurled bombs. Sexton squirted his bullets at them while rushing towards them, and killed or captured the whole platoon. Except for a thin line in places the Battalion was now still farther behind the barrage, the "shorts" as well as the wire having delayed several. A small clump of trees suddenly appeared from out the smoke. That upright, fearless small figure that had somehow got through still more wire, and that was the centre of attraction and admiration to all within sight, ran into the clump by himself and, killing several, sent another dozen back as prisoners.

Now came the breasting of the ridge and stronger opposition which occupied a deal of time in spite of so many gallant deeds against it. Capt. W. Parsonage, M.C., was wounded by a bomb while leading his company across a belt of wire against a strongpost. The other heroic deeds will not lose by letting the story take its course.

Continuing down the slope beyond, "B" swung round to its left in order to junction with the 15th, who had been very successful. The smoke had cleared and "B" found themselves under the direct short-range fire of two German Field Guns and four Minenwerfers. Any advance past them in action was impossible, and a frontal attack on their strong position required careful consideration. Sexton, who seemed to be wherever the greatest obstacles were, saw one of the guns in action, and other Germans manning a bank nearby. It was like a tonic to him, if indeed, he required any more than the fire of battle. His eyes flashed, he rushed like a whirlwind towards them, jumping a trench and tearing his clothes free from barbs which threatened to hold his back, firing short bursts as he rushed, killed the gunners at the Field Gun, and sent the others scurrying into their dugouts. Two machine-guns opened on him as he dashed across a flat near Mill Spinney, but did not deter him from the new trench he was running at, and in which he killed 12 who hesitated to put their hands up. He now ran back to the bank near the field gun and fired down dugouts until he heard cries of "Kamrad!" "Come up, then," he called out, and, as they made their exit, he sent them back, 30 of them, including a Battalion Commander.

Cpl. A. Edwards joined Sexton in the glory of the capture of a Field Gun, the second for the Bn., which he did by reckless gallantry and Lewis-gun efficiency. He was a source of strength and inspiration to his company all that day, being awarded the D.C.M. But "B" hadn't waited to watch either him or Sexton complete his job, but had hurried to join the 15th immediately these men had silenced the opposition.

Meanwhile on the right the 48th Bn. had been held up and a gap developed between them and "C" Company. "A" immediately went forward on the right of "C", worked south a little and joined with the 48th, Capts. Turner and Turnbull setting splendid examples of inspiring leadership.

"C" was on its objective at 6.30 a.m., "B" and "A" arriving a little later. Until Zero plus 185 (8.25) all dug, the halting barrage protecting them and giving them the proper line. Then they made ready to advance again—the Second Phase.

At 8.30 the barrage again moved forward, following closely by the 13th, with the 45th and 15th on their flanks. The halt had been too long,—two hours,—for it enabled the enemy to remove his heavy guns and to increase his supply of Machine Guns. However the barrage was now more accurate on our front, and all were in tremendous heart because of such great success so far. Strong opposition was again struck, especially on the right, where Lt. Harry Baker was the Battalion guide. This splendid officer repeatedly went ahead into the smoke to reconnoitre. Collins Copse was proving a hard nut until Baker went into it and located the enemy, at whom he threw bombs until 20 surrendered, and walked back ahead of him. He had also located another enemy trench, the position of which he now pointed out to a party, spread them out, and, after a shower of bombs, led them in a rush, capturing the position and another score of prisoners. A few moments later he charged a machine gun and crew of 5, firing his revolver while running until the remaining 3 surrendered. This prompt and most daring action undoubtedly saved many lives. Be it also remembered that Baker was suffering intensely from a wound in the leg received half-an-hour previously, refusing to evacuate until his men were safely dug in on the Red Line,—the second objective. This tall, slim, fine looking officer, by his magnificent bravery, coolness, resourcefulness and constant courtesy to all, proved himself an inpiring leader indeed, and well deserved the D.S.O. awarded him for the day and previous similar work. Not only the right, but the whole of the Battalion struck tremendous opposition in mounting the Red Line Spur. There were many posts surrounded by barbed belts of great width, the strongest of a dozen being Coronet Post and Ascension Farm, with a system in between. The memory of the heroism, in addition to Baker's, with which these posts were captured will never fade from the minds of members of the Two Blues. All agree that Sexton's fearless figure was again an inspiration. Two machine guns on his right and one on his left again held up his company. A platoon was lying, or kneeling, firing at the left gun, but this did not suit Sexton, who calmly stood up to get a better target, and silenced the gun. He certainly was leading a charmed life, for the other two guns were still pouring lead into the platoon and around him, the spiteful pinging and the thudding into the ground or bodies making all seek shelter. All except Sexton. He remained standing up and firing into the guns until he put both out of action. The platoon rose and rushed ahead after Sexton, when another trenchful of Huns bobbed their heads and rifles up, and fired rapidly. Sexton, nearest to them, instantly jumped into the trench, killed all slow at "kamerading" and sent back 5 more prisoners. Surely this was enough for one day for anyone. Not for Sexton. His officers had advised him over and over again to take less risk. "You've only got to die once," was his reply. Three more machine-gun posts and trenches he rushed that morning before the Red Line was consolidated. During the digging-in another machine gun swept across his company's front from a post 70 yards out. Again he killed the crew, and a few minutes later strolled down the Sunken Road and brought back 15 prisoners. Marks was so astounded at the almost incredible reports of Sexton's doings that he minutely questioned dozens of all ranks concerning each deed before sending in the recommendation for a V.C. And surely no V.C. was ever better merited.

Alongside Sexton's the deeds of other heroes in this epic battle may seemed dwarfed except to those who saw them and knew the men. Sgt. J. Lihou, D.C.M., M.M. again shines out, even in such company. He and his small section hugged the barrage, and, on one occasion, got right ahead of their company. A machine gun opened onto them from behind. Lihou threw a bomb, which killed 3, and rushed the post, capturing 5. This delay gave another machine gun time to fire into his party. Lihou again threw a bomb and jumped into the trench along side the gun and captured its crew of 5. He then led his party down their trench, along the Brown Line, and saw the post that was holding up the 48th Bn. Unhesitatingly he climbed out of the trench by himself, and charged a gun and post of 20 Germans, but unfortunately it was his last charge. He died as such a man would die, giving his life to save others, being awarded posthumously a Bar to his M.M. So passed well-beloved Jimmy Lihou, D.C.M., M.M. (and Bar).

Sgt. F. Darke organised a platoon from several small parties of lost men and, on his own initiative, did splendid work on the critical Right Flank, leading the way into a network of trenches and capturing many prisoners, winning his M.M. and commission.

Pte. E. Wick's mates and small bodies of other platoons, having lost all their Nco's, and being delayed by the smoke and wire, became confused when they came to a heavily-shelled area. Wicks, seeing the importance of advancing, rapidly organised the men and led them through the barrage to their proper position on the final objective, deservedly winning the Bar to his M.M.

After the death of Lt. McGuire, Sgt. F. Sheppard took charge of the Company Sigs. and Runners. In the smoke he suddenly found himself in a trench with Huns on both sides of him fighting like tigers and firing into the backs of our advanced men. Although it was 18 against 6 Sheppard managed to push them back until help arrived, when all surrendered. Sheppard received his M.M.

When we were consolidating the Brown Line Cpl. J. Duncan, with one man, went out ahead to reconnoitre, and brought back valuable information and 12 prisoners. During the Second Phase he was sent to locate the 45th Bn., and again came across Germans who attempted to escape; but Duncan, by a great sprint, headed and brought back 50 of them. His 4 men were certainly splendid, especially C. Allen. Duncan received a M.M., Sgt. H. Townsend, M.M. and Cpl. R. Miles (O.P.) cut tracks through several belts of wire in the face of the enemy, during which Miles rushed a Post and captured a machine gun and 5 prisoners. Sgt. A. Acton received the D.C.M. for specially distinguished leadership and patrol work on this great day. For almost two years this popular Scout had shown consistent gallantry and enthusiasm for dangerous stunts, and had won the admiration of all, especially for the quiet manner in which he did the most glorious deeds.

Pte. L. McInnes, another scout, volunteered on three occasions to deal with posts holding up his platoon, rushing out ahead as he exclaimed "Let me go!" without raiting to hear his officer's reply.

Cpl. W. McDonald, after rushing and capturing 12 Germans, gave his life attempting to repeat the deed, being awarded a posthumous M.M.

By 9.30 a.m. "A", "C", "B" and "D" were in position from right to left on the Battalion's Objective, the Red Line, and Col. Marks had moved his Hqrs. forward to beyond the Brown Line.

Runner T. Denny, returning to the front line after delivering a message, found 6 men lost in the fog and took charge of them to lead them to the line. The part he arrived at however, happened to be a gap between two companies, still in possession of the enemy. Denny immediately attacked, using his own and many German bombs, bombing down and then up their trench to our men on both flanks, capturing over 100 prisoners and 7 machine guns. His D.C.M. was well earned. But accounts even of such glorious deeds, become wearisome.

Lewis-gunners Cpl. J. Banks, H. Martyn, K. Miller, W. Edgar, G. Cowell all captured prisoners and machine guns by their dash, courage and initiative, the former three receiving M.M's.

Sgt. T. Stevens, L. Climpson, W. Brown had all been splendidly cheerful, reliable and courageous for a long time, and continued their fine work in this Battle, Climpson receiving the M.M. The ever gallant Ptes. A. Cornell, and H. Forster repeated their deeds of heroism, Cornell receiving his M.M. Signallers K. Chambers and F. Warner carried heavy loads and repaired lines for hours after being painfully wounded, saying nothing of their injuries until collapsing from loss of blood. Chambers received his M.M. Cpl. J. Richards dressed wounds for 36 hours under shellfire, a typical example of the usual devotion of the staff of our R.A.P. R.Q.M.S., J. Mitchell and Sgt. R. Hill received M.S.M's. for long conscientious attention to records and work in the line in the interests of their mates.

The prisoners stated that they had received orders to hold their positions at all costs, and that they had determined to do so, which they generally did until face to face with the attackers. This fact makes the work of our men all the more glorious. For a Battle Strength of 18 officers and 397 other ranks our captures amounted to 560 unwounded prisoners, including 2 Colonels; 2 field-guns, 8 minenwerfers, and 30 machine-guns in good order and about 20 destroyed. Our losses were 109, of whom 11 were killed. Among the wounded were Lts. J. White, M.M. and J. Marsh, both recently promoted from the ranks for good work, and who did splendid work this day.

At Zero plus 269 (9.49) a.m. the 14th leapfrogged the 13th and 15th. They fought all day against great odds and had not reached their objective, the Blue Line, by night fall. The Artillery arranged to help them, and at 11 p.m. under a barrage, the 14th completed their task, —a memorable performance for troops so tired and wet, for it rained again during the day. On the night of the 20th the 13th relieved the 14th. We had a company of the 16th attached to us. Immediately after taking over, our patrols pushed out, followed by strong parties who established and consolidated a line of Posts 500 yards ahead of the Blue Line, and commanding the bridges over the Canal

The death of the gallant Cpl. A. Dawson (O.P.) on the 20th seemed especially sad as he was leaving for Australia the next day, on account of long service, with other Originals— Sgt. W. Pearce and McKnight and Cpls. R. Miles and S. Gow. These had fought well from first to last.

On the night of the 21st, after moving a little to the right, we were relieved by the 4th Leicesters, and, footsore and weary, trudged several miles back to near Tincourt, remaining there next day. The 13th had fought its Last Battle, without, however, dreaming that it was so. And, like its first battle, it had, notwithstanding every possible preparation and supervision on the part of the Colonel and Generals, been a Soldiers' Battle, a series of a hundred glorious little battles in valleys, trenches and copses, where the quick decision and self-careless action of the individual,—man, Nco, or platoon officer,—meant all the difference between victory and defeat. The fact that all were taken into their Commander's confidence regarding the design and aim of the battle, and that all were intelligent enough to appreciate the varying situations, certainly meant a great deal.

This Battle of the 18th September proved that the 13th of the 25th April, 1915 had not deteriorated. Perhaps,—very probably, indeed,—the early members left their influence behind them. There were not many of these members left at Le Verguier, whole platoons containing not one man who had been on Gallipoli. Records show that at Villers Bretonneux in June only 143 of all ranks of the 750 then in the Battalion had even seen Gallipoli. There was, however, the continuity of personnel, with all that it means, in the Battalion. There were always "Old Hands" in every platoon to influence the reinforcements, and among the officers there was a constant sprinkling of Gallipoli heroes, and the Commanding Officers, after Burnage,— Tilney, Durrant, Marks, Murray and Allen were all with the Battalion on the Peninsula. Other officers who gained positions of influence in the 13th on the Western Front, like H. D. Pulling, T. Wells, D. P. Wells, R. H. Browning, W. S. Bone, R. Henderson, R. A. McKillop, A. W. Davis only did so after long meritorious service in the line with the Battalion. Still Sexton had not seen the enemy before February, 1917, Lihou before October, 1916, Baker (after service with the A.A.M.C.) before August, 1917, and many others in action for the first time in our last battles distinguished themselves in a manner that won instant comparison with the conduct of the Originals at the Landing.

Our M.O., Mjr. C. R. Merrillees, performed splendid work during this final period. One of our bravest and ablest young offiers, Lt. H. B. Davis, had, as a Bde. officer during the past few months, won his M.C. He was killed 2nd October.

In thinking over the names of heroes not mentioned in these pages I call to mind, without effort, scores. I determined to write their names, but the writing of each calls up several others, and I also recognise that there are as many even the names of whom I have not had the honor of knowing. These heroes and their relations, however, may rest assured that their names remain in the minds and conversation of their comrades, and will be handed down by them in legends of the Fighting 13th while Australians remain the Australians of these great years, and may therefore in the future receive their dues more equitably than it has been my power to write them.

There were other heroes too, in their quiet way. In Rouen hospitals at least 5 of the 13th gave their blood to save the lives of others, and one gave lumps of his flesh. Records of such cases seldom reached the Battalion, as some never rejoined. One healthy man, who had been given 14 days' leave, did not return for 6 weeks, being marked in our records as A.W.L. He had visited some mates in Harefield Hospital, and, learning that a Digger of the 20th Bn. could only be saved by transfusion of blood, had there and then offered himself to be tested, and, being found healthy, had been accepted. He left hospital ten days later, rather weak, but with 21 days' special leave. When Col. Durrant complimented him on his sacrifice he remarked: "Don't make a fuss over it, Sir; there are three others in "D" now who have done the same." Where one case came under the Bn's. notice there were probably a dozen whose heroism was simply recorded in the papers of the various hospitals.

The end of the War found the 13th possessing the following glorious record of decorations awarded:—

V.C.—2—Murray, Sexton.

C.B.—1—Burnage.

C.M.G.—3—Durrant, Murray, Wray,

D.S.O.—6—Tilney, Durrant, Murray, Marks, Marper, Baker.

Bar to D.S.O.—1—Murray.

M.C.—33—

Bar to M.C.—1—Henderson.

D.C.M—31—

M.M.—188—

Bar to M.M.—7—

M.S.M.—6—

Foreign Decorations:—Serbian, 4; French, 4; Belgian, 1.

A total of 288.

General Brand's query, "Can any battalion point to a finer record?" is answered.

There were also approximately 300 Despatches and Corps Mentions. Sexton's was the eighth V.C. won by the 4th Brigade. The 5th Division also won eight, the 3rd Division 7.

Recommendations by the Commanding Officer to Brigade numbered over 4,000, which would probably mean considerably over 16,000 recommendations by Company Commanders to Colonels. Some are known to have received six recommendations without an award. Their reward is in the knowledge of service nobly done.

After the Armistice Lt. W. Noble, Sgt. S. Harrison, C.Q.M.S. J. McDonald and Cpl. T. Cooper were mentioned in Despatches for long meritorious war srvice. Capt. T. White was congratulated by General Monash in Orders for gallantry, and Pte. A. Stevenson awarded his M.S.M. for gallant self-sacrifice in attending to prisoners of war in a German hospital, especially during the influenza epidemic, even remaining behind in Germany after his time to leave in order to continue his good work.

APPENDIX.

What the 13th paid towards Victory (excluding evacuations through illness from gas or other causes):—

Gallipoli—

	Deceased.	Wounded.	Totals.
Officers	15	46	61
O.R.	385	666	1051
	400	712	1112

Western Front—

	Deceased.	Wounded.	Totals.
Officers	39	85	124
O.R.	660	1760	2420
	699	1845*	2544

*Including 114 evacuated as "Gassed."

Totals for the War:—

	Gave their Lives.	Wounded.	Totals.
Officers	54	131	185
Other Ranks	1045	2426	3471
Total ..	1099	2557	3656

Including those who died in Australia because of war injuries, it can safely be said that over 1200 of the 13th gave their lives.

Lost as prisoners:—Gallipoli, nil; Western Front, 13 officers, 280 other ranks. The majority of these were also wounded.

Chapter XXXIII.—From Picquigny to Belgium, and Home.

AFTER a bivouac at Biaches and a reveille at 4.30 a.m., we were taken by 'buses on the 24th September to Picquigny, arriving there after a six-hours' journey. Here we remained most comfortably until the 13th November, all making good friends among the villagers. During this period a big batch of the members of the Battalion with the longest service, including Col. Marks, Mjr. A. W. Davis (Adjt.), Capt. E. Plucknett (Q.M.) and other distinguished members, bade farewell on their departure for Australia on leave. They were the recipients of unanimous congratulations and the best of good wishes, and were greatly missed indeed. A few who, instead of returning to Australia, took "Blighty leave, came back after their 70 days.

Training was carried on as usual, Mjr. T. Wells, M.C., being in command, but the programmes were hampered in November by the rains. Mjr. Wells carried out a system of competitions in the training—guard-mounting, route-marching, shooting, etc., all entering keenly into the competitive spirit. One competition was a route-march in full pack for over seven miles, followed by shooting at service targets.

On the 1st November (All Saints Day), the Brigade assembled at the invitation of the residents, and, accompanied by them and their children, loaded with flowers and wreaths, marched to the British Cemetery, where the children marched along the lines of graves, knelt reverently and covered the mounds with the flowers. It was a touching sight indeed and brought unashamed tears to eyes of many old soldiers. The Cure of the parish, schoolmaster and a French officer made eloquent addresses which were interpreted by Chaplain Harper and a French interpreter, and the children sang the British and French National Anthems, our bands playing both again before dismissal. We all felt that the graves of our mates would be well tended after our return to Australia.

On the 9th we received orders to move forward again, and expected to take part in the big battle then going on, but the move was postponed from day to day until the 13th, in the meantime, on the 11th, news of the Armistice being received. Great joy was evinced by the French and Diggers who assembled in the Square to hear the news. Australia was near at last; but still there was a tinge of sadness and disappointment in the celebrations, sadness at the thought of absent comrades, and disappointment at the knowledge that the "old Batt" with all its associations would soon be a thing of the past.

On the 13th, at 8 p.m., we left Picquigny and marched 17 kilometres to Saleux, the night being clear and frosty, making marching a pleasure. At Saleux, after a hot tea, all settled down in the trucks to sleep. We left early next morning by train, and reached Epehy at 5 p.m., after an interesting journey past some of our old battlefields. At Epehy we occupied tents for the night. [See map with Chapter XXV.]

On the 15th we marched to Templeux-le-Gerard, and entrained on decauville for Brancourt, whence we marched to Fresnoy-le-Grand, having passed during the day through the whole width of the Hindenburg Line—its systems of wire, trenches and forts being far more amazing than we had ever imagined.

Before leaving Picquigny all sewed on new color-patches after ripping off their old ones. The latter were immediately picked up by the ladies in each place, several of whom remarked: "Bons souvenirs de bons soldats!" It was indeed touching to see how our friends treasured our colors, explaining as they placed them safely away, often in their bosoms, "Vous etes si gentils." Many a patch of the Two Blues is still regarded and remembered warmly throughout Northern France and Belgium.

At Fresnoy for a week we had football matches daily, and a few interesting route marches—one to Fonsommes, the source of the Somme, a tiny trickle. Our football teams were still doing well at Rugby and Soccer, although they had lost so many of our most famous players, men like Sgt. W. Roger Bradley, Capt. "Dos" Wallach, Capt. D'A. Irvine, and Lt. J. Cooney. Col. Allen, however, played a splendid game and took his place regularly in matches, and Capt. Swinburne, Lt. McRae, F. Theiring, J. O'Neill, Morris, "Snowy" Lancaster and Carter upheld the Battalion's reputation. "Professor" Doody was an assiduous trainer too.

At Fresnoy we had 50 Germans to do our fatigues of cleaning up, helping cooks, etc.

On the 21st Lt.-Col. A. S. Allen, D.S.O., assumed command. Originally with the 13th for a period of 1915, he had gone to the 45th, where he had won high distinction and great popularity The war being over, his work consisted mainly in keeping up the morale of the men anxious to return home, watching their health and arranging education facilities for those desirous of same. Mjr. Wells, assisted by Chaplain Durnford, M.C., and the more highly educated members of the Battalion of all ranks, had commenced a fine course of educational work at Picquigny, and Col. Allen continued the good work, after a break due to moving, at Florennes. At Picquigny also Padre Durnford and the author had commenced a Battalion newspaper, "The Two Blues," and the Signallers had issued the opposition journal, "Orts." Great interest was displayed in these babies while paper was available, but the shortage became so acute that operations had to be curtailed.

The French inhabitants of this and our next areas, and the Belgians later, welcomed us joyously and told pitiful tales of German barbarism. Again and again they wept at the thoughtfulness and kindness of the Diggers towards them. "How we welcomed those young boys of England, such young boys when they first appeared by ones and twos coming out of the woods!" said one old lady of Prisches, referring to the Tommies. A letter from the citizens of Monceau-les-Leups was received by our General, containing the following passage:—"I beg to have the honor of saluting our deliverers through you. We have been suffering so much since the beginning of the war that the sight of your gallant troops has been to us as the glorious sight of the new arising of the sun of Liberty." Practically all of every town we visited testified to the inhuman treatment to which they had been subjected, details of which are not for these pages. But one feels proud that these liberated peoples retain warm hearts for the men of the Sunny South. "Silenrieux retains the fondest memories of the Australians." "Fresnoy-le-Grand will conserve the fondest memories of the passage of the Australian troops. God bless you," and "Homage to the valiant Australian army that has so greatly contributed to the liberation of poor Belgium. We shall long retain fond memories of the amiable officers of the 13th Australian Battalion. The several days spent with them have been marked by true sympathy and real friendship. We will remember our hosts." These are the expressed feelings—in writing—of these people concerning the visit of our Battalion to their towns, and we are rightly as proud of such tributes as of our victories.

On the 23rd we camped in tents at St. Souplet after a march of 15 kilometres, passing en route litter of every description cast away by the Hun, and illustrative of his demoralised condition. After a day at Prisches we reached Sains du Nord on the 26th. The roads were sloppy, but were still picturesque. Apple orchards abounded, but all were very poor, even destitute, all their stock and poultry having been taken by the Hun. "The Bosche stole them all, stole everything," we were repeatedly told.

On reaching Sains, after 22 kilos, we were complimented by the Brigade Major on having presented such a fine appearance on the march. On the 29th Gen. Drake-Brockman addressed the Brigade in one of the big woollen mills in Sains on repatriation, touching on the following points:—1. The possibility of the 4th Brigade relieving the Canadians on the Rhine; 2. Length of time required to ship the A.I.F. home; 3. Intention of Allies to carry on as though a state of war still existed; 4. Chances of the enemy faithfully carrying out the terms of the Armistice; 5. The drawback of landing 200,000 men in Australia at about the same time; 6. A.I.F. Education scheme; 7. Diggers' wives in Britain, and their voyage to Australia; 8. The intention, as far as possible to send units, or parts of units, back to Australia together. His address was a fine one and was listened to most attentively.

Leaving Sains we marched through Sivry, just across the Belgian border, Silenrieux and Phillipville, where Napoleon spent the night after Waterloo, to Florennes, south of Charleroi, where we had very comfortable billets for several weeks, and where we spent a most enjoyable Christmas. The people treated all with remarkable kindness. Light training, plenty of sport, and education filled in the winter days, which, mainly on account of the good billets, were the most cosy winter days we spent on the Western Front. Christmas dinner was spread in big rooms in the large Jesuit monastery. Sports were held on Boxing and New Year's Day.

At Florennes the Prince of Wales visited the Brigade, making himself extremely popular by his happy manner and interest in individual men.

Many were now leaving for educational work in other parts, many going to England. Several also returned to Australia. Consequently our strength dwindled until we were less than half-strength.

The 13th was certainly now finishing its career as a battalion. Keen students still attended classes to improve themselves, the subjects dealt with being English, Mathematics, Book-keeping, French, Shorthand, Typewriting, Electrical Engineering, Carpentry, Tailoring, Sign-writing, Geography and History; voluntary and able instructors being found from all ranks. Lts. A. N. Brierley and W. Edgar, who had both good service in the firing line, were the leading spirits and organisers in this work, and they were helped by Cpls. Green, Hepworth and Gleeson and Ptes. Martin, Sweet, Manning and Bishop.

In November great interest was taken in the Brigade in the question of regimental colors. At Sains we received two small flags, simply the two blues, from Mrs. W. M. Hughes on behalf of the Australian women in London, and Col. Allen arranged for their presentation by Gen. Drake-Brockman who, after an impressive ceremony, addressed the Battalion on Regimental Colors of British regiments, and advocated similar methods of perpetuating the glorious history of the battalions of the 4th Brigade, particularly so, as the A.I.F. battalions were to be regarded, according to Government proposals, as the Reserve Battalions of their respective regiments. This parade marks the beginning of an attempt to preserve for future generations the traditions of our glorious battalion in historical colors, all ranks being filled with the idea, little dreaming that on account of A.M.F. regulations—as if the A.I.F. were not worthy of its own regulations in this matter—their self-sacrifice and efforts would result so disappointingly. A purely voluntary subscription list was opened, and, within a few days, members of the Battalion had subscribed £128 for these colors. The Agent-General in London displayed keen interest in and devoted much time to the preliminary arrangements and formalities, such as the designing, painting, obtaining approval and ordering, and the Commonwealth Government was written to for what was then considered as merely formal consent. A water-color by H. Burke, C.B., C.V.O., F.S.A., Norroy King of Arms and Inspector of Regimental Colors, and specifications for King's and Regimental Colors were soon received and approved. Burke had arranged with the Heralds' College. The Agent-General then notified that he had arranged with the Royal School of Art Needlework to do the work at an estimated cost of £44 for King's, and £88 for Regimental Colors. The C.O. arranged for the extra outlay of £13 over the subscriptions. It was at this stage that opposition from A.I.F. Headquarters was met, and it transpired that the Commonwealth had already considered Regimental Colors and fixed a standard design for all units as follows:—Color, green; unit titles in gold on a red circle; A.I.F. badge on crimson; badge to be of gold and the scroll of silver with gold lettering; the crimson background to show the Crown. How could such a display ever lend itself to perpetuate the history of the "Two Blues" or of any other of our famous units? What principles were observed in drawing up such specifications? Certainly not those observed by Imperial Regiments. Our beloved colors were to be omitted from our Regimental Colors! What A.I.F. Battalion will feel pride in following this flag in preference to the colors they carried in every action, and wearing which so many of their comrades died? The colors that are still treasured in France and Belgium!

The War Office had also arranged for the presentation of King's Colors; hence our order for them was cancelled, but, as the work on our Regimental Colors was in process, there was no alternative but to complete them, those interested feeling that, once these colors were in Australia, a more sympathetic note would be found. Also, in reply to a very concise and clear communication by the Agent-General a letter was received from the Minister about this time which mentioned that the War Office was presenting King's Colors, but did not refer to Regimental Colors. The consent so formally and clearly asked for was therefore not actually obtained, but the correspondence very definitely supplied no objections, and the situation was fully appreciated by the Battalion.

During the correspondence the majority of the subscribers left for home, and to consider the refund of £30 balance on account of the cancellation of King's Colors to subscribers was out of question; and Col. Allen arranged for lithographs of the colors at a cost of £36, the £6 being arranged privately; subscribers reachable having received these lithos from Lt. Blythman, who kindly consented to look after them. Both Col. Allen and the Adjutant, Lt. Webster, left England before the Colors were ready. However they arrived in Sydney in March, 1920, the freight, etc., being paid privately. Since then Lt Blythman has made several efforts to obtain official recognition of them, but unsuccessfully. They remain stored in the Technological Museum.

On account of the various educational and repatriation schemes the Battalion could not come home as a unit, small groups arriving on each boat during 1919. On arrival old members found Col. Marks waiting to welcome them. He was a civilian now, but found time to visit Anzac Buffet on the arrival of the boats. Then men were hurried away among crowds of loving and longing relatives. They had finished with the A.I.F. All felt that they and their colors, with all they stand for, would soon be officially recognised as a powerful, even if Reserve, influence in the Defence Schemes of Australia, but years have passed, members are scattered, and the belief they had in politicians and their National outlook has dwindled.

From Florennes the remainder of the Battalion moved to Hansinelle, nearer to Charleroi, where we stayed some weeks, continuing our sports, amusements and education. Here again, as in all our billets after the Armistice, we entertained the civilian population. That the people appreciated our efforts may be judged from a typical address written and read in English by the schoolmaster of Hansinelle at our Farewell Ball on the 29th March, 1919:—"Gentlemen and Dear Allies,—A French proverb says: 'Aux Seigneurs les Honneurs'—Give honor where honor is due.—Therefore, thank you, the organisers of these magnificent balls, for the excellent time spent in your agreeable company. Thank you also, Messieurs Artists, Musicians and Singers, for the fine, well-performed pieces. We, inhabitants of Hansinelle, certainly understand little of your Mother tongue, but the harmony of your well-cultivated voices and the dancing itself will always bring pleasant memories of these unforgettable hours. Thank you, Messieurs soldiers, for the dumb lessons given to us—exquisite civility, perfect and true harmony amongst yourselves, and the excellent comradeship that exists between officers and men. Thanks in short to the Australian Nation that has sent her best sons to deliver us from the Prussian boot, from the tyrannic yoke of the Bosche. Alas! many will never see their beloved parents of the beautiful Australian continent again. Before their graves, too prematurely opened we bow profoundly and respectfully, and cover them with myositis, the flower of remembrance exclaiming, "Forget—Never!" No, the Belgians know only too well that the democratic Australian Army was a model and picked army. They know also that its motto was always and everywhere: 'Advance—Yes! Fall back—No!' Besides they know that neither the dangers of the sea nor the long separation from the loved ones, nor the thousand tortures of our climate, nor the numerous evils of the war, in short, nothing could stop its magnificent spring. Honour and glory to it! In the name of the inhabitants of Hansinelle and the whole of the Belgian Nation, I address you my warm and hearty thanks. Dear friends and brothers, your sacrifices were not sown on the sterile fields of ingratitude. In consequence do I need to add that if once Australia were invaded by a foreign nation, your dead heroes left amongst us would cause to rise up from all parts of Belgium legions of volunteers who would flow to your aid with the cry of 'Everything for our dear Australian Allies!' Officers, soldiers and Australian people, thank you! A thousand times thank you!"

At Hansinelle it was decided that a composite battalion from the four battalions of the Brigade, should be formed, the staff and equipment of the 13th to be used. We moved to Bouffioulx, part of Charleroi, where the equipment of the 14th, 15th and 16th Battalions was handed in. Col. Allen remained C.O. of the 4th Brigade Battalion. Gradually the 4th Brigade Battalion was depleted by repatriation, and we absorbed the remnants of the 12th and 13th Brigades, becoming the 4th Division Composite Battalion, still controlled by the staff and machinery of the 13th Battalion. This continued until there remained only 500 of the 4th Division, when the last of the 1st Division joined us. It was a strenuous time keeping the men's spirits up to the last as their friends went, but owing to the tradition of the 13th and the fact that the whole of the 13th Headquarters staff volunteered to remain to the last, the job was easier than it would probably have been otherwise.

Now came the finale of the A.I.F. in Belgium. The last quota of the two famous divisions, 1st and 4th, numbering 1,000 left for England. A few more details of the A.I.F. were still to leave, but this quota was the last large one to leave France.

The 13th, the first Battalion of the 4th Division, and with the first of the A.I.F. in action, had the honor of being responsible to the last in seeing the last of these two fighting divisions safely away from the countries in which they had so wonderfully proved themselves. Our Headquarters staff remained intact until landing in Australia, forming, with addition, the ship's staff on the "Suevic."

Old members meet each other in all parts of the State and yarn delightedly over stirring times and old comrades and Battalion identities like "Old Dad," Sgt. Bloomquist, Sgt. J. Grady "Lofty," the barber, "Haircut Johnny" and his mule clippers, "the man who paid the 13th," etc., for in every district of the State are to be found representatives of the 13th, who in most cases have repatriated themselves, proving themselves men in peace as in war. Young families are growing up proud of their dads, so the influence of the 13th, the "Old Batt," will not die despite the apathy of politcians. For years to come children will eagerly gather round the winter fires to hear Dad or Grandad tell the story of the Landing, Bloody Angle Australia Valley, Hill 60, Bois Grenier, Pozieres, Mouquet Farm, Voormezeele, Stormy Trench, Bullecourt, Messines, Ploegsteert, Polygon Wood, Passchendaele, Hollebeke, Ypres, Hebuterne, Villers Bretonneux, Hamel, 8th of August, Le Verguier and the Hindenburg Line, and of Harry Murray and the hundreds of other heroes, many of them known only to the tellers. Far more interesting stories than I have had the honor to attempt will be told and truer to the life of the Battalion will they probably be. I candidly feel that my humble efforts have fallen short. Records have been unobtainable, hidden away among a hundred tons of papers still unsorted in England and Australia. A future writer may be able to add many names I have unfortunately had to miss. When the Grand Reveille sounds, and the final Fall-in takes place, if manliness, gallantry, patriotism, sincerity, generosity and self-sacrifice count for anything, there will be a full muster of the old Two Blues up there.

At the end of January, 1920, those who had served with him were truly grieved to hear of the death of Col. Doug. Marks, who gave his life in a gallant attempt to rescue a stranger from the undertow at Palm Beach. They were proud of him and always will remain so.

Practically every member of the 13th within travelling distance of Sydney was present at his Memorial Service in St. James' Church, but none of his comrades-in-arms felt his loss more than his bosom friend and ardent admirer, Col. H. Murray. He gave his life as willingly as he knew any of his Two Blues would.

> "Life may go so honor stay—
> The deeds you wrought are not in vain."

ENVOI.

It has been an effort to condense and to do proportionate justice to the events in our history and the heroes of the Battalion. Every chapter could have been enlarged considerably, to the greater satisfaction, perhaps, of those specially interested in certain periods. Still it is hoped that those with the 13th even for a very short period will find that period treated as complete in itself, which desire has been responsible for a certain amount of repetition. An effort has been made to tell the story as simply as possible in order that the humblest member may follow it without effort. The story is simply for members of the 13th A.I.F., and of its namesake in the A.M.F. and of their friends and relatives. Members of other units are asked to read it in this light, if they do read it.

If one, after reading the story, feels that the 13th had four years of terrific muscle and nerve strain—correct. If he feels a little sympathy for the few who tried and failed to be the superman their heroic comrades were the author shares that sympathy with him from the bottom of his heart. If he knows a Digger who remained solid for four years, three years, two years, aye, even for one period in a strafed line, and then began to soil his record, let him at once stretch out the hand of sympathetic fellowship, and grip. A Digger who slipped after years of splendid service is penalised more than enough by the feeling of shame that possesses him when he thinks back, thinks of his splendid comrades and their mutual deeds—and then of his red-ink entries on his previously honorable sheet. So whether such a Digger slipped while a Digger or on his return to civil life, please recognise that no one who faced the hells he faced for such periods can be expected to be his old sterling self again for years, or maybe, for this life. If I have any special ambition regarding this story it is that it may be the means of arousing even a little of this sympathy in such cases.

T.A.W.

Several other 13th stories and incidents have been told in "Diggers Abroad" (Angus & Robertson).